CRIME LABORATORY MANAGEMENT

CRIME LABORATORY MANAGEMENT

Jami J. St. Clair

with contributions by
Jo Ann Given *and* Michael W. St Clair

ACADEMIC PRESS
An imprint of Elsevier Science

Amsterdam Boston London New York Oxford Paris
San Diego San Francisco Singapore Sydney Tokyo

ACADEMIC PRESS
An imprint of Elsevier Science
84 Theobald's Road, London WC1X 8RR, UK
http://www.academicpress.com

ACADEMIC PRESS
An imprint of Elsevier Science
525 B Street, Suite 1900, San Diego, California 92101-4495, USA
http://www.academicpress.com

ISBN 0-12-664051-3

Library of Congress Control Number 2002113742
A catalogue record for this book is available from the British Library

Typeset by Kenneth Burnley, Wirral, Cheshire, England
Printed in Great Britain by MPG Books, Bodmin, Cornwall
02 03 04 05 06 07 MP 9 8 7 6 5 4 3 2 1

CONTENTS

In memory of my father,
James Franklin Jackson,
who, when he learned that I wanted to work in
a crime laboratory, surmised that I'd always have work;
and with love to my husband, Mike,
who has supported me and the "work" ever since

PREFACE

Many crime laboratory supervisors are promoted not on their management abilities but on their analytical abilities. They quickly learn that the position requires an entirely different set of abilities. While training programs are mandated to teach a new forensic scientist how to perform DNA analysis, few laboratories require new supervisors to fulfill a training program on effective laboratory management. General management classes can be applied to the crime laboratory setting but there are often idiosyncrasies that exist for crime laboratories that are not taught in these classes. Therefore, new laboratory supervisors must learn by trial and error. They learn a little here and pick up some more there. After several years, they have acquired the skills to respond effectively to situations that commonly occur in the crime laboratory.

This text endeavors to fulfill several objectives. It attempts to fill in some of the gaps that exist in the training for new laboratory supervisors and provide new perspectives to experienced directors. It may also give an overview of crime laboratory operations to non-science administrators that oversee laboratories as well as others interested in crime laboratory operations. Finally the text provides many subjects useful to crime laboratory analysts that aspire to become supervisors or just wish to know more about laboratory management.

Crime Laboratory Management is broken into nine chapters where classical management theories proposed by such notables as Steven Covey and Ken Blanchard are applied to crime laboratory management. Accompanying the theoretical discussions are practical applications and scenarios that can be adapted by forensic laboratory managers for use in their own laboratories.

Chapter 1, "The Role of the Crime Laboratory", details the crime laboratory's responsibility to various segments of society and addresses why laboratories must be accountable to suspects as well as victims. Laboratories may operate as an independent public agency, as a unit within a law enforcement agency or as a commercial enterprise. Regardless of their organizational structure, laboratories share common operational elements and require similar personnel positions to fulfill their missions. The duties of the positions and the requirements of the individuals that fill the positions are discussed.

The most important task of a crime laboratory director is discussed in

Chapter 2, "Human Resource Management". Initially, personal leadership is stressed because only through self-awareness of one's own strengths and weaknesses can one effectively manage others. This awareness can also make a manager aware of the needs of the individuals that they manage. For a crime laboratory supervisor to ensure that the laboratory is operating to its maximum potential, they need to understand how to fulfill their employee's needs. This chapter also addresses practical tips for hiring the right individuals as well as developing and evaluating employees.

It is commonly accepted that employees of crime laboratories are held to a higher standard than those in other careers. New crime laboratory employees must pass a barrage of tests to ensure that their past behavior is free of illegal or unethical acts. While it is expected that their past behavior will be indicative of their future actions, this is not always the case. Chapter 3, "Ethics", explores the common reasons why unethical acts are committed. If these reasons are identified, they can be addressed and prevented. Models for ethical decision-making as well as practical training scenarios that can be used to teach forensic scientists how to resolve conflicts are also presented.

The need for crime laboratories to ensure a high-quality work product has been illustrated time after time in recent years. Many within the forensics community promote accreditation of laboratories and certification of analysts as a measure of quality. Chapter 4, "Quality in Crime Laboratories", is written by Jo Ann Given, a past chair of ASCLD/LAB®, the United States' most recognized crime laboratory accrediting body. Ms. Given provides a thorough discussion of the various accrediting, certifying and standard-setting bodies active in the United States and in the international community.

Crime laboratories are faced with daily changes to their operations. Chapter 5, "Strategic Management", addresses how laboratory managers can prepare for future trends and respond to events that affect the laboratory's operations by developing and managing from a strategic plan. The chapter also discusses the various management programs that have been adopted by organizations, including total quality management and balanced scorecard. While these programs vary, they share many common elements such as a customer focus, employee participation, and a continuous improvement of processes. These elements are highlighted and discussed.

The day-to-day activities of crime laboratories are usually well established. However, changes in environment, such as the passage of a new law, often require that the laboratory address these changes in order to maintain the effective operation of the laboratory. A "project" is undertaken to determine the need for the change, determine the best alternative, and implement the selected processes. Chapter 6, "Project Management", discusses the steps necessary to successfully complete a project. The chapter also gives practical tips for managing a project as it progresses and evaluating its results to ensure that it achieves the desired outcomes.

All crime laboratories, both public and private, operate with scarce resources. Funds that are used for one purpose are not available for another. Therefore, the effective use of budgetary resources is necessary to ensure that the crime laboratory continues to operate in alignment with its goals and objectives. As many crime laboratories are public agencies, Chapter 7, "Resource Management", discusses classical theories regarding public budgeting, including how agencies operate with limited funds, as well as how they determine which processes to eliminate if funding is reduced to a critical level. The chapter also presents a practical discussion regarding how crime laboratories can supplement their budgets, including where to seek grants and how to successfully write a proposal.

One of the skills that new laboratory supervisors must develop quickly is communication. The ability to effectively communicate to employees, administrators and external stakeholders is essential to gaining the support necessary to fulfill the laboratory's goals and objectives. Chapter 8, "Effective Communications", gives practical information on various aspects of communications. Practical tips regarding public speaking and written correspondence are presented, and because today's crime laboratory directors must be politically astute, this chapter provides a practical discussion regarding the US political process. It addresses how a laboratory manager can actively promote their laboratory's needs or those of the forensic community to elected officials. The National Forensic Science Improvement Act provides an illustrative example of the theories discussed.

Finally, crime laboratory managers must ensure that their laboratories operate as safely as possible. The safety of their employees should be considered with day-to-day operations as well as when new processes are instituted. Chapter 9, "Safety in the Forensic Laboratory", is written by Michael St Clair, Certified Safety Professional, and outlines general safety precautions for the crime laboratory. The chapter includes practical discussions regarding common physical and chemical hazards, chemical management, spill control, biological hazards, facility safety equipment, and personal protective equipment.

On a personal note, the production of this text has allowed me to research many aspects of crime laboratory management. It does not in any way imply that I am the ideal laboratory manager; just ask my employees. I, like all other managers, strive each day to learn new processes and approaches that will improve the operations of the crime laboratory. I get ideas from professional managers employed in forensics as well as other public and private careers.

I take advantage of opportunities to attend management workshops and hear about new management techniques. Mostly I have learned from experience, including trial and error: a lot of error. This text reflects some of what I have learned in the past 20 years of formal and informal learning. While I have attempted to include what I consider to be the most important aspects of crime laboratory management, it does not and cannot cover every situation that a manager will face.

Crime laboratory management is an evolving art. The same approaches that were successful 20 years ago will not produce the same results today. Individuals can continue to grow and improve only through constant learning and adaptation to new information. It is my hope that the reader will gain new information from this text that will help them to improve their own management abilities as well as the operation of their organization.

ABOUT THE AUTHORS

Jami J. St Clair has over twenty years of experience in local and state crime laboratories and private forensic laboratories. Ms St Clair holds a Bachelor of Science degree in Forensic Science from Eastern Kentucky University and a Master of Arts degree in Public Policy and Management from The Ohio State University. She served as President of the American Society of Crime Laboratory Directors in 1998 and is currently the Crime Laboratory Director for the Columbus Police Crime Laboratory in Columbus, Ohio.

Jo Ann Given has many years of experience in private research, and state and federal forensic laboratories. She holds a Bachelor's degree in Chemistry and a Masters degree in Analytical/Organic Chemistry from Old Dominion University. Ms Given served as President of the American Society of Crime Laboratory Directors in 1989 and served two terms as Chair of the American Society of Crime Laboratory Directors/Laboratory Accreditation Board (ASCLD/LAB). She has served on several scientific working groups and is presently ASCLD/LAB's representative to the National Cooperation for Laboratory Accreditation (NACLA). Ms Given is currently the Director of the Naval Criminal Investigative Service Laboratory in Norfolk, VA.

Michael St Clair has over eighteen years of experience in the environmental health and safety field. He is a Certified Safety Professional in Comprehensive Practice as affirmed by the Board of Certified Safety Professionals. His experience includes personnel exposure monitoring, biological exposure monitoring, sampling for chemical and biological contaminants, emergency response and management of an extensive environmental compliance program. Mr St Clair's field experience includes oversight, as well as health and safety responsibilities on environmental remediation projects.

CHAPTER 1

THE ROLE OF THE
CRIME LABORATORY

If you want a place in the sun, prepare to put up with a few blisters.

(Abigail van Buren)

THE "GLAMOROUS" CRIME LABORATORY

In the past several years, crime laboratories have taken on a glamorous air of mystery. People are led to believe that crime laboratories are exciting places. There is something new happening every day. Analysts are beautiful people involved in every step of criminal investigations including crime scene processing, evidence collection, interviewing witnesses, collecting body fluids, crime re-enactments, bench analysis of every type of evidence using the most sophisticated instrumentation available, arresting the suspect, and prosecuting the guilty. They work 24 hours without tiring because they love their job. And why not? They can solve any crime single-handedly in 48 minutes and still have time for a beer with the guys. The truth is much more mundane and considerably more frustrating.

The glamour of working in a crime laboratory quickly fades for a new employee who is faced with analyzing 15 "crack" or "meth" cases a day, every day for months on end. They stand on their feet in a windowless laboratory with antiquated and inadequate instrumentation. The only time they leave the laboratory is to travel three hours to testify in court. They get assigned a ten-year-old unmarked cruiser that only has an AM radio but does have 100,000 miles and was used by a cigarette-smoking overweight narcotics agent. When they arrive at court they find that the case settled yesterday and "we forgot to call."

The analysts and managers that have chosen to make this life a profession are highly adaptable individuals. They realize the budgetary limitations of government work. They accept the ethical requirements of their positions both on and off the job. They accept the demands on their time by law enforcement and the courts. They are willing to work for less than they are worth and with no recognition for their efforts. They fight for funding for instrumentation when their agency would rather fund cruisers. And they absorb the criticism thrust on them by opposing attorneys, defense experts and journalists.

Life in the crime laboratory is often boring, with occasional bursts of frustration. But it is a vital function in the criminal justice process. Without forensic testing, the guilty would walk free and the innocent would be imprisoned. Even with all the frustrations, lack of recognition and inadequate salaries, it is this realization that provides forensic examiners with the satisfaction to continue to perform their duties with integrity.

Crime laboratory management is an often-overlooked discipline of forensic science. Without effective management, crime laboratory analysts become overly frustrated and leave employment. Crime laboratory staff commit ethical violations or criminal acts. Laboratory procedures and scientists stagnate and lose pace with national standards. Case completion slows and backlogs grow to unmanageable levels.

To effectively manage a crime laboratory, managers must understand the roles of their crime laboratories and their responsibilities within the system. They must accept their obligations to their employees, their superiors, the law enforcement community, prosecutors, victims, suspects, and the public. They must understand the importance of fiscal accountability and ethical responsibility. In short, they must be able to balance the needs of all the people all of the time with limited resources.

ROLE OF THE CRIME LABORATORY IN SOCIETY

From the collection of evidence through the sentencing of the convicted, the crime laboratory plays an integral role in the criminal justice process. The crime scene investigators are either part of a laboratory or they have received extensive training from one. Of course, all the examination and analysis of the physical evidence is performed at the crime laboratory. Most courts will not proceed with indictment, much less prosecution, if the laboratory analysis is not complete. And finally many sentences in drug cases rely upon the weight of the controlled substance that is provided by the crime laboratory.

Regardless of a crime laboratory's role or level of involvement, they have a responsibility to perform services in a manner responsive to the demands of their stakeholders. While these demands may vary between segments of the population, many elements remain the same. For example, forensic scientists are expected to approach every situation in an objective, scientific manner with a high degree of integrity. A crime laboratory's challenge is to meet the various expectations of its stakeholders with the same high level of responsiveness.

Jo Coleman

Information Update Service

Butterworth-Heinemann

FREEPOST SCE 5435

Oxford

Oxon

OX2 8BR

UK

Keep up-to-date with the latest books in your field.

Visit our website and register now for our FREE e-mail update service, or join our mailing list and enter our monthly prize draw to win £100 worth of books. Just complete the form below and return it to us now! (FREEPOST if you are based in the UK)

www.bh.com

Please Complete In Block Capitals

Title of book you have purchased:..

....

Subject area of interest:..

Name:..

Job title:...

Business sector (if relevant):..

Street:...

Town:... County:...

Country:... Postcode:...

Email:..

Telephone:..

How would you prefer to be contacted: Post ☐   e-mail ☐   Both ☐

Signature:... Date:...

☐ Please arrange for me to be kept informed of other books and information services on this and related subjects (✔ box if not required). This information is being collected on behalf of Reed Elsevier plc group and may be used to supply information about products by companies within the group.

FOR OFFICE USE ONLY

Butterworth-Heinemann,
a division of Reed Educational
& Professional Publishing Limited.
Registered office: 25 Victoria Street,
London SW1H 0EX.
Registered in England 3099304.
VAT number GB: 663 3472 30.

BUTTERWORTH
HEINEMANN

A member of the Reed Elsevier plc group

RESPONSIBILITY TO THE POLICE

By their very nature, crime laboratories have a close relationship with law enforcement agencies. The physical evidence upon which they perform analysis is collected or seized by police officers. Forensic scientists often meet with officers to discuss circumstances surrounding casework. These discussions assist both officer and analyst in determining the significance of the evidence. If a suspect and victim are known to have an intimate relationship, the presence of semen may not be significant. However, if they are estranged, it can be very important. Arguably, these meetings can be valuable in the efficient and effective analysis of cases.

A common point of discussion and often disagreement among supporters and critics of crime laboratories is how close a relationship should forensic scientists have with the police. While communication is important, it is equally important that a forensic scientist remains objective. Many people outside the criminal justice system infer that crime laboratories that reside in police departments owe their primary allegiance to their employer. While it is important that a crime laboratory assists the police, it is equally important that forensic scientists do not view themselves as "cops in lab coats." When forensic scientists align themselves with police and seek to support law enforcement's theories above all else, unethical practices are prone to happen. It is the responsibility of crime laboratory management to ensure that forensic scientists do not view themselves only as instruments of the police.

RESPONSIBILITY TO THE PROSECUTION

The necessity for detailed notes and overall quality in analysis becomes apparent in the courtroom. It is not at all uncommon for a forensic scientist to be criticized while on the witness stand for something that should have been recorded but was not. It is therefore the crime laboratory management's responsibility to ensure that the prosecution can rely upon the quality of their analysis.

Impartiality is important in this stage of the criminal justice process as well. An expert witness wields a great deal of influence over a jury. The jury believes that they are unbiased scientists beyond reproach. If they testify to findings that were obtained in a manner that was less than objective or to conclusions that are beyond what the evidence allowed, the jury could be swayed to find an individual guilty for a crime that they did not commit. On the other hand, if cross-examination reveals a bias, the jury may disallow the testimony of the forensic scientist and allow a guilty individual to be set free.

RESPONSIBILITY TO THE VICTIM

An often-repeated dogma among those who investigate homicides is that they speak for the victims who can no longer speak for themselves. Also, a forensic scientist has an obligation to a homicide victim and their family and friends to perform a comprehensive analysis of the evidence. The physical evidence may be the only way of identifying a killer. This same concept applies to all victims of violent crime.

Forensic scientists also have a responsibility to those who are not yet victims. By thoroughly analyzing evidence from one rape case, a suspect can be identified and prosecuted, thereby preventing them from raping again. Also, by identifying controlled substances in a white powder, the forensic scientist assists in prosecuting a drug addict who may resort to burglary or more violent crimes in order to obtain money to buy more drugs.

As with other stakeholders in the criminal justice process, forensic scientists must not align themselves too closely with the victim. In doing so, they risk obscuring their objectivity. They may also be tempted to stretch their conclusions to assist in prosecuting a suspect to provide closure to a victim or to their loved ones.

RESPONSIBILITY TO THE SUSPECT

While assisting to identify the guilty is a primary function of crime laboratories, it is equally important to identify the innocent. With the prevalence of DNA analysis in casework, a suspect is exonerated a large percentage of the time analysis is performed. Many convicted offenders are being released as post-conviction DNA testing reveals that the body fluid originally used to convict them is not theirs. Exonerations not only lie within the domain of DNA analysis: vindication also regularly occurs when a bullet does not match a firearm or a white powder fails to show the presence of a controlled substance.

It is also the crime laboratory's obligation to the suspect to provide results in an expeditious manner. By quickly analyzing the evidence, an innocent suspect will be able to quickly resume a normal life without undue stress.

RESPONSIBILITY TO SOCIETY

In addition to the roles that a crime laboratory plays in the criminal justice process, they also play an important role outside the process. Generally, crime laboratories are supported through taxes. As a public agency, a crime laboratory is responsible for operating efficiently and effectively. This includes careful consideration of all functions, from prudent budgeting to fair treatment of personnel.

As a public agency, the crime laboratory must be responsive to the public's request for information. Crime laboratories often fill the role of teacher. The field of forensic science has interested students for many years. Crime laboratories are often asked to allow students to shadow employees or they may receive requests to provide presentations to local schools. Also, journalists often approach laboratories for the opportunity to provide interesting stories for print, radio or television. While these can mean significant interruptions to the daily operations, the requests to provide training should be balanced with the laboratories' other responsibilities.

LABORATORY OPERATIONS

There is no "average" crime laboratory. Crime laboratories operate within many different environments. While there are some private laboratories, most crime laboratories are supported by public funds. Authority may come from the local municipal level, regional or the federal level. Laboratories may operate as a division of a law enforcement agency, prosecutor's office, or medical examiner's office – or they may be independently operated. Although the primary goal of all laboratories is the same, the span of operation of the laboratories differs.

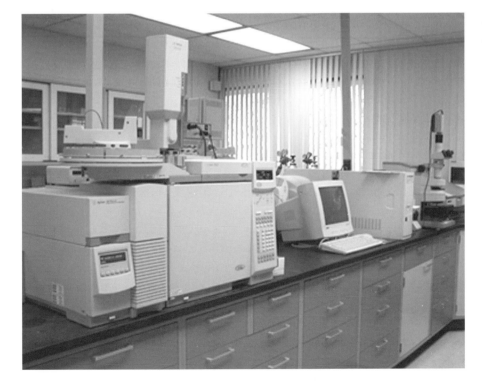

Figure 1.1

Many crime laboratories offer analyses in numerous disciplines.

Not only do environments differ, but also the type of work that crime laboratories perform differs. Crime laboratories are often envisioned as capable of performing analysis in many different disciplines – controlled substances, DNA, firearms, trace evidence, etc. However, that is not always the case. Laboratories may specialize in one discipline. For example, a fire marshal's laboratory may only perform testing for accelerants or a medical examiners' office may have a laboratory that only performs toxicology testing. Private laboratories may operate for the sole purpose of performing DNA testing on convicted offender samples. The Drug Enforcement Administration even has a "Special Testing" laboratory whose sole purpose is to perform research on controlled substances.

PUBLIC LABORATORIES

By definition, public laboratories operate as bureaucracies. Bureaucracies are generally located within the executive branch of the government and are found at the federal, state, and local levels of government. Simplistically, bureaucracies are charged with ensuring execution of laws. However, when laws are passed, they lack the detail needed for implementation. Therefore the bureaucracies must create the policy used to implement and monitor the laws.

As bureaucracies, public crime laboratories must implement policies to ensure compliance with laws. For example, when legislation is enacted to make an abused substance illegal, the crime laboratory must develop a procedure to identify that substance. State crime laboratories may also have responsibility for instituting administrative rules. Often state departments of health control rules regulating the analysis conducted to determine intoxication while operating a motor vehicle. A state laboratory may also set rules governing collection of DNA standards for entry into databases.

In setting rules, the agency must consider the spirit of the law for which the rules apply and apply them equally to all stakeholders of the law. The laws governing the collection of DNA standards for entry into databases vary from jurisdiction to jurisdiction. The coordinators for the databases must ensure that the collection protocols strictly comply with these laws. In addition, there should be no exceptions to the protocol. Regardless of one's standing in society, if they meet the requirements they should be included in the database. Conversely, if they do not meet the requirements, they should not be included.

As do all bureaucracies, crime laboratories experience a high level of fiscal accountability. Government crime laboratories must be responsive to fiscal inquiries from their parent agencies as well as the public. Crime laboratories are expected to operate in an efficient manner. The government watchdogs demand that public money is not squandered. As tax revenues decrease and funding becomes more competitive between public agencies, more crime laboratories are undergoing increased scrutiny regarding their operations. Laboratories are being questioned on the prudence of maintaining processes that can be performed by others more efficiently.

In addition to operating in an efficient manner, government crime laboratories are expected to operate in an effective manner. In other words, crime laboratory operations should produce a product valuable to the public. Most laboratories have no problem convincing the public that their service is valuable; however, crime laboratory employees should not assume that effectiveness by itself is enough to gain funding to fulfill all its desires. In public funding issues, effectiveness goes hand in hand with efficiency. It is important for a public agency that, while producing a valuable service, it is doing so with efficiency.

Finally, a public agency is expected to treat everyone fairly. Equal treatment of the public as well as employees is demanded of crime laboratories in the same way as other public agencies. With respect to service to the public, discrimination is not acceptable in any public agency. Forensic scientists must not allow the race, age, sex, or wealth of a suspect or victim to influence the thoroughness of their analysis or the scientific conclusions reached. Above all, forensic scientists must be scientists who approach their work in an objective manner and should never assume guilt or innocence. Further, forensic scientists must not allow the fact that they receive payment from a law enforcement agency to influence their conclusions.

Employees within public agencies are expected also to receive fair treatment. Laws and policies are in place to ensure this occurs. Many crime laboratories follow hiring policies put in place by Civil Service Commissions. These policies outline what may or may not be asked during interviews as well as the factors that can eliminate candidates from being hired as forensic scientists. Throughout their careers, agency policies, bargaining units and employee contracts, as well as legislation, ensure equal treatment and due process in disciplining and dismissing employees.

In addition to practicing equity with individuals, a public agency is expected to treat businesses fairly. Public crime laboratories receive funding from the government level within which they operate. They operate within approved budgets, and spending is strictly controlled. Generally, the purchasing process for public laboratories is complex and time consuming. When seeking purchases, crime laboratories may have independent spending authority or may be required to obtain approval through their agency or advisory board. Most public laboratories must request authorization for purchases beyond a set level. For major purchases, a public laboratory often is required to obtain bids from several vendors. This complicated process ensures that all businesses have fair access to the jurisdiction's business.

SPAN OF OPERATION

The level of government at which a public laboratory operates, as well as its dependency status, has a great deal to do with how easily funding is made available, how efficiently it operates, and the opportunities to which it has access. Laboratories that operate within a larger agency often have little authority over their own budget. They are required to share the agency's resources with other units. They compete for supplies, equipment, personnel, and training. Independent laboratories have greater control over planning for and making purchases. They can increase fees if they plan to invest in equipment or facilities in the future. However, being a part of a larger agency does allow an umbrella for emergencies. Independent crime laboratories dependent on their own budget may not have reserve funds should an immediate need arise. However, a laboratory that is located within a larger agency can call upon the resources of the overall agency for assistance.

Local laboratories

Local laboratories often operate with greater efficiency than do larger state laboratories. One reason for this is that the jurisdiction which they serve is smaller. They are familiar with the requirements of the local court system, and the court system is familiar with them. Often the forensic scientists are not required to provide testimony on cases, and when they are, they do not have far to travel.

Often it is necessary for forensic scientists to work closely with the law enforcement officers. Forensic scientists who work within police agencies often are familiar with the investigating officers. This allows for easier communication and results in more efficient and effective use of resources. When questions arise during analysis, the detective is readily accessible. While ease of communication is important in terms of efficiency, it must always be noted that forensic examiners should not allow themselves to become overly accommodating to the desires of the detectives.

Crime laboratories that are located within medical examiner's offices can confer with the pathologist when questions arise regarding homicide investigations. In return, the forensic scientist is available for consultation when the pathologist has questions. Collection of blood standards and other evidence is streamlined.

Regional laboratories may also operate under a law enforcement agency, a prosecutor's office or as an independent agency. Generally, these laboratories perform analysis for several law enforcement agencies and do so on a contractual basis. Operational funds may come from the fees paid by these agencies or from taxes generated from the counties in which the agencies reside. The forensic scientists with regional laboratories are still familiar with the limited number of officers and local medical examiners with whom they work, and often these laboratories maintain the same high level of throughput as does a local laboratory.

State laboratories

State laboratories are generally part of a state police system, an Attorney's General Office, or as an independent agency. Often the chief executive of the organization is an elected official or has been appointed by one. This influence often provides them greater access to grants and additional funding opportunities.

State laboratory systems are usually composed of several laboratories that operate as regional laboratories. In this way they are similar to most local and independent regional laboratories in that they are familiar with the officers who frequent the laboratory. However, they receive a wide range of analytical requests. They typically receive the casework that local laboratories are incapable of performing. These cases are generally more complex and time consuming and therefore reduce the efficiency of the crime laboratory.

Forensic scientists who work for a statewide agency often have less contact with both the law enforcement officers and the medical examiner's office. This lack of communication works to their disadvantage when information is required to perform analysis. Often there is a delay in contacting the officer due to differing schedules that cause considerable delay in performing the analysis. When this happens often, large backlogs of cases develop.

When a case goes to court, it may be in a county that is not familiar with a particular forensic scientist. Therefore the analyst is asked to appear more frequently than their local counterparts. This is especially time consuming for forensic scientists who work in a large state with minimal population and only one crime laboratory. For example, a forensic scientist in Alaska is often required to fly to court in remote villages. A trip to court in Alaska consumes at least one day and often more. The same trip to court for an analyst in Detroit takes an hour. The time required for court appearances is a major contributing factor to backlogs in state crime laboratories.

Federal and international laboratories

Laboratories that operate within federal agencies are envisioned to have lots of money and expertise. They are believed to have all the funds that they need to perform any test required. Federal crime laboratories know that this is not the case. However, like any laboratory that operates within a larger agency, they have the opportunity to draw on additional resources as required in an emergency. Additionally, because they operate at a federal level, they are often responsible to assist in the investigation of high profile cases. When this occurs

Congress can choose to appropriate additional funds to help the laboratory accomplish its task.

International laboratories generally operate in the same manner as do laboratories in the United States. There are local, regional, state, and national laboratories. Funding comes from contracts with individual law enforcement agencies or from taxation. They too are concerned about quality processes and are required to be responsive to the public for their actions. International laboratories, especially in Europe, have the added challenge of interacting with laboratories and law enforcement agencies from neighboring countries. These agencies not only operate under different government philosophies but also with different languages. Sharing information regarding individual criminals and crimes requires organized coordination and cooperation.

Private laboratories

Private laboratories are those that perform analysis for fees and either operate as not-for-profit or for-profit. These laboratories may work solely for law enforcement or as independent examiners for the defense bar. The "laboratory" may be one individual with minimal equipment such as a document examiner, or it may employ several hundred examiners with a broad range of expertise. It may also exist for the sole purpose of assisting insurance investigators with determining the cause of a fire or explosion or analyzing DNA database samples.

Often the individuals in public laboratories are skeptical of the training and abilities of those employed by private laboratories. This usually stems from the fact that these examiners are testifying against their findings or provide criticism or arguments to defense attorneys to "muddy the waters." Private examiners operating for the defense bar have an image of unethical individuals willing to accept cases for which they possess minimal expertise only to derive income. However, with available certification and accreditation, these laboratories and examiners can demonstrate that they only perform within their expertise and produce an ethical product.

CRIME LABORATORY ORGANIZATIONAL STRUCTURE

All employees of the crime laboratory play vital roles in fulfilling the mission of the organization. Their job tasks may differ significantly or overlap. The most common position in the crime laboratory is that of forensic scientist. The forensic scientist generally analyzes physical evidence in one of many scientific disciplines. In addition to the forensic scientist, evidence handling personnel receive, release and ensure that the evidence is properly maintained while in their custody. Clerical personnel type and maintain crime laboratory reports in a retrievable manner as well as direct telephone inquiries to the appropriate persons. Supervisory personnel are responsible for overseeing the daily and long-term operations of the laboratory. Regardless of the specific tasks to which they are assigned, all crime laboratory employees are responsible for the quality of the casework that is reported. No one can afford to say that it is "not my job." All tasks contribute to the overall quality of the forensic services provided by the laboratory and employees must be able accept their responsibility to quality rather than passing it to other employees.

The titles and responsibilities of crime laboratory staff and leadership vary greatly from organization to organization. Depending on the size of the organization, a crime laboratory may have one manager that oversees all the laboratory personnel, manages budgetary matters, and represents the laboratory to outside stakeholders. In large organizations with multiple laboratories, there will likely be several layers of management with specific responsibilities. In all crime laboratory organizations, one individual will have ultimate responsibility for the effective and efficient operation of the laboratory. Most forensic organizations have many employees responsible for all aspects of forensic analysis and management as outlined in Figure 1.2.

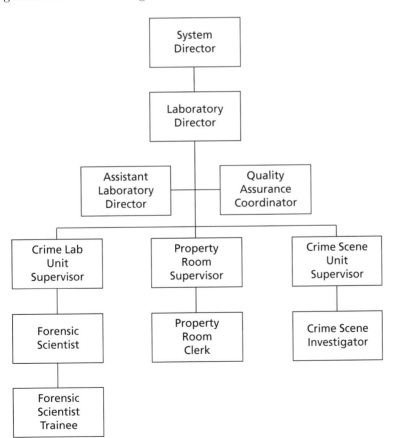

Figure 1.2

Forensic laboratory organization.

FORENSIC SCIENTIST TRAINEE

Often a scientist is hired into a crime laboratory in a forensic scientist trainee position. The new employee requires training before they are competent to perform analysis on evidence and testify to their findings. A crime laboratory may have a formal "trainee" position or the trainee is hired directly into a forensic scientist position. Crime laboratories may give a generic term of "Forensic Scientist" or "Criminalist" to these positions. Some laboratories may have specific job titles for a specific position such as "Forensic Scientist – Toxicologist" or "Latent Fingerprint Examiner."

Often, the employee has just completed their college degree. Unless their degree program included an internship with a crime laboratory, they may not have any experience with forensic analyses. Most crime laboratories require that new forensic scientists possess a minimum education consisting of a baccalaureate degree in a natural science such as chemistry, biology, or forensic science. Often requirements may include specific classes and/or training. The DNA Advisory Board (1998) requires that analysts performing DNA analysis "must have successfully completed college course work (graduate or undergraduate level) covering the subject areas of biochemistry, genetics, and molecular biology (i.e., molecular genetics, recombinant DNA technology) or other subjects which provide a basic understanding of the foundation of forensic DNA analysis, as well as course work and/or training in statistics and population genetics as it applies to forensic DNA analysis." A trainee may be required to possess this coursework prior to being hired, or the laboratory may require that the trainee obtain the necessary education requirements during their training period.

New employees are generally required to undergo an extensive screening prior to being hired. They may be required to undergo comprehensive background investigations that probe their personal as well as employment history. Investigations focus on improprieties of a criminal or unethical nature. Applicants are asked to disclose information of past criminal conduct such as traffic violations including speeding, driving under the influence of alcohol, drug use and thefts. Additionally, acts that can influence future misconduct such as credit problems, excessive alcohol use, and deviant sexual practices are explored. As well, applicants are often required to pass pre-employment polygraph examinations and drug screens. Finally, they may have to undergo a series of interviews before obtaining the position of trainee.

Most laboratories will have a formalized training program for each discipline. The program should include stated objectives and demonstrations of competency. A forensic training program may require several months or years. A trainee may spend only a few months to become competent with controlled substance analysis or several years to become competent with document examinations. Trainees are usually assigned to a more experienced analyst during their training period. This mentor provides feedback to the trainee through their training period as well as to the laboratory supervisor regarding the trainee's progress.

FORENSIC SCIENTIST

After a specified period of time and accomplishing performance objectives that include demonstrations of competency, the individual is allowed to report and testify to casework. The individual may continue to perform bench analysis for many years. Their competency at performing work increases with experience. A forensic scientist may stay within the same discipline or train in another discipline. If they choose to transfer to another discipline, while they will have to complete another training program a forensic scientist generally is not demoted to the "trainee" position and retains their salary.

Most crime laboratories offer a series of forensic scientist positions through which employees may progress. General terms for these positions are Forensic Scientist I and Forensic Scientist II or Criminalist I and Criminalist II. Based upon their experience and expertise, the steps are usually promotional in nature. More senior analysts are expected to have achieved the knowledge necessary to perform complex tasks and analyses. The more senior the analyst, the greater their responsibility becomes. They may not only perform the more complicated casework but also serve as a valuable source of information to management. Senior analysts are intimately familiar with the operations and needs of the discipline within which they work. Senior analysts may be relied upon to assist in purchasing decisions or to act as supervisor in the absence of the regular supervisor. They may also be asked to design and conduct training programs for other analysts or law enforcement officers and to act as mentors to new analysts within the discipline.

In addition to the technical knowledge required, certain abilities are necessary for forensic scientists. The skills required for a forensic scientist as well as a forensic scientist trainee include the ability to establish and maintain working relationships with other laboratory employees, as well as others within the criminal justice system. Forensic scientists must be able to maintain detailed documentation regarding their analysis and clearly communicate their conclusions in both written and oral forms. They must be able to testify in court using appropriate courtroom demeanor. Senior forensic scientists must be able to work independently and apply appropriate problem-solving techniques to resolve technical and procedural difficulties.

UNIT SUPERVISOR

At some point, a forensic scientist may decide to seek advancement. The analyst may be promoted based on a number of factors. A good analyst has proven their ability to approach a situation with scientific objectivity, think through and resolve any problems and reach a conclusion. When they are promoted into management, they face a whole new set of problems. Most problems are not as objective as the chemistry they have been performing throughout their career. Often, a new supervisor is put into the position with little or no training on personnel management, arguably the most important and challenging part of their job.

The first supervisory position is usually over a specific discipline. The position may hold a title indicating a working supervisor. Titles may be a continuation in the Forensic Scientist or Criminalist series, such as Forensic Scientist III, Criminalist III, or Senior Forensic Scientist or Senior Criminalist. The title may also reflect the supervisory nature of the position such as Forensic Science Supervisor or Criminalist Supervisor. Many individuals in this position may perform analytical analyses as well as managerial tasks. The supervisor is looked upon as an individual with considerable technical expertise and may serve as training coordinator for new analysts.

A supervisor may be hired from outside the laboratory or promoted from within. Both situations result in unique challenges for the newly promoted supervisor. If a supervisor is hired from outside the laboratory, the analysts that they supervise may not recognize their expertise in the discipline or management. Employees may challenge their authority as supervisor, especially if they had also sought the supervisory position.

When an analyst is promoted to supervisor from within the laboratory, they face a whole new set of challenges. As an analyst in the laboratory they are familiar where opportunities for improvement exist. The other analysts recognize their expertise and may more readily accept their suggestions. However, the new supervisor will also find themselves in the awkward position of supervising their friends. When they are required to discipline an analyst, there may be accusations of turning their back on friends or playing favorites by disciplining one analyst but allowing a "friend" to perform the same act without discipline.

Unit supervisors often oversee the personnel in the section. In this role, they may direct training of new analysts and perform performance evaluations for all analysts that they supervise. They may act as quality assurance coordinator for the discipline where they are responsible for technical reviews of casework, auditing processes, and validation of new procedures. They may be responsible for ensuring that instrumentation is maintained in proper working order and recommend purchase when new instrumentation is required. As a senior analyst with significant knowledge of the discipline, they may still be required to perform casework and maintain competency in the discipline.

In addition to the comprehensive knowledge of a forensic discipline and other skills acquired as forensic scientists, unit supervisors require abilities necessary for supervising personnel. The skills required by a supervisor not only include the ability to establish and maintain working relationships with others but also the ability to coordinate the activities of the unit. This ability to effectively communicate with others is essential for a unit supervisor to ensure that the unit operates smoothly. Additionally, unit supervisors must have the ability to recognize the need for new processes as well as the initiative to implement the improvements.

EVIDENCE CONTROL

In all crime laboratories, evidence control is a critical function. The manner in which evidence is submitted and stored can affect the results of analysis. Most laboratories have individuals who accept and release evidence to the law enforcement officers that they service. These individuals may carry the title of Evidence Custodian, Property Custodian, Evidence Technician, Evidence Technician or Evidence Receiving Technician. Individuals in this position are responsible for ensuring that evidence is received in a sealed condition per laboratory requirements and appropriately stored (Figure 1.3). They are also

Figure 1.3

Appropriate storage in property rooms is key to maintaining evidence control.

responsible for establishing a chain of custody and other documentation essential to maintaining control of the evidence. Evidence custodians require the same background investigation as forensic scientists. Their integrity is important as they are exposed to not only evidence but also money and other valuable items.

Skills required by an evidence custodian include an ability to maintain effective working relationships with the laboratory staff and the law enforcement officers with which they constantly interact. The evidence custodian interacts with more external individuals than do most others in the laboratory. They are commonly the first employee that an officer meets and their courtesy and demeanor determine if the officer has a positive or negative impression of the laboratory. As with others in the laboratory, they must possess the ability to maintain detailed and complete evidence documentation. When receiving or releasing evidence, they must ensure that all items are accounted for.

If a crime laboratory falls within a larger law enforcement agency, the evidence custodians may not be assigned to the crime laboratory but to a property room with a separate chain of command. A property room maintains property other than the evidence that requires forensic analysis. They receive lost and found items as well as items for which no forensic analysis will ever be requested. When the property room is separate from the laboratory, it is the responsibility of the crime laboratory to work closely with the property room to ensure that the evidence custodians are aware of the importance of protecting evidence against loss and maintaining a secure chain of custody.

In other laboratory organizations, the property control function for the entire agency falls under the purview of the crime laboratory. This creates an opportunity for the crime laboratory director to closely monitor the quality of the evidence handling. If training is necessary, the director can take immediate steps to correct the situation.

There are also challenges when this agency function falls to the crime laboratory. Generally, unlike crime laboratories, police department property rooms operate and must be staffed on a 24-hour basis. This type of operation demands that a supervisor be assigned for the sole purpose of overseeing this operation. Whether overseeing a police agency's property control function or the control function in a large crime laboratory, an individual in this position must possess similar abilities to other unit supervisors. To ensure that coverage is available 24 hours they must be able to instill a team atmosphere for their unit. If property custodians are unwilling to work overtime to cover for an absent employee, dissatisfaction can occur and the operation will not be as effective as possible.

CRIME SCENE INVESTIGATION

Since the O. J. Simpson case, the importance of proper evidence collection and storage has been in the spotlight. The proper training of the individuals in the crime scene investigation unit as well as the effective operation of the unit itself will prevent errors that can affect the laboratory's ability to properly analyze the material.

In some organizations, the crime scene investigation function falls within the crime laboratory. The individuals that process crime scenes may be commissioned law enforcement officers or trained civilians. One of the major job functions of the crime scene investigators includes documenting the crime scene. Documentation may be in the form of notes, photography, line drawing, and/or drawing software. Crime scene investigators are also responsible for identifying and collecting physical evidence at crime scenes. Crime scene investigators are usually responsible for processing the crime scenes for fingerprints and must therefore be familiar with the appropriate development method for each substrate. They must ensure that the evidence is properly secured and free from contamination. The crime scene investigator begins the chain of custody and ensures that the evidence is properly stored. They are also required to testify as to the processes used at the crime scene.

The requirements for a crime scene investigator vary. If the position is occupied by commissioned law enforcement officers, there may be no prerequisites required for transferring to the Crime Scene Unit. While some law enforcement agencies may take exceptional qualifications such as education into account, others may consider only the seniority of the officer.

If the position is civilian, a more structured process may exist. While crime scene investigators need to be aware of the abilities and limitations of the laboratory, they do not need to possess the extensive education required for forensic scientists. The requirements, therefore, may not be as restrictive as required for forensic scientists. However, if the crime scene investigation position is used as a career path to forensic examiner, the individual hired for the position may have the same educational background as laboratory analysts.

Specialized skills such as a detailed knowledge of photography may be beneficial to those seeking a position in crime scene investigation. Another skill that is necessary in this position is the ability to maintain detailed and complete documentation. Since some interaction with victims is common, crime scene investigators must also display courtesy and empathy.

As with the property control function, the crime scene unit must operate on a 24-hour basis. In large law enforcement agencies, this requires that personnel staff the unit at all times. In smaller agencies, it is possible to have an investigator on call in case a crime occurs. A supervisor is required for the unit if it is staffed on a continuous basis. A supervisor in this unit should possess the same ability to motivate a "team" atmosphere as does a property control supervisor.

QUALITY ASSURANCE COORDINATOR

Most laboratories have an individual designated as the Quality Assurance Coordinator. The duties of this position include oversight of quality processes in the laboratory. In smaller laboratories, there may not be a separate position for assumption of quality assurance duties. Instead the duties may be incorporated into the responsibilities of a forensic scientist or even the crime laboratory director. If an individual holds this office in a full-time capacity, they must have access to the laboratory director or a manager with the authority to set policy and act on the recommendations made by the quality assurance coordinator.

The individual who fills the role of quality assurance coordinator must have a detailed understanding of the importance of quality processes in the overall operation of the crime laboratory. Generally this requires specific training in quality assurance concepts. Also, the individual should have knowledge of crime laboratory operations. This is not a position where a recent college graduate should be placed. Not only do they not have the necessary knowledge but will they not be recognized by others as an authority. ASCLD-LAB® lists a number of responsibilities for a quality manager. These are listed in Figure 1.4.

In addition to maintaining necessary documentation, the quality assurance coordinator must be able to offer suggestions for improvements to forensic scientists and their supervisors. They are often required to train employees on

Figure 1.4
ASCLD-LAB® responsibilities of quality manager.

- Maintain and update the quality manual.
- Monitor laboratory practices to verify continuing compliance with policies and procedures.
- Evaluate instrument calibration and maintenance records.
- Periodically assess the adequacy of report review activities.
- Ensure the validation of new technical procedures.
- Investigate technical problems, propose remedial actions, and verify their implementation.
- Administer proficiency testing and evaluate results.
- Select, train, and evaluate internal auditors.
- Schedule and coordinate quality system audits.
- Maintain training records of laboratory personnel.
- Recommend training to improve the quality of laboratory staff.
- Propose corrections and improvement in the quality system.

required procedures. The position requires extensive communication and negotiation skills.

Often this position is given a secondary responsibility to safety coordinator. As such, the individual assuming this position should have knowledge regarding chemical and biological safety. They would also be responsible for providing appropriate training to the laboratory analysts.

CRIME LABORATORY DIRECTOR

Eventually, a supervisor becomes proficient with the duties of their position. When this happens, they are promoted to another position. Often this is over a number of disciplines. Other times, it is over an entire laboratory. They may no longer be responsible for performance reviews and quality assurance audits, but they will take on many other duties. For example, they will probably be responsible for proposing and managing a budget – a duty for which they may have no previous experience. They may have to decide which of two needs is greater or if the cost of a particular examination exceeds its value and should be discontinued.

Generally, an individual who has the responsibility of managing an entire laboratory is designated a Crime Laboratory Director. Again, job titles may vary. Other names used are Crime Laboratory Manager, Crime Laboratory Supervisor, Forensic Laboratory Supervisor, or Chief Criminalist.

In addition to overall responsibilities for the direction of the laboratory, other duties of a crime laboratory director include budget oversight and approval of spending recommendations. The laboratory director will also evaluate personnel needs and select or approve which individuals are hired. They are responsible for ensuring that the laboratory effectively addresses the needs and concerns of their stakeholders by developing ongoing relationships with the criminal justice community and public.

A recent development in the necessary duties of all crime laboratory directors is the knowledge of the legislative process. While this was always an important role for crime laboratory system directors, the increased activity of all laboratory directors in the process has required them to become knowledgeable with how they can influence legislation that affects the laboratory's operation.

Most crime laboratories do not require a managerial degree for the crime laboratory director position. If the laboratory has supervisory positions, the individual promoted could have some supervisory skills but may still lack managerial skills such as budgeting. New laboratory directors without management knowledge should seek training that will provide them with the required information.

While it is desirable that a laboratory director should be intimate with the operations of a crime laboratory, the decision to hire individuals outside of the forensic community may also be considered. This individual may bring an entirely different management perspective to the laboratory. If this is the route chosen by the laboratory administration, the new director will need extensive cooperation from their assistants who have forensic experience.

In some laboratories, an assistant crime laboratory director position may exist that assists a laboratory director with the management of the laboratory. However, the laboratory director still retains the primary responsibility for the goals of the crime laboratory. Various delineations of duties may exist that complement each other. For example, the assistant laboratory director may perform much of the day-to-day tasks such as personnel and purchasing matters, while the crime laboratory director focuses on strategic planning and securing resources to facilitate laboratory operations.

LABORATORY SYSTEM DIRECTOR

Often crime laboratories are part of a multi-laboratory system. Laboratories may be located throughout a region, state or country. While each laboratory within the system will have a laboratory director, the system will have a system director. Each laboratory director reports to the system director. The system director has little to do with the day-to-day operations of the laboratory but provide direction for the laboratory as a leader. They determine the priorities of the organization and ensure that their vision is embraced by all in the organization.

A system director must be very active in establishing the relationships that facilitate the effective operation of the crime laboratory system. The system director ensures that all laboratories within the system cooperate and work together toward the same goals. Though usually assigned to "headquarters," the system director must make frequent trips to all the system's laboratories. This ensures that the director is perceived as approachable and that they are concerned not only about the headquarters laboratory but also about all the laboratories within the system.

When the crime laboratory system is the primary provider of forensic services for the state, the system director must be involved with legislators to promote legislation and funding. They must promote themselves as the voice for forensic sciences within the state that they represent.

While all crime laboratory directors feel political pressure from their administrators, a crime laboratory system director is especially vulnerable to this pressure. Often the crime laboratory system operates under the purview of an elected state official. Because this official is so visible and is especially concerned about their political future (retaining their office through re-election) they may make demands of the crime laboratory director. The demand may only be to perform analysis on a case immediately as a favor to a politically connected sheriff. However, laboratory system directors must have a clear sense of ethical principles and be willing to stand by them should they be asked to do something that can be viewed by others as unethical.

SUMMARY

The popular media portrays crime laboratories to be institutions where miracles occur daily. The truth is far less glamorous and far more mundane. Crime laboratories operate under various structures and may be public or private and may be federal, state, or local. Regardless of their span of influence, they all seek to provide quality analysis to the jurisdictions that they serve.

Rigorous controls are required for both forensic analysts and the forensic testing to be accepted in the criminal justice system. Compliance with these requirements is the responsibility of all the employees of the crime laboratory. Additionally, public crime laboratories are required to be responsive to the citizens that they serve by operating in an effective and efficient manner with regard to the funding derived from tax revenues.

REFERENCES

ASCLD/LAB® (2001) Accreditation Manual, ASCLD/LAB, Garner, NC.

DNA Advisory Board (2000) Quality Assurance Standards for Forensic DNA Testing Laboratories. *Forensic Science Communications.* 2(3). Federal Bureau of Investigation, Washington, DC.

Meier, Kenneth J. (1993) *Politics and the Bureaucracy* (third edition). Wadsworth Publishing Company, Belmont, CA.

Wilson, James Q. (1995) Constraints on Public Managers. In: Cigler, Allan J. and Loomis, Burdett A. (eds) *American Politics.* Houghton Mifflin Co., Boston, MA. 419–434.

CHAPTER 2

HUMAN RESOURCE MANAGEMENT

The study of leadership isn't nearly as exact as, say, the study of chemistry. For one thing, the social world isn't nearly as orderly as the physical world, nor is it susceptible to rules. For another, people, unlike solids, fluids, and gases, are anything but uniform and anything but predictable.
(Warren Bennis)

I will pay more for the ability to deal with people than for any other ability under the sun.
(John D. Rockefeller)

INTRODUCTION

The single most important task of the crime laboratory manager is human resource management. The personnel who work in any organization determine if that organization will be successful. In a crime laboratory, the *quantity* of persons employed help determine if cases are worked in a timely manner; but the *quality* of the persons employed determines if they are worked in a quality manner. The character of the person determines how they will approach an assignment and determines if they will take shortcuts that will affect quality when under pressure. While their character is developed from childhood, their development as employees is influenced through their work experiences.

Personnel are the backbone of any organization. How they feel about their job plays a vital role in how the organization runs. Good and bad attitudes directly affect the environment of the workplace. If they are satisfied with the respect, support, and opportunities given to them, if the work environment is pleasant and production expectations reasonable, they will reflect a positive attitude. They will be proud of their work. When asked to do more, they will gladly do it. However, if employees lack motivation or feel betrayed by the leadership, they may develop a negative attitude that will likely spread to others in the laboratory. If they are dissatisfied, they will look for reasons not to be at work. They may take shortcuts or engage in other unethical behavior. They will look for ways to retaliate such as engaging in work slowdowns. When asked to do more, they will refuse or attempt to justify why they can't.

People have many experiences throughout their lifetime, beginning at birth. Social scientists have theorized on why people behave as they do. Genetics, birth order, childhood discipline and trauma, and wealth have all been theorized to be influential factors. In reality, all these play a role in building a person's character traits. Certain traits are generally considered more desirable for forensic scientists than others. Obviously, someone who seeks recognition above all else may be well suited for acting. But as a forensic scientist, they may be willing to call a match with insufficient evidence just to be recognized for their contribution to solving a crime. While a laboratory director cannot influence a person's core character, they can influence employees in either positive or negative ways. They have the power to produce productive and ethical employees. Conversely, they also have the power to produce indifferent employees who work only toward retirement.

An organization reflects the character of its leader. The organizational culture in different agencies can be traced to their leaders. In a crime laboratory, if a laboratory director is perceived as inflexible and disgruntled, employees will also develop these traits. If a laboratory director is perceived as proactive, the forensic scientists may be more willing to try new techniques. If the director is approachable, the forensic scientists will be more eager to approach them with new ideas. The attitude of the director influences a laboratory long after they are gone. When a crime laboratory director retires or leaves, their attitude is perpetuated for many years in those that they influenced as they are promoted into leadership positions.

PERSONAL LEADERSHIP

Bennis and Nanus (1985) discuss the difference between managers and leaders. "Managers," they say, "are people who do things right and leaders are people who do the right thing." Managers, they say, seek to maximize efficiency – task-oriented activities. Leaders on the other hand seek to maximize effectiveness – goal-oriented activities. The Gallagher-Westfall Group conducts training for law enforcement organizations. They summarize the difference as outlined in Table 2.1. They conclude that "Managers care for the body of the organization; leaders care for the spirit; but truly great leadership does both."

Leaders develop a vision for their organization. Bennis and Nanus interviewed 90 individuals that they considered to be leaders. They found through these interviews that all possessed a compelling vision that drew people to them. A leader is passionate about their vision. They are focused on the outcomes that will fulfill their vision. A crime laboratory director's vision may be to change a mediocre laboratory into one that is recognized for its analytical accomplishments. To make this vision reality they must take specific actions.

Managers	Leaders
Managers do things right	Leaders do the right thing
Managers focus on the tangibles within the organization	Leaders focus on the intangibles within the organization
Managers are referees	Leaders are coaches and cheerleaders
Managers focus on what to do	Leaders focus on how to do it
Managers pronounce	Leaders facilitate
Managers are responsible	Leaders are responsive
Managers have a view on the mission	Leaders have a vision of the mission
Managers view the world from the organization	Leaders view the organization from the world
Managers manage from the chateau	Leaders lead from the trenches
Managers focus on what to say	Leaders focus on how to say it
Managers lack a gut stake in the enterprise	Leaders have a gut stake in the enterprise
Managers are preserving life	Leaders have a passion for life
Managers are driven by constraints	Leaders are driven by goals
Managers look for things done wrong	Leaders look for things done right
Managers run a cost center	Leaders run an effort center
Managers are quantitative	Leaders are qualitative
Managers are program-centered	Leaders are principle-centered
Managers initiate programs	Leaders initiate on-going, never-ending processes
Managers develop programs	Leaders develop people
Managers are concerned with efficiency	Leaders are concerned with efficacy
Managers sometimes play the hero	Leaders play the hero no more

True leaders share their vision with their employees. Their enthusiasm for the vision encourages others to embrace it as well. Their employees are aware of what the leader feels is important for the organization to run effectively. In 1998, the American Society of Crime Laboratory Directors bestowed its Briggs J. White Award for "Excellence through leadership in Forensic Science Management" to Bruce Vander Kolk of the Illinois State Police Forensic Sciences Command. Vander Kolk was nominated by his employees based on his vision for excellence that propelled the Illinois State Police system to one of the most highly regarded in the country. The supervisors and forensic scientists who work for Vander Kolk are encouraged to participate in professional organizations. Many go on to hold leadership positions in those organizations.

While Vander Kolk shared his vision and led the Illinois laboratory system into a place of great esteem, other states lack an executive who encourages others to follow them. They may not participate in outside organizations or encourage their staff to do so. These laboratory systems may lag behind in advancing new technologies as professional organizations provide opportunities for training as well as networking. Employees participating in organizations will likely provide suggestions on techniques utilized by other laboratories that can improve in their own.

Table 2.1

Managers and leaders.

Leaders are committed to their vision. Their commitment to making the vision reality compels their daily behaviors to be consistent with the vision. As they share the vision with their employees, the employees always know that the leader will respond in a consistent manner. This consistency establishes the trust that is essential to an effective organization. Forensic scientists who trust that their laboratory director will be open to ideas on improvement because this is consistent with their vision to be more willing to communicate their ideas and concerns. Through this open exchange, the laboratory director can take steps to improve the laboratory and be true to their vision.

SELF-AWARENESS

Before a crime laboratory director can lead others, they must know themselves. Throughout history, philosophers have reiterated this philosophy. In *The Art of War* (1983), Sun Tzu states, "So it is said that if you know others and know yourself, you will not be imperiled in a hundred battles." Shakespeare advises "To thine own self be true." In a modern management text, Bennis and Nanus (1985) state that leaders generally recognize their strengths and compensate for their weaknesses. A common myth is that leaders are born. In reality, the skills possessed by leaders can be learned. Individual strengths can be emphasized and weaknesses compensated for. Knowing this makes it possible to change. The realization that people possess shortcomings and that change is possible, is fundamental to personal growth.

It takes more than self-awareness to overcome weaknesses. Action must follow realization. People must realize that unless they change, they cannot be as effective as they desire in either their professional or personal lives. With this realization, initiative must be added. This initiative often takes courage. It is not easy to step out of a comfort zone and it is much easier to allow a mediocre situation to exist than it is to change it. However, a laboratory cannot become an excellent working environment without constant attention by the laboratory director. In order for the director to focus attention on the laboratory, they must be familiar with their own tendencies of behavior.

Everyone has preferred tendencies of behavior. These preferred tendencies both strengthen and weaken the ability to perform specific tasks. Behavioral tendencies that weaken job performance can be strengthened through actions. For example, some tasks such as public speaking require extroverted tendencies. If an individual accepts a position where they must often speak in public and they are aware that they are introverted, they can take small steps to become more extroverted. This may involve finding courage to speak out in a meeting or speaking directly to someone rather than relying on e-mail.

Many make the traditional New Year's resolution to overcome weaknesses, and most break them shortly thereafter. Whether the resolution is to exercise every day or to lose weight, they quickly fall into their old habits. It is said that new behaviors take 21 days to become habits. If not practiced every day, people return to habits that they have developed in the past. It is much easier to keep the same habits than to change. If a person can continue to function with a weakness, they will not seek to improve it. This supports the supposition that people will not change until the pain of staying the same is greater than that of changing. If a laboratory director is confronted with a crisis borne from their own bad habits or poor judgment, personal change takes on a new urgency not previously present.

All people have control over some things but no control over others. While the weather cannot be controlled, a person's own behavior definitely can be. While there are circumstances in which people find themselves that they certainly did not choose, they do have a choice in how they respond to these situations. Positive behavior during these incidences earns respect from others.

Often people find themselves in difficult situations due to decisions that they make. When this occurs, respect is earned when they accept the consequences of their actions and learn from their mistakes. If the unethical actions of a laboratory employee place the laboratory in an embarrassing situation, the crime laboratory director is faced with many choices. They may try to cover it up, justify the employee's actions, or accept the situation and use it as an opportunity for improvement. If their own action or inaction contributed to the situation, they gain the respect of others by admitting their contribution and accepting the consequences. Individuals and organizations profit when permanent change is undertaken to improve a bad situation.

Myers-Briggs

In order to achieve permanent changes in behaviors, it must first be determined what needs to be changed in order to improve deficiencies. There are many diagnostic tests available to determine personal behavioral profiles. The tests usually involve responding to a series of questions that categorize particular traits. The Myers-Briggs categorizes individuals by their preferences for performing certain tasks. Using Myers-Briggs, individuals are broken into one of 16 different profiles based upon four basic preferences: *Energizing* (where people get their energy); *Attending* (what people pay attention to when they get information); *Deciding* (what system people use to make decisions) and *Living* (what type of life people adopt).

An individual's Energizing preference may be introversion or extraversion. Introverts draw on energy from inside themselves while extraverts draw from outside themselves. Introverts are not inclined to share their thoughts and ideas while extraverts enjoy sharing what's on their mind. In the book, *Lifetypes,*

Sandra Hirsh and Jean Kummerow (1989) distinguish between the Energizing preferences as presented in Table 2.2. Introverts prefer "quiet time" and feel drained when they are required to participate in a number of events. Extroverts, on the other hand, feel energized when they are busy with activities. Extroverts are happiest in careers where there is a lot of interaction between people. Introverts tend to choose careers that allow them time to individually concentrate on facts. For this reason, many introverts are drawn to the sciences, and a crime laboratory may employ more introverts than extroverts.

Table 2.2

Energizing preferences: how and where energy is obtained.

Extrovert	Introvert
Projects energy out; making actions easy for all to see	Keeps energy inside, making it difficult for others to know them
Absorbs self in activities	Absorbs self in thought
Focuses outwardly toward activity and action	Focuses inwardly toward thoughts and ideas
Speaks freely and vocally	Hesitates before speaking and proceeds cautiously
Tolerates crowds and noise	Avoids crowds and seeks quiet
Easily distracted	Concentrates well
Meets people readily and participates in many activities	Proceeds cautiously in meeting people and participates in selected activities
Enjoys a public arena with lots of activity	Enjoys a private arena where they can be alone
Becomes restless without involvement with people or activities	Gets agitated without enough time alone or undisturbed
Acts quickly	Reflects and acts in careful way

An individual's Attending preferences, how they get information, are sensing and intuition. Sensing relies on obtaining information using only the five senses, whereas intuition refers to consideration of what might be or could be. Hirsh and Kummerow describe Sensors as using "a realistic pragmatic and exact standard when accepting information." Intuitives tend to pay more attention to their internal instincts. Table 2.3 shows the Attending preferences as outlined by Hirsh and Kummerow. Whereas Sensors tend to enjoy professions that require attention to details, Intuitives often enjoy the professions that rely more on using ideas to develop paths for the future and building relationships. Good decision-making requires that both preferences be utilized. If a crime laboratory has all Sensors, although there will be great attention to detail, there may be a lack of employees who naturally seek creative solutions for the future.

Sensing	Intuition
Uses direct observation and first-hand experiences	Uses "intuitive flashes"
Learns new things through imitation and observation	Learns new things through general concepts
Values solid, recognizable attainments, achieved in a step-by-step manner	Values different or unusual attainments, achieved via inspiration
Focuses on actual experience, discounting information that comes through the imagination	Focuses on possibilities and inferences, discounting information that comes through direct observation
Trusts five senses and experiences to know what is and is governed by that	Trusts inspirations and hunches to reveal what might be and is governed by that
Is content, accepting life as it is and makes changes as reality dictates	Is restless, seeing how life can be different and tries to modify it
Gets annoyed when things are left too much to chance, preferring precise and exact information	Gets annoyed when things are too clearly defined, preferring approximations and generalizations.
Appreciates and enjoys traditional and familiar ground	Appreciates and enjoys new and different experiences
Behaves practically	Behaves imaginatively
Becomes creative through effort and perspiration	Becomes creative through insight and inspiration

Table 2.3

Attending preferences: information-gathering techniques.

An individual's Deciding preferences may be thinking or feeling. Decision-making using the thinking preference involves a logical and objective approach whereas the Feeling preference involves a personal approach. Hirst and Kummerow distinguish between the types in that "Thinking types use an impersonal, objective ordering system in order to find a standard of truth. Feeling types tend to be concerned with finding what is of value or what is important to themselves or others." The Deciding preferences as outlined by Hirsh and Kummerow are presented in Table 2.4. Thinkers tend to select careers where analytical analysis is preferred whereas Feelers select careers where value is placed on personal interactions. Crime laboratories will generally attract Thinkers because of the need to rely on empirical data to reach legally defensible conclusions. An interesting note regarding the Deciding preferences is that two-thirds of women prefer the Feeling preference. With the large infusion of women into the forensic sciences, it will be imperative for a crime laboratory director to interact with Feeling types as well as Thinking types in order to ensure an effective working environment for all. Presenting only objective data to employees to support managerial decisions will not be sufficient for those who prefer value-based decisions. Or, if a laboratory director is themself a Feeler, they must be prepared to present data to support their value-based decisions.

Table 2.4

Deciding preferences: decision-making system.

Thinking	Feeling
Has truth as objective	Has harmony as objective
Decides more with their head	Decides more with their heart
Prefers on principle to question others' findings, believing their findings may be inaccurate	Prefers to agree with others' findings, believing people are worth listening to
Views encounters with others as having a purpose	Views encounters with others as friendly and important in themselves
Notices ineffective reasoning	Notices when people need support
Chooses truthfulness over tactfulness	Chooses tactfulness over truthfulness
Critiques and points out the negatives, overlooking the positive	Overlooks people's negatives points, stressing areas of agreement
Focuses attention on universal principles	Focuses attention on personal motives
Deals with people firmly as required	Deals with people compassionately
Expects world to run on logical principles	Expects the world to recognize individual differences

Finally, the Living preferences, what lifestyle a person adopts, are judgment and perception. Judgment refers to living a planned and organized life and perception is living in a more spontaneous and flexible manner. Hirsh and Kummerow state that "Judgers set a course of action and run their lives accordingly," whereas "Perceptive types like to adapt and move with the flow of life and they prefer a tentative approach to it." Their outline of Living preferences are presented in Table 2.5. The working styles of each type differ in that Judgers prefer structured, organized work settings while Perceptives enjoy more flexibility. Many forensic disciplines exist that satisfy both of the Living preferences. Judgers may prefer a position analyzing controlled substances because the large volume of work allows for planning of work activities. Perceptives may enjoy a crime scene investigation position where their schedule and priorities change with each telephone call.

Table 2.5

Living preferences: type of life that is adopted.

Judgment	Perception
Prefers life to be decisive, imposing their will upon it.	Seeks to adapt their life and experience what comes along
Works for settled life, with their plans in order	Keeps life as flexible as possible so that nothing will be missed
Prefers to reach conclusions	Prefers to keep things open
Uses words such as "should" and "ought" liberally, on themselves and others	Uses words such as "perhaps," "could be," and "maybe" in regard to themselves and others
Enjoys finishing things	Enjoys starting things
Desires to be right, to do the right thing	Desires to have many experiences and miss nothing
Regiments themselves and is purposeful and exacting	Is tolerant and adaptable

Myers-Briggs' individual behavioral tendencies are based on combining one of each of the four preferences. While details of each of the 16 types is beyond the scope of this text, many references exist that elaborate on the individual types. No type is any better or worse than another. When an individual relies on one tendency over another, it can lead to shortcomings in personal or professional skills. If any behavior is extreme, the opportunity exists for improvement by minimizing the reliance on that behavioral tendency.

DISC

Another widely used behavioral profile system is the DISC (Dimensions of Behavior Personal Profile) System. DISC categorizes behavioral tendencies in four categories. DISC is an acronym for the four categories of behavioral tendencies that the system distinguishes between: Dominance, Influence, Steadiness, and Compliant. As with the Meyers-Briggs tendencies, all DISC tendencies have strengths and weaknesses. To determine their own behavioral tendencies, individuals choose words that most closely relate to them. Individuals are rated as high or low in a specific category depending on their tendency to use the behavior. Individuals may rely on more than one of the behavioral categories. For example, an individual may be a "DC" if they equally use both Dominance and Compliant behavioral tendencies.

According to the DISC personal profile system, the Dominance tendency refers to placing emphasis on "shaping the environment by overcoming opposition to accomplish results." Individuals that rate high in the Dominance category are fast-paced and results-oriented. They seek authority and take command of situations. They make fast decisions to solve problems. Often however, those who rate high in the Dominance category do not recognize the needs of others and may come across as demanding. Additionally, they may make decisions too quickly without consideration of all necessary data. Using the original *Star Trek* series as a basis for examples, Captain Kirk is an example of a high "D." He enjoyed the freedom of operating light years away from Star Fleet command and often violated the "Prime Directive" in order to accomplish a goal. It is often advantageous for a leader to have high Dominance tendencies in a military setting or one in which quick decisions are imperative. However, a crime laboratory director who exhibits too much Dominance tendencies can be perceived as autocratic and opinionated.

The Influence tendency puts emphasis on "shaping the environment by influencing or persuading others." Individuals high in the Influence category are fast-paced and people-oriented. They tend to be very outgoing and enjoy participating in a group. They have an optimistic attitude and are enthusiastic about projects. However, Influencing individuals are not detail-oriented and often over-delegate a project. Often their projects are not completed either because they do not pay attention to the details or because they have spent too much time socializing. Dr. McCoy is a high "I." McCoy enjoyed interacting with other crew members and was quick to share his thoughts, whether they were requested or not. In a crime laboratory, employees with high Influencing tendencies may spend a lot of time talking to others and require close oversight to ensure that they have sufficiently documented their casework. They can also be the informal leaders of the laboratory because of their charisma: others are drawn to them and may embrace their opinions. Laboratory directors should work to ensure that these employees share their vision instead of opposing it.

The Steadiness tendency places emphasis on "cooperating with others to carry out the task." These individuals are slow-paced and people-oriented. They are very hard working and work well with others. They are considerate and make excellent instructors because of their patience. However, individuals high in the Steadiness category can be highly possessive of information and resist change. The *Enterprise*'s chief engineer, Scottie, is a high "S." Scottie was a hard worker and always came through in a pinch. He preferred to repair the equipment himself or as part of a team rather than delegating the work. In a crime laboratory, employees with Steadiness tendencies are the team players and are considered to be "nice" due to their desire to please others. While they may resist change, they also avoid confrontation and are likely to perform all assigned tasks. This also can make them vulnerable to the will of others and less likely to share their opinions about an unacceptably bad situation with their supervisor.

The Compliant (also referred to as Competent, or Conscientious) tendency places emphasis on "working conscientiously within existing circumstances to ensure quality and accuracy." Individuals in this category are generally slow-paced and results-oriented. They are analytical in their approach to problem-solving and tend to collect a lot of data. Often this makes them reluctant in reaching decisions. While they will delegate a task, they tend to micromanage to ensure that it is done "correctly." Spock was the high "C" of the *Star Trek* crew. He logically reached decisions by collecting analytical data. A lot of forensic scientists have Compliant tendencies. While they can be relied upon to follow the rules and carefully document casework, they may feel a need to collect an over-abundance of data prior to reaching a decision and be slower at completing their duties. Crime laboratory directors with high Compliant tendencies must be aware of their tendency to micromanage others. When overused, this tendency can result in a lack of trust among employees and damage the working environment.

Behavioral profiles not only let people understand themselves but also allow them to better understand the differences of others. It is important to understand that everyone in the crime laboratory is different from everyone else. When the crime laboratory employees all realize that everyone's strengths and weaknesses differ, they are willing to compensate for someone else's weaknesses and accept that someone else will compensate for their own. They also realize that others add to the overall success of the laboratory in a way that is different from their own. Not any better or worse, just different.

There is no best behavioral type for a particular situation or career position. Everyone has specific tendencies that can make tasks seem easy or hard. One very important requirement for forensic scientists is analytical ability. While some may find it easy to record every detail of an examination in a systematic manner, it may be a challenge for others. On the other hand, these non-analytical individuals may be very creative and devise new procedures for approaching problems. It is the laboratory director's challenge to ensure that the "non-analytical" forensic scientist takes detailed notes but it is equally important to challenge the "analytical" forensic scientist to think creatively.

In a crime laboratory, as with any work environment, there are many different types of people: not just outward appearances but also behavioral types. Organizational effectiveness is achieved when people are aware of their tendencies, as well as the tendencies of others. It is important that each recognizes the contributions of the others. Teams made up of different types of people that are respective and appreciative of the varied strengths that the others bring to the unit can be very productive and overcome the weaknesses intrinsic in each other.

TIME MANAGEMENT

Crime laboratory directors are faced with many demands for their time. The demands include daily, weekly, and long-term decisions and tasks. Examples of daily or short-term tasks include answering routine questions from employees, administrators, law enforcement officers, prosecutors, students, and other internal or external stakeholders. Other daily tasks may include prioritizing, assigning, and reviewing casework, ensuring coverage for technical and administrative tasks, and general troubleshooting of "emergencies." Weekly, monthly, or medium-term tasks may include overseeing purchases, personnel training needs, compiling and issuing administrative reports. Long-term tasks include planning and overseeing facility improvements or construction as well as achieving strategic plan objectives and goals.

In order to accomplish everything, a laboratory director must manage their time. Their time management process may be an informal list-making process of all tasks that need to be completed or it could utilize a complex computerized program that reminds them when tasks are due. Because of the wide range of tasks that require attention, the most popular time management systems include a prioritization of tasks. While listing activities on a daily basis helps to accomplish the short-term activities, it often ignores the medium and long-term activities that demand completion.

Stephen Covey presents a time management matrix for scheduling priorities, not prioritizing schedules. The matrix is based upon the urgency and importance of the task. Tasks that are "urgent" seek immediate attention but are not always important. Tasks that are "important" contribute to accomplishing goals and

	Urgent	Not urgent
Important	**Quadrant 1 tasks** Rush cases Cases with court dates Crime scene investigations Personnel misconduct	**Quadrant 2 tasks** Strategic planning Instrument preventative maintenance Routine casework Training/employee development Stress-reduction activities
Not important	**Quadrant 3 tasks** Some requests for information Some mail/telephone calls Interruptions	**Quadrant 4 tasks** Time-wasting activities Some mail/telephone calls Gossip

Figure 2.1

Covey time management matrix as a basis for common crime laboratory tasks.

make a difference but are not always urgent. Figure 2.1 illustrates how Covey's time management matrix accommodates common crime laboratory tasks.

The matrix is broken into four quadrants. Quadrant 1 tasks are urgent and important and are composed of crises and pressing problems. When an individual spends too much time on these activities, they may become highly stressed and may quickly burn out. Examples of the Quadrant 1 tasks that crime laboratories commonly encounter are responding to frequent requests for rush cases because of large backlogs or providing knowledgeable personnel to immediately respond to crime scenes.

Quadrant 2 is composed of tasks that are not urgent but are important. These usually are preventative or planning activities. They also include building relationships with others. Because they are not urgent they are commonly forgotten in lieu of other, more pressing problems. When planning is not accomplished, more Quadrant 1 tasks may develop. If planning is not performed to reduce the backlog, a laboratory will continue to respond to requests for rushes which will result in employee burnout. Regardless of the temptation to put these tasks on the back burner, performing Quadrant 2 tasks may minimize future crises.

Quadrant 3 tasks are urgent but not important. These usually involve requests from others. Often, answering a telephone fits into this quadrant. The ringing telephone seems to require an urgent response, but often the telephone call is not important. Focusing on these tasks results in feeling out of control and individuals constantly find themselves taking care of incidents moment to moment. Any planning that may have taken place is ignored because there is no time for it.

Quadrant 4 activities are neither urgent nor important. They may be pleasant but essentially waste time. If too much time is spent on these tasks, nothing will be accomplished. These activities include idle gossip or unnecessary busy work. In order to make the most of the time available, Covey promotes using discipline to avoid the unimportant tasks found in Quadrants 3 and 4. He endorses spending time on the non-urgent but important activities as found in Quadrant 2 to minimize the urgent and important ones in Quadrant 1.

Regardless of the time management system selected, all crime laboratory managers should utilize a system. In addition, they should promote its use to the other employees in the crime laboratory. Whether the individual is balancing time between administrative reporting and personnel evaluations or between casework and quality assurance processes, they must have an organizational process to ensure that all tasks are completed as required.

STRESS MANAGEMENT

Stress management is another technique important for all crime laboratory employees. No matter how much planning is undertaken to prevent incidents from occurring, there will always be events that cannot be controlled and will cause stress. The breakdown of a critical piece of instrumentation just when it is needed for a high-profile rush case can cause stress on both the analysts and the laboratory director.

An individual's nature will influence how they respond to stress. Some may allow it to overwhelm them while others seem to have little concern for it. Others claim that they do their best work under pressure. Everyone has their own way to relieve stress; some good and some bad. Ethical concerns can arise when stress is reduced through destructive techniques such as excessive alcohol consumption.

Sewell (2000) suggests that in order for stress reduction programs to be successful they must include:

- proper diet and nutrition to maximize the body's capacity to handle stress;
- cardiovascular fitness to reduce the impact of stress and to foster the body's proper response to stress;
- outlets outside the job, such as hobbies or travel, to allow an emotional and psychological escape from job issues;
- sufficient rest and relaxation to allow the body's restoration from stress; and
- stress-reduction techniques such as relaxation responses, yoga, or tai chi, which can restore emotional balance.

A crime laboratory's administration can help its employees positively counter stress in a number of ways. Many organizations have access to generalized training programs available to jurisdictional employees. Many city and state governments have training units whose primary function is to provide training. These units can be secured to provide stress management training to all members of the crime laboratory.

Additionally, a crime laboratory can provide organized outlets for exercise and teambuilding by organizing activities outside of the work environment. These activities may include team sports such as softball or volleyball teams that compete against other community groups. If the laboratory or its parent organization is large enough, they may also organize a "tournament" where units compete with each other. The laboratory administration should actively support their team by encouraging participation and recognizing its successes.

It is important for crime laboratory employees to take advantage of vacation leave in order to restore their energies. Most crime laboratories have at least one employee that does not fully utilize their vacation time. These employees risk burnout when they spend all their time at the laboratory. A crime laboratory director should encourage employees to use their vacation time.

Finally, many public agencies have access to Employee Assistance Programs. These units provide crime laboratory employees with assistance for many concerns. They provide counselors to assist individual employees with financial, addiction, or other psychological issues. Employee Assistance Programs can be equally valuable in helping a unit or entire laboratory deal with a tragic incident such as sudden death or violence in the workplace.

HIRING

One of the most difficult tasks that a crime laboratory director must do is to hire employees. While one would like to believe that there is a foolproof technique that will achieve acquiring the perfect employee, there is no guarantee. While experience is often sought for new employees, it is usually a person's basic character traits that will make them a good employee. The way that they approach casework and cooperate with others may be more important in the long run than whether they can immediately begin performing case analysis. Many of the traits that are consistent to outstanding employees are not taught in classes but are an intrinsic part of the individual.

When a vacancy occurs in a crime laboratory, it is the beginning of a difficult process for the crime laboratory director, staff, and applicants. Since most crime laboratories are public agencies, the hiring process is rigorous and long. The process may take as long as six months or a year. Most include many steps that an applicant must successful pass in order to be considered for a position. The steps may include submitting a resume, completing an application, passing a written knowledge examination, undergoing a personal history background investigation, passing a polygraph examination, passing a pre-employment drug screen, and participating in one or more interviews with various staff members.

Many applicants who begin the process do not complete it. A candidate may decide that the position is not worth the work required to obtain it. In this case, it is possible that the candidate may not be willing to do the work required of them after they are hired, and the laboratory may not be the ideal environment for them. Also, the laboratory management may determine that the applicant is not suitable for the position based upon the results of the background investigation or other phase of the application process. Because of the large number of applicants required to fill one position, it is important to recruit as many individuals as possible for a vacancy.

Recruitment for a position can be accomplished in many media. Advertisements in local media such as newspapers, radio and television are traditional means of attracting applicants. However, this recruitment approach has many limitations. The focus may be too broad and the individuals not of sufficient education and background for the position. Also the pool of candidates will be limited to those within a certain geographical radius and may not provide an adequate number of suitable candidates for a highly specialized position such as forensic scientist. To reach a more focused audience over a broader geographical area, a crime laboratory director should seek recruitment opportunities in professional publications, colleges with forensic science programs, and forensic science Internet sites.

The evaluation of candidates begins from the first contact. If a candidate's mother calls to get information regarding the position, this may be an indication that the applicant is either too timid or not willing to perform the work necessary to be an effective employee. If the applicant's resume has errors, it may be an indication that they are not detail-oriented. On the other hand, if the candidate's application is overly detailed, it can be an indication that they will be slow employees with a tendency to over-document or to over-scrutinize every decision.

Agencies may require that applicants pass a basic knowledge written examination before or during consideration for a position. There are positive and negative aspects to this approach. The test provides an objective measurement of knowledge because all applicants are required to answer the same questions. However, the questions must be sufficiently broad to avoid excluding acceptable candidates. Most scientist positions in crime laboratories have general descriptions such as forensic scientist or criminalist. Entry-level positions require one of several natural science degrees. If a standardized examination is given to all applicants for all forensic scientist positions, it cannot be weighted with biology questions specific to DNA analysis or chemistry questions specific to drug identification.

A laboratory can instead choose to prepare examinations for specific positions. Applicants for DNA positions would be asked questions concerning molecular biology and applicants for drug identification would answer questions concerning mass spectrometry. The questions still must be broad enough to allow those with no specific experience in a crime laboratory to have an equal chance to compete for entry-level positions.

Standardized tests can also limit the pool of applicants available for a position. In some jurisdictions, applicants must pass a competitive examination presented by a civil service administration during a specific period of time. Only the applicants who have participated and passed this test are eligible for a position. The laboratory director must interview and rule all applicants unacceptable before another test can be given. This process limits the laboratory's ability to hire candidates for a specific discipline.

Most crime laboratories require other "tests" in addition to the interview. Background investigations, polygraphs, and drug testing are common requirements for applicants. If an applicant's performance at any phase reveals unacceptable behaviors, they can be eliminated from consideration. It is not at all uncommon that 50 percent of applicants do not complete the selection process.

PREPARING FOR THE INTERVIEW

Yate (1994) describes that employees should be able to perform the job, willing to perform the job, and can be managed while performing the job. One's ability to perform the job is measured through their education and experience. Often this is the sole factor on which employment decisions are based. However, many laboratory directors have been disappointed to find that the "most qualified" applicant has negative qualities that make them difficult to manage. In addition to being able to perform the job, they must be willing to do the job. The stereotypical government employee is one who does only what is required for only the time that is required. Laboratory directors understand that much more is required from a forensic scientist. Employees must be more than able to do a job, they must be willing to work with others to complete a case, and go out of their way to offer assistance and advice to law enforcement officers. Finally, even if an individual is able and willing to perform the job, if they can't accept advice or criticism or if they don't communicate important issues to management, they may prove to be too difficult to manage.

In evaluating an applicant's ability to do the job, an interviewer should consider how an applicant's previous experience contributes to the responsibilities of the position. An applicant for a forensic scientist position should be able to relate how their previous experience is applicable. Many entry-level applicants have little more than a college degree. Their only experience with the instrumentation is in a teaching laboratory. It is important to establish if these applicants truly understand the theory behind the instruments and their overall role in the analysis of physical evidence. If an applicant has had an internship with a crime laboratory, they should be able to expound on the theory of the instrumentation as well as understand its role in the analysis.

The educational background required for a position in a crime laboratory will vary depending on which discipline the position is in. In the past, forensic scientists performed analyses in several areas. When laboratories operated in this way a general degree was beneficial. As the analyses became more complex and the legal scrutiny more intense, the need for specialization arose. In today's crime laboratory, forensic scientists may spend several years learning a discipline before ever signing a case report. If an applicant is hired to fill a specific position, it is advantageous for them to be satisfied with the position. If their education has prepared them for a DNA position, they may not be satisfied with a drug analysis position. This dissatisfaction could result in their resignation from the laboratory or their transfer to the DNA section. Either situation results in an unnecessary training period.

The educational requirements for analysts performing casework have also become more stringent. Federal guidelines set by the DNA Advisory Board require that analysts performing DNA analysis have classes in genetics, biochemistry, and molecular biology. Scientific working groups in all disciplines have published recommendations for analysts working in specific disciplines. While a new employee may be permitted to take required courses early in their career, it is advantageous for them to possess the education upon taking the position.

An applicant's communication skills are vitally important to their ability to be a successful crime laboratory employee. A forensic scientist must be willing and able to share information with their supervisor and fellow employees. They cannot be timid about asking for help nor can they be officious in demanding it. One of the most important duties for a forensic scientist is to present their findings in a court of law. The individual not only must not be afraid of public speaking, they must also be able to explain complex scientific concepts in lay terms.

Communication skills are important for other employees of the laboratory as well. Evidence intake employees are the first and most frequent contacts for law enforcement officers submitting evidence. If these individuals are rude, they reflect poorly on the laboratory. The same is true for all laboratory employees who interact with the public. Receptionists, secretaries, and property room staff must be courteous and be aware of the need for proper customer service.

In order to determine if an applicant is willing to do the job, questions must be asked to determine if they are willing to do the whole job. Some candidates apply based on television shows or other fantasy ideas of what a forensic scientist does. When confronted with the actual job duties, they may be less than willing to accept the limitations. If the applicant believes that they will assist at crime scenes, they may be dissatisfied with a position in which they rarely leave the laboratory. If they believe that they will strictly be conducting casework, they will be dissatisfied when they are also required to perform instrument maintenance.

In addition to the routine duties applicants must be willing to perform, they must also be willing to follow the quality assurance guidelines of the job. An applicant must be made aware of the documentation required in the position. If the applicant is not detail-oriented, they may not see a need to fulfill these strict requirements. If this is the case, they will need constant oversight to ensure that they are complying with the requirements. This will be frustrating for both the supervisor and the employee and could lead to a poor working relationship.

All employees must be able to work as a team and be willing to assist others as necessary. If an applicant prefers to work alone or feels that they do not need the assistance of others, their attitude may create an uncomfortable working environment. Their lack of communication will cause others to avoid communicating with them. This will isolate them even further and create a poor working environment.

Applicants must be willing to operate under stressful conditions in an organized fashion. Forensic scientists are often put in a position of completing an analysis in an expedited manner. This requires that they work with other sections to complete all the required analysis on an item of evidence. If they are not willing to cooperate or cannot cope with stress, they can damage the analysis and fail to provide useful information that will lead to the identification or arrest of a guilty party.

Finally, applicants must be willing to make their own decisions that could lead to the conviction and possibly affect the life of another. The results issued by forensic scientists affect the lives of suspects and victims. While convictions are not solely based on their findings, physical evidence plays an increasingly important role. An applicant must take this role seriously. They cannot be over-zealous and make identifications for which insufficient evidence exists just to secure a conviction. Nor can they be over-timid and fail to make a call just to secure an acquittal.

All crime laboratory directors must be concerned with how easily an employee can be managed. Applicants should be hired on the supervisor's ability to manage them. As with marriage, a supervisor should not expect that an employee can or will change. If a manager prefers that others operate independently, they should avoid those who need constant encouragement. If they prefer to be deeply involved in processes, they should avoid those who prefer to work alone. The personality traits that individuals possess are an intrinsic part of them. Most are neither good nor bad even though they may conflict with a manager's traits. Careful consideration should then be given to an applicant's behavioral needs and the supervisor's ability to respond to them.

Investigating why an applicant is seeking employment can reveal important insight into an applicant's ability, willingness, and managability to perform the job. If an individual is currently working in another crime laboratory, this line of questioning can reveal areas of concern. Disagreements with their current supervisor may indicate future discontent with any supervisor's decisions. If they are unhappy with the quantity of work they are required to perform, it may indicate an unwillingness or inability to perform an acceptable amount of work in any laboratory. Disagreements with fellow employees could indicate that they will have difficulty with any fellow employees.

If the applicant was previously employed at a crime laboratory but is now working elsewhere, it is important to determine why and how they left employment. Terminations as well as simply seeking another position may reveal either lack of ability to perform the job or differences with management. Both should be of concern to a crime laboratory director. Whether or not the applicant is forthcoming with reason, it is important to hold a discussion with previous employers. Checking with references may lead to the discovery of additional information about the candidate.

Yate outlines personality traits to evaluate when hiring an employee. Depending on the position, some of the traits may be more important than others. For example, a forensic scientist must have highly developed analytical skills. It is important that they are able to follow precise procedures in a detailed manner. And while a forensic scientist supervisor must also have analytical skills, it is arguably as important that they possess outstanding communication skills.

Yate breaks down these traits into Personal, Professional, and Business Profiles. These traits are presented in Figure 2.2. The Personal Profile reveals an individual's basic character. Among these traits are drive, motivation, communication, chemistry, energy, determination, and confidence. The Professional Profile reflects on an individual's ability to behave in a professional manner and includes reliability, integrity, dedication, pride, analytical skills, and listening skills. The traits that compose the Business Profile reflect an individual's awareness of business operations. Those traits that make up the business profile include efficiency, economy, procedures and profit.

Due to low salaries, many crime laboratories hire mostly recent college graduates. These applicants are seeking a position that will allow them to utilize their education. Most of these applicants have minimal work experience and

Personal profile traits

- *Drive* – Does the individual have the desire to get things done? Do they focus on the goal rather than tasks? Can they break down overwhelming tasks? Do they avoid busy work? Can they make a decision?
- *Motivation* – Does the individual have enthusiasm for the job? Are they willing to ask questions? Can they motivate others to do a good job through their own interest?
- *Communication* – Can they talk and write to people at all levels?
- *Chemistry* – Do they have a positive attitude? Do they accept responsibility for their own actions? Do they cooperate with others and draw a team together?
- *Energy* – Do they apply extra effort in small as well as important matters?
- *Determination* – Can they cope and continue during difficult times? Can they be assertive yet not aggressive?
- *Confidence* – Are they friendly and honest with all employees? Can they keep a secret when appropriate?

Professional profile traits

- *Reliability* – Is the individual self-reliant yet keeps management informed? Do they not rely on others to ensure that a job is well done?
- *Integrity* – Do they take responsibility for own actions, whether good or bad? Do they make decisions in the best interests of the organization, not for personal achievement?
- *Dedication* – Does the individual follow through on their commitment to tasks and projects and do what is necessary to complete the project on time?
- *Pride* – Does the individual have pride in their profession? Are they willing to pay attention to the details and ensure high quality work?
- *Analytical skills* – Does the individual carefully analyze a situation and consider all solutions including short and long-term benefits and negatives before selection? Does the person possess the perception required that leads to good judgment?
- *Listening skills* – Does the individual possess good listening skills? Are they attentive?

Business profile traits

- *Efficiency* – Is the individual conscience of resources and minimizes wastages of time and money?
- *Economy* – Can the individual differentiate between expensive and cheap solutions to problems?
- *Procedures* – Will the individual work within the established procedures? Are they willing to keep management informed and follow the chain of command? Will they not implement their own "improved" procedures or organize others to do the same?
- *Profit* – For private laboratories, are they aware that this is what keeps the laboratory in business?

Figure 2.2

Personality traits to consider with applicants.

many have never even seen a crime laboratory. Some may have been researching job opportunities and thought that a crime laboratory may be an "interesting" place in which to work without any knowledge of what will be expected of them. It is very difficult to judge these individuals' willingness and manageability. It is important not to base hiring decisions strictly on grades earned in school. Grades may provide a false indication of their true value as an employee and should only be considered as a part of the equation. Interview questions should address their understanding of crime laboratory operation and expectations. Applicants should be asked to provide examples from the past when they exhibited initiative either in school or other jobs as well as what their goals are for the future and what they have done to achieve the goals. Also, their analytical approach to problem-solving can be revealed in many aspects of their life.

Interviewing applicants can take many forms. Initially a telephone conversation with the applicant can be used to determine if further interviewing is worthwhile. An individual's communication style as well as interest in the position can be determined. The interview should also answer questions that the applicant may have. Based upon the answers, the applicant may withdraw themself from the process.

Prior to interviewing, a crime laboratory director must determine the most important traits that the position requires in addition to the basic education and experience requirements. The questions asked during the interview should draw out the traits that are important for the position. For example, if an analytical approach to problem-solving is important, the director may ask the applicant to give an example of a problem that they faced. The question should always be followed up with why they found it difficult, where they turned for help, and how they overcame the problem. Particular attention should be given to the approach that was taken when resolving the problem.

CONDUCTING INTERVIEWS

Once a crime laboratory director has determined what traits and knowledge is important for a candidate, they should design the interview. Where the interviews take place can be as important as what questions are asked. If the interview is held in the crime laboratory, the forensic scientists who will be working with the candidate have the opportunity to interview them in a laboratory setting. This can provide insight into how comfortable they are with their surroundings as well as their future fellow employees. They will be aware of the conditions into which they will be coming to work.

The interview participants may include the laboratory director, a personnel specialist with knowledge of legal restrictions on interviewing, a law enforcement administrator if the laboratory is located within a law enforcement agency, the unit's senior forensic scientist or supervisor, or other analysts. For other positions, such as the position of crime laboratory director, it may be advantageous to invite other directors to assist with the interview. This provides external opinions and is useful if the agency is looking to change the direction in which the crime laboratory is currently progressing.

The questions asked of applicants should be thought through and aimed at soliciting responses that will provide insight to the traits that the director feels are important for the position. If the laboratory director feels that integrity is the most important trait, they should ask questions that requires the applicant to provide examples of ethical decision-making.

During the interview, closed-ended questions such as "Do you work well with others?" should be avoided. Instead, open-ended questions such as "Tell me about a time when you had to work with others as a team" should be used. Follow up with questions about which persons with whom they worked well, and why; also, persons with whom they had conflicts, and why. Be careful not to ask too many questions at once but follow one with the other. Closed-ended questions can be asked if they are followed by open-ended ones. "Do you consider yourself to be an organized person?" should be followed with "Tell me about a time when you were faced with a number of competing priorities." And if they do not include how they resolved the situation, ask as a second follow-up question.

When phrased properly, questions provide insight into how an applicant has reacted in the past in similar situations. This likely will dictate how they will react in the future. If you are interested in how easily an individual can be managed, ask a question such as "Tell me about an incident in which a decision that you made was questioned by your supervisor?" or "Tell me about a decision that your supervisor made with which you disagreed." Be sure to follow the question with ones that will draw out the specific traits in which you are really interested: "How did you react? Why did you disagree? Did you tell him/her your point of view?"

Often, when faced with these types of questions, an applicant will hesitate to answer. They should be given time to think about the question. Most people are uncomfortable with silence and will be prompted to provide an answer. The answer given under these conditions will be one that they have not rehearsed. Instead of framing the answer to be what they believe you want to hear, it will be a more honest response on how they feel about a situation.

An applicant's answers may beg for more explanation. For example, an applicant may announce that they disagreed with an employer's evaluation. One way to obtain more information is to rephrase the question and wait. "So you felt that the evaluation didn't properly reflect your work?" Usually, the candidate will expound without additional questions. If the applicant's response reveals a major concern, asking about a similar situation may confirm the belief.

Another widely used technique is to ask loaded questions in which the applicant must decide between two similar choices. This technique is useful in determining how a forensic scientist may respond to an ethical dilemma. "How would you respond if an officer needed a test result for a toxicological procedure quickly but the controls were outside laboratory guidelines?" The director should be wary of the applicant who responds that they would let the supervisor decide. They may find themselves continually making decisions for this employee. Another loaded question that reveals how an applicant would behave in general is, "Do you tend to make decisions too quickly or too slowly?" An applicant is faced with revealing a negative about themselves and will generally hesitate before answering. Those who say they tend to make decisions too slowly may need to be prompted to completing tasks more quickly. Those who make decisions too quickly may be less aware of details and require extra oversight to insure that they are thoroughly documenting data.

An interviewer should always practice good listening skills. After a question is asked, allow the applicant sufficient time to think about the question and answer. Some candidates may be overly talkative. The interview can be progressed by interrupting the candidate with a response such as, "That makes me want to ask you about . . ." A talkative candidate should be handled with care. Be aware that should this individual be hired, their tendency to talk a lot may present problems in the future.

If a face-to-face interview is desirable, a number of techniques may be employed. The applicant may be asked to perform some aspect of the job while on a tour of the facilities. Entry-level candidates who are being considered for controlled substance analysis may be asked to assist with an instrumental procedure to determine how easily they take instruction. Candidates with experience can be asked to conduct a more detailed examination if time permits, such as identifying an unknown fiber. Another situational exercise for an applicant would be to describe the operation of a familiar instrument as if they were testifying in court.

When interviewing candidates for police officer posts, many law enforcement agencies subject the candidates to stressful situations. The questions are presented in an adversarial way to provoke a reaction from the applicant. The interviewer then evaluates the candidate's behavior under stress. While this technique may be used with forensic scientist applicants, they are rarely under the same stress as police officers and it may not be as applicable.

The behavioral style of employees is very important to assure that they will fit with the existing personnel. Through careful observation and thorough questioning, the basic character of a person can be revealed. Many interviewers believe that neatness and accuracy in completing paperwork reflect on a person's attitude toward the job. An applicant who submits a resume with many mistakes may not be sufficiently focused on details. As this is an important factor for forensic scientists, managers should be wary of these individuals or be prepared to accept their limitations.

There is no singular best type of person to hire as a forensic scientist. All people have strengths and weaknesses to add to an organization. It is important that the other employees recognize the strengths of others. The individuals who are not detail-oriented tend to be more creative. These individuals have great ideas but sometimes lack the desire and ability to carry them out. However, too many detailed persons in a crime laboratory may hinder the creative process. Additionally, they tend to operate slower than the creative individuals and may increase the backlog that exists in most laboratories.

LEGAL CONSIDERATIONS

In the United States, federal legislation applies to hiring requirements for individuals. Included in this legislation is Title VII of the Civil Rights Act of 1964, the Americans with Disability Act of 1990, and the Age Discrimination Act of 1967. Many crime laboratory directors employ or have access to human resource professionals who are familiar with these requirements. Figure 2.3 lists questions that should be avoided in order to comply with the federal requirements.

Figure 2.3

Interview questions to avoid.

What religion are you?

What church do you attend?

Are you married?

Do you have children?

Do you plan to start a family?

Are you a citizen?

What country do you come from?

What is your maiden name?

Do you have a disability that will prevent you from doing this job?

Will your disability interfere with your ability to do this job?

How many days were you sick last year?

Do you have (name of disease)?

How old are you?

When did you graduate from high school or college?

In addition to these federal requirements, each jurisdiction has specific requirements that their agencies, local, and state governments mandate. Hiring practices of laboratories vary from simple consideration of resumes and interviews to written examinations, polygraphs, and drug screens.

Most laboratories require a particular level of education prior to employment. However, if a laboratory is located within a law enforcement agency, there may be positions that have historically been filled by sworn officers. This is especially true for firearms and latent fingerprint examiners. In this situation, the laboratory director may be required to follow rules of placement that govern officers. Generally this consists primarily of seniority, although special qualifications may sometimes be considered.

Laboratory directors may also be faced with the "political" hire. This sometimes occurs when an administrator or elected official has a friend or relative who seeks employment. While this can be a unique situation, the individual should be required to meet the same entry requirements as any applicant. Once hired, they should be held to the same standards as other employees.

TRAINING

After an employee is hired, a significant factor in their development is training. A general training program must be developed for all new hires. This should cover all administrative, safety, and quality assurance processes at the laboratory. It should be general enough for clerical as well as technical employees. Some of the things to be addressed are safety orientation, understanding of policies, evidence handling, property transfer protocols, accreditation requirements, contamination control.

When establishing training programs, employees must meet specified performance objectives. A training program must consist of performance objectives to be met, outline how the objectives will be taught, including specific learning activities such as reading and exercises, and finally, a demonstration of competence to exhibit that the employee has learned the performance objectives. Individual development plans can be useful in the employee training process. A development plan includes goals, measurements, actions, and assistance.

Goals should be clear and specific. A goal for a new forensic scientist should go beyond "completing casework independently." A goal should include what knowledge, skills, and abilities an employee will have developed when they reach the goal. Goals for a forensic drug analyst may include knowledge of instrumentation theory, laws governing drug analysis, and quality requirements.

Measures are the standards which indicate that the person has met the goals.

For example, a measurement that would indicate that a forensic scientist has achieved the goal of instrument operational knowledge would be for the analyst to perform routine maintenance independently.

Actions are the tasks performed that will assist an individual to develop the knowledge, skills, and abilities required to achieve their goals. An analyst striving to become competent in instrument operation would observe others performing maintenance, read instructional manuals, perform maintenance under close supervision, and finally independently perform the task.

Assistance includes what the mentor or supervisor needs to do to help the employee with development. This may include on-the-job training, external training programs, or feedback about their progress.

A discipline-specific training program must be established for all employees. This training program will be used for new hires as well as transfers from other disciplines and those in need of remedial training. Items in this program should include procedures commonly used in this section. Some of the things to be addressed are principles of methods and instrumentation, interpretation of results, maintenance of instrumentation, references to read, practicals to perform, legislation pertaining to discipline, competency tests to demonstrate competency, mock trials, and a formal recognition of training.

For new hires with little experience, it is advantageous to assign a senior analyst to mentor the individual. This could be the section supervisor or another analyst who has considerable experience in the section. The individual who acts as a mentor should be approachable so that the trainee is comfortable asking questions or bringing problems to them. The mentor should also be comfortable in sharing their feelings about the trainee with the laboratory director. The director needs to be aware of problems as soon as possible so that they can be corrected. Unfortunately, some problems may be uncovered that cannot be corrected. If the individual has problems that cannot be corrected, management should take steps early on to terminate the individual. Most agencies have a probationary period. Once the probationary period has expired, it is more difficult to dismiss an employee. Management should therefore begin the termination process during the probationary period.

Mentors should also possess a positive attitude toward the goals of the laboratory and management. New hires will develop the same attitudes as their mentor. If the mentor talks positively of the administration, new employees will be satisfied with their situation. On the other hand, if they hear constant criticism of the administration, the negative attitude will be perpetuated in this employee as well. In addition to their trainer, the new employee will make friends with other analysts in the laboratory. They too will be influential with the new employee. Understanding this makes it important for a crime laboratory director to address negative issues as they arise.

In smaller laboratories, the situation may occur where there is only one knowledgeable analyst in a discipline. Should that person leave the laboratory, a new hire would not have the opportunity to have a mentor. In these situations, it is necessary to either hire a technically knowledgeable analyst who has had training elsewhere or to ensure that a mentor from another agency is available to a lesser experienced analyst. Even if a new hire has training from elsewhere it is worthwhile to establish a relationship with a more knowledgeable analyst so that questions can be asked and ideas can be shared.

During the training process, the new hire should be exposed to outside training as well as on-the-job training. This provides an analyst with an opportunity to discuss techniques with forensic scientists from other laboratories with different perspectives on analytical procedures. There are many training opportunities at regional and national forensic science meetings and workshops. However, with limited training budgets, this is sometimes difficult to accomplish. Some meetings can be extremely expensive to attend and may not provide the level of training necessary for an inexperienced analyst. Meetings should be evaluated based on the level of training necessary for the analyst requesting to attend. It may be more valuable for a new analyst to attend a more expensive one-week course that focuses on one instrument than for them to attend a less expensive two-day regional forensic science meeting where various papers are presented that do not present in-depth training.

Another option to reduce costs but yet provide specialized training is to share the costs of regional training with several laboratories. The Forensic Science Institute of Ohio is an organization primarily composed of crime laboratory directors and created for the sole purpose of providing quality training for Ohio's forensic scientists. The organization identifies a need within the member laboratories and arranges for instructors to present training. Often costs are low because the training is held at a member laboratory and travel costs are minimal.

Often training can be included in the purchase of an instrument. Most instrument purchases include a short familiarization session. A crime laboratory director may consider including a week-long course for all analysts on theory and operation with the purchase of the instrumentation. If a federal grant is used to purchase instrumentation, the grant application should include sufficient funding to provide training on theory and operation of the instrument.

Many laboratories take advantage of local colleges and universities to provide training opportunities for analysts. Analysts may be permitted to audit courses in exchange for instruction in others. The placing of interns may also be the basis for exchanges. Many organizations also have tuition reimbursement programs for employees. Employees who take work-related coursework at a local university receive reimbursement for the tuition. Forensic scientists can either take a single course or work toward an advanced degree using this benefit.

Distance learning via the Internet or correspondence is a developing training opportunity. As there is no travel, costs are kept low. Students have the opportunity to ask questions through chat rooms or e-mail. Many college courses are provided in this manner. If college credit is provided for these courses, tuition may be covered through an agency's tuition reimbursement program.

Agencies must establish policies regarding college coursework. Agencies may or may not allow personnel to attend classes during work hours. If they do not, it may be necessary to vary hours in order to allow an analyst to attend a course that will be beneficial for both the analyst and the laboratory.

DEVELOPING PEOPLE

As an employee develops in their job performance, they will progress through various degrees of ability and attitude. Because of the changes employees experience at each developmental stage, they require different management approaches. Forensic scientists who have many years of experience should not need the same level of oversight as new hires. Blanchard and Hersey (1982) theorized that the leadership style of the manager varies according to the development level of the employee. They termed this "situational leadership." Table 2.6 outlines the appropriate leadership style for each level of development.

Development level	Appropriate leadership level
D1 Low competence High commitment	**S1** DIRECTING Structure, organize, teach and supervise
D2 Some to low competence Low commitment	**S2** COACHING Direct and support
D3 Moderate to high competence Variable commitment	**S3** SUPPORTING Praise, listen and facilitate
D4 High competence High commitment	**S4** DELEGATING Turn over responsibility for day-to-day decision-making

Table 2.6

Leadership styles appropriate for the various development levels.

The development level is based on competence and commitment. New employees with little experience have high commitment but low competence (D1). They are excited to start a new job and perhaps a new career. They have a lot of confidence and a lot of motivation and interest in the position. However, they do not have the knowledge and skills that they need to perform the job. A lot of oversight and direct supervision are required at this level. This "directing" style of leadership (S1) involves teaching in a structured manner with specific directions and close monitoring. During this stage of development, a mentor should work closely with the employee and an individual development plan should be adopted. Employees at this stage of development require a great deal of feedback concerning their job performance. Honest feedback corrects concerns quickly and, if given in a positive manner, perpetuates the employee's high level of commitment.

As the employee progresses, they will face challenges. They may fail a competency test or have challenging cases and lose confidence in their abilities. Their commitment may decrease to moderate or low and their competence remains low to moderate (D2). At this level, the manager needs to coach the employee with both a directing and supportive style (S2). At this level it is important to closely monitor the employee but also to provide support by recognizing accomplishments and asking for input from the employee. Supervised delegation of simple tasks should have more guidelines and require frequent updates. If errors are made, consequences should be immediate.

Long-term employees who are highly competent with their jobs may lose motivation due to being overburdened or under-recognized. Many crime laboratory employees are at a high competence, low commitment level (D3). Because they are competent in their jobs, they do not need close direction but only need to be supported in their duties. A manager needs to recognize and support the accomplishments of these individuals with a "supporting" leadership style (S3). They should also be provided with the opportunity to assist in laboratory decision-making as recognition that they are considered to be valuable to the organization. Additionally, if they are not already overburdened, their job duties can be made more interesting and their commitment level raised by assigning them challenging new tasks.

The individuals at a high competence and high commitment level (D4) need very little direction and independently find motivation without constant recognition. A "delegating" style (S4) is appropriate for these individuals. While occasional monitoring and support are necessary, daily decision-making can be turned over to these employees, as they require little of the manager's time. A manager can delegate complex tasks with few guidelines and less frequent reporting requirements to these individuals.

The leadership needs of an individual may change depending on the task.

An experienced forensic scientist who is changing disciplines may require a "directing" style on scientific procedures but "delegating" for chain of custody, evidence handling, and administrative tasks. Managers should be aware that for all new tasks, an employee needs a higher level of direction. They should also be aware that even forensic scientists with high commitment and competence can lose commitment if not recognized occasionally for their service.

DELEGATION

As an employee develops in their job performance, a manager should be able to increasingly trust them to perform routine tasks. A manager may also delegate special projects to employees to assist with their development. When delegating to employees with low competency levels, there are several steps that should be followed to ensure that the task will be completed to the manager's satisfaction.

First, the manager should clearly communicate what the goal of the project is and what the successful completion of the project will consist of. The manager should also clarify why the task is necessary, and its importance. The employee should be informed of any complications that they may experience during the performance of the task.

Second, the manager should grant the employee authority required to perform the task. This will allow the employee to perform the task without challenges from others. The manager should also provide the employee with the resources that they will need to complete the task. In addition to financial resources, the employee may need additional training or other avenues of obtaining information.

Finally, the manager should obtain the employee's commitment for the project. The manager should ensure the employee understands their expectations for the successful completion of the task, including any timelines for completion. Even when delegating to an employee with a high competence level, a director should ensure that they understand what is necessary for successful completion.

EVALUATIONS

Most crime laboratories require that employees be rated on their performance. Often salaries and promotions are tied to these performance evaluations. Appraisals often include ratings on quality of work, quantity of work, cooperation with others, and initiative. If the crime laboratory is part of a larger organization, the evaluation form may be very general in nature. The laboratory director should include tasks within the broad categories that are specific to the crime laboratory. ASCLD/LAB® accreditation requires that the testimony of each analyst be monitored. This can be incorporated into the evaluation of a forensic scientist. Testimony evaluations may include the analyst's ability to convey scientific concepts in an understandable manner, appearance, demeanor, confidence, voice, eye contact, technical competence. Care should be taken to ensure that the analyst doesn't overstate their qualifications or conclusions. Further new employees should be observed by a supervisor or a more experienced analyst. More experienced analysts can be evaluated by an officer of the court such as a judge, prosecutor or defense attorney. It should be noted that prosecutors and defense attorneys often may evaluate an expert witness based on the benefit 00to their side of the argument. A prosecutor may give higher marks to an analyst if they win the case. If too much weight is placed on the testimony evaluation, it can tempt an analyst to present biased information to get a positive evaluation. Because of this, it is beneficial for even experienced analysts to be evaluated by supervisors at times.

Employees should be initially directed on what is expected from them. This should consist of written performance objectives. These goals should reflect the mission of the organization. The performance objectives should be mutually agreed upon by both the laboratory administration and the employees whose work will be judged against them. The objectives should be such that a manager can evaluate a forensic scientist's competence and commitment based on these objectives. Much consideration should go into setting the objectives, as this will determine what activities are set as priorities. If an employee is only judged on the number of cases they work, they will work a lot of cases. It is possible that the quality of the analysis will suffer or other tasks such as instrument maintenance or procedure development will not be performed.

Evaluations can be intimidating to both the reviewer as well as the employee. The employee may be concerned that they will not fulfill the expectations of their supervisor and the supervisor may be concerned that the employee will be dissatisfied and conflict will occur. An evaluation should not be the first indication to an employee that they are not performing well. At that point, the employee does not have time to correct a deficiency before it appears on a permanent record. A supervisor should confront a problem situation early so that the employee has an opportunity to correct it and to prevent it from growing into an uncontrollable problem.

Performance appraisals can take many forms. While the traditional process is an appraisal from a superior, many new evaluation processes have evolved. An appraisal may include input from peers as well as other stakeholders such as police officers and prosecutors. They may include self-appraisals or, for supervisors, input from employees.

Blanchard and Johnson (1983) discuss one-minute praisings and reprimands. This approach allows immediate recognition of good and bad behavior.

The steps presented by Blanchard and Johnson are listed in Figure 2.4. Blanchard *et al.* (1985) tie praisings and reprimands into the situational leadership model. They say, "Praisings foster improvements in the development level of individuals and permit a manager to gradually change his/her leadership style from more direction (directing) to less direction and more support (coaching and supporting) to less direction and less support (delegating)." They go on to say that new employees need praise and recognition when they are "approximately right." When training a new employee they should be recognized at many steps in their progress. They will lose commitment if they are not praised until the end of their training period.

One-minute praisings
1. Tell people up front that you are going to let them know how they are doing.
2. Praise people immediately.
3. Tell people what they did right – be specific.
4. Tell people how good you feel about what they did right, and how it helps the organization and the other people who work there.
5. Stop for a moment of silence to let them "feel" how good you feel.
6. Encourage them to do more of the same.
7. Shake hands or touch people in a way that makes it clear that you support their success in the organization.

One-minute reprimands
1. Tell people beforehand that you are going to let them know how they are doing and in no uncertain terms.
2. Reprimand people immediately.
3. Tell people what they did wrong – be specific.
4. Tell people how you feel about what they did wrong, and in no uncertain terms.
5. Stop for a few seconds of uncomfortable silence to let them "feel" how you feel.
6. Shake hands or touch people in a way that lets them know that you are on their side.
7. Remind them how much you value them.
8. Reaffirm that you think well of them but not their performance in this situation.
9. Realize that when the reprimand is over, it's over.

Figure 2.4

One-minute praisings and one-minute reprimands.

Blanchard *et al.* (1985) state that "Reprimands stop poor performance and may mean that a manager has to gradually move back from less direction and less support (delegating) to more support (supporting) or more direction (coaching and directing)."

Another way to evaluate employee performance is based on the Johari

Figure 2.5
Johari Window

	Known to self	Unknown to self
Known to others	Public	Blind
Unknown to others	Hidden	Unknown

Window. The Johari Window (Figure 2.5) was developed by Joseph Luft and Harry Ingham to describe the dynamics of communication and trust.

When conducting evaluations, an employee should initially be asked to list their strengths. Most of the ones that they list will be known to the supervisor. This information falls in the "Public" square and can be easily agreed upon since it is known by both the employee and the supervisor. A supervisor's recognition of these mutually agreed upon strengths affirms the employee's belief of their level of competence. For example, a forensic scientist's belief in their ability to take detailed notes will be supported by the supervisor's recognition of the same attribute. When these easily-agreed-upon strengths are initially discussed, they allow the evaluation to begin on a positive note.

While most of the strengths fall in the "Public" square, there will be some strengths that the supervisor is aware of that the employee had not considered. These constitute "Blind" information. When the supervisor brings these up, they will continue to build the employee's confidence in their abilities.

After the employee's strengths are discussed, the evaluation should shift to opportunities for improvement. When the employee is asked to list where they believe room for improvement exists, there will be some "Public" information where both the employee and the supervisor agree. There will also be some areas that the employee discloses that the supervisor was unaware ("Hidden" information). The supervisor and employee should agree on goals for improvement for both the "Public" as well as "Hidden" items.

There will also be "Blind" areas of improvement which the supervisor is aware of that the employee did not list either because they are unaware of the area or they fail to interpret it as a concern. If the supervisor brings up their concerns, the employee may become defensive or may discount the concern as an opportunity for improvement. Therefore, unless the behavior is harmful to the organization, it may not be advantageous for the supervisor to raise the concern. Instead, they should set a plan to improve mutually agreed upon opportunities for improvement.

The last square of the Johari Window includes "Unknown" information that is unknown to all parties. It includes information that has yet to be discovered and, until revealed, no action can be taken to address it.

TROUBLE-SHOOTING PERFORMANCE PROBLEMS

Poor performance and unacceptable behavior should be identified and corrected as soon as possible. If allowed to continue, the managerial acceptance of the performance/behavior will set precedence with other employees that the behavior is acceptable. Common practice of an unacceptable behavior will then decrease the effectiveness of the workplace.

If a significant problem is observed during an employee's probation, the crime laboratory management faces a difficult decision. If they honestly believe that the behavior should be corrected, corrective action should be taken at the first sign to concern. However, they should also not be afraid to use the probationary period as it is meant to be used: as part of the selection process. Intense pre-employment screening usually ensures that forensic scientists meet high standards of integrity and conduct. However, it cannot always be predicted how a person will interact with others or behave after being hired.

After a performance or behavioral problem has been identified, the manager should evaluate the situation and determine what steps should be taken. Effective decision-making involves several steps. First, the nature of the problem should be clearly defined. Performance problems and behavioral problems may be handled in entirely different manners. When clarifying the problem the contributions of all involved parties should be considered.

Second, collection of reliable information is imperative to reaching a defensible decision. In order to adequately collect information, a manager may have to interview others and gather appropriate documentation.

Next, all possible decision options that will solve the identified problem should be considered. During this stage, it may be advantageous to discuss the situation with other managers to expand the available options. The manager should be conscious of the confidentiality issues surrounding the situation and use caution when determining with whom they discuss the matter.

The manager should then decide on an option to pursue. They should be aware of their own pre-existing biases that may influence their decision. Decisions regarding personnel always allow an opportunity for review by others, including the employee; or, if discipline is involved, by others involved in the disciplinary process. Therefore, the manager should document the factors used in reaching the decision and possibly why other factors were not considered to be significant in reaching a decision.

After the decision is implemented, the manager should evaluate the decision. If it involves a series of steps, the decision should be evaluated at intervals in the process. If the decision is not having the desired corrective effect, it should be re-evaluated and additional information considered.

When a performance problem is identified, the manager should ask a series of questions in determining what steps to take.

1. *What is the nature of the problem?*

   The problem should be well understood to the manager.

2. *Does the person have the knowledge/skills to do the work?*

   The manager should identify the skills needed, including technical and organizational skills. If the employee lacks these skills, training should be provided to them. Additionally, they should be provided with an opportunity to obtain experience on performing the task with the help of a mentor to provide feedback regarding their progress. The manager should set short, progressive deadlines for the employee to exhibit that they are acquiring the necessary knowledge and skills.

3. *Does the person have the attitude/belief to perform the work?*

   If this is a concern, the manager should provide the analyst with a role model to work with them to increase their confidence.

4. *Does the person have the emotional capacity/motivation to do the work?*

   This is a difficult area for a manager to effect improvement. The manager will be required to provide considerable coaching to the analyst giving immediate feedback on what is and is not acceptable. Additionally, the employee has to be willing to improve.

5. *Does the person have the ability to learn the work?*

   If not, the manager should be prepared to terminate or compensate for the employee. If the deficiency is discovered during their probationary period, termination will be easier than if it is discovered later on. However, if the manager has set progressive deadlines, they may have collected the documentation required to support termination. If termination is not an option, the manager may consider reassigning them to another position. However, the manager should be aware that other employees in that section will be unwilling to compensate for the employee, just as the employees in the first section had probably been.

6. *Does the employee have the tools necessary to do the work?*

   If not, the manager should give the employee the tools or devise a way around it.

7. *Does the employee have positive incentive for doing the work?*

   If not, the manager should build incentives into the system or, at least, remove disincentives from interfering with the work.

Behavioral problems should be considered differently from performance problems. When behavioral problems are identified, Carr and Fletcher (1990) suggest that a manager ask the following questions when considering appropriate action.

1. *Exactly what unacceptable behavior is the employee/organization exhibiting?*
   It is important to clarify the exact nature of the behavior in order to adequately address it.

2. *Is the behavior serious or merely irritating?*
   If the behavior is not serious, the manager should caution the employee or group that it is not appropriate, and if it doesn't improve, stronger measures will have to be taken. The manager should document all warnings in preparation for future discipline. If the situation does not improve and begins to have a noticeable effect on the unit, the manager should be prepared to implement more serious measures.

3. *Is the employee/organization aware of the rules in this area?*
   If not, the employee should be informed regarding the rules and the consequences for not following those rules. Again, the warning should be documented.

4. *Is the behavior critical to the organization or to the safety/well-being of other people?*
   If the behavior puts people in immediate danger, the manager should do whatever is necessary to protect the safety of others, including calling the police. Once the situation is under control, termination or other appropriate discipline should be sought.

5. *Does the behavior undermine your authority or the basic supervisor/subordinate relationship?*
   If the behavior cannot be corrected through counseling or discipline, it may be necessary to transfer or terminate the employee in order to avoid further challenges to the manager's authority.

6. *Is the behavior deliberate?*
   If the deliberate behavior is more than simply irritating although not critical to organizational effectiveness or employee safety, the manager should take steps to correct the behavior through counseling and ultimately through the disciplinary process.

In order to improve an employee's behavior or performance, the employee and the manager should agree on an individual development plan. The plan can be implemented either as part of a performance appraisal or upon the identification of a behavioral or performance concern. The plan should include a timeline for completion of specific tasks or review of the employee's behavior that will indicate compliance to the plan. If the employee does not comply with the due dates assigned, the manager should first assume that the problem was with the plan. The manager should meet with the employee and clarify their expectations and ensure that the employee understands what is required. The manager should document all meetings in which the plan is discussed.

If the employee still has difficulty meeting the manager's expectations, the manager should again discuss the situation with the employee. At this point they should consider the system in which the employee is operating. If there are obstacles to completion, such as a lack of training, the manager should work to remove these obstacles. Additional timelines for completion should then be set and documented.

If the employee still does not improve, they represent a serious threat to maintaining the effectiveness of the organization and the manager must be prepared to undertake assertive problem-solving. This may include "last chance" due dates and progressive discipline. Most public crime laboratory managers must meet a number of requirements in order to justify termination of employees. Generally the disciplinary process is detailed and time-consuming. By following the above plan, the manager will already have several issues of non-compliance documented and the termination process can be expedited.

RESOLVING CONFLICT

Many forensic scientists are represented by bargaining units or unions to negotiate for benefits as well as to handle grievances with management. These bargaining units represent interesting situations for the crime laboratory director. Their primary purpose is to ensure fair treatment for their members. Often their ideal of fairness differs from management's ideal. Even if forensic scientists are not represented by a bargaining unit, a crime laboratory director must often work with employees to resolve a conflict of opinion.

When two sides with differing opinions must agree on one outcome, the best solution that will satisfy all parties is likely different from either original idea. This mutually beneficial outcome is generally referred to as a win/win solution. A high level of trust must exist in order for win/win solutions to be reached. If either party does not trust the other, they are likely to feel that any solution proposed will be harmful to them while benefiting the other party. This will lead them to become defensive and unwilling to resolve differences.

When attempting to settle a disagreement, negotiation often takes place between parties. In order to successfully negotiate a mutually beneficial solution, both parties must see the problem from the other party's point of view. This may take considerable communication and time. Often the positions held by each party are addressed where the issues and concerns are not. This is discussed later in this chapter. When the concerns and issues have been identi-fied, the parties can then determine what results would be acceptable to both. In order to reach these results, new options can be presented. This can be done by brainstorming or other creative techniques.

Established goals provide objective measurements for an employee to strive for. But what if the employee does not agree on the goal. It is possible and highly probable that an employee does not agree with the goal. This may be either a quantitative number of cases or discontinuation of an "unacceptable" behavior. How does a supervisor enforce a goal that the employee truly believes is unreasonable?

At these times it is important to "negotiate" with the employee. When negotiations are undertaken, the supervisor should be willing to enter into them with an open mind. If the supervisor is open to understanding the employee's opinion, the employee may be willing to be open to the supervisor's opinion. This openness is difficult for all parties. There may be a lack of trust that will contribute to the difficulties.

In order to successfully negotiate with another party, Fisher and Ury (1991) cite four steps to be followed. These include separation of the people from the problem; focusing on interests, not positions; inventing options for mutual gain; and insisting on using objective criteria.

SEPARATE THE PERSON FROM THE PROBLEM

The first and most important point is to separate the person from the problem. It is important to focus on the problem, not on the people presenting the problem. It is important to remember that everyone is human, with human emotions. Most people come from different backgrounds and hold different values. They react differently and may react unpredictably when they feel that a threat has been made against them or something they hold valuable.

Negotiation can be difficult when one person perceives a situation differently from another. In order to effectively negotiate a solution, each must understand how the other perceives the situation, as well as how they perceive the other person and their motives. If they feel that they are being treated unfairly, they will look for evidence to support their beliefs. When a crime laboratory director is in a negotiating situation, they should put themselves in the shoes of the other person to understand why they feel that way. Additionally, the manager should look for opportunities to act inconsistently with the other person's beliefs. It is helpful to discuss the perceptions that are held by both sides. This will help both sides understand the other. Perceptions will not change overnight just by discussing them. To change other people's perceptions, actions should continually challenge beliefs.

Negotiations can be successful even if there is a lack of trust. However, relationships that have been built on trust and respect over time can make negotiation smoother. When individuals work together to reach a solution that embraces the values of both, they will be more inclined to accept the proposed solution.

Because individuals hold deeply held beliefs, when threatened, they can become emotional. They may raise their voice or become quiet, they may even cry. Each must allow the other to express their emotions. When one person expresses that they feel unfairly treated and why they feel this way, they should be allowed to talk without interruption. The negotiator doesn't have to agree with their position, just try to understand it from their point of view.

FOCUS ON INTERESTS, NOT POSITIONS

Second, the focus of negotiations should be on the interests of the parties, not the positions that they represent. While positions may be opposite, the underlying interests may be the same. The underlying interest of a forensic scientist and a supervisor is a high-quality work product. However, the forensic scientist may believe that this is not possible if they have to work a certain number of cases per month. When negotiating a solution, the focus should be on the quality of the analysis. Both sides will have alternative solutions among which there may be a mutually beneficial solution.

Determining the interest behind the position is similar to peeling an onion. The position presented may represent several interests. When determining what interests a position represents, it is important to ask why a position is supported. Based upon their beliefs, an employee's interests may not be the same as the director's. However, when considering interests, the basic human needs are often at the base of all positions. These include:

- Security.
- Economic well-being.
- Sense of belonging.
- Recognition.
- Control over one's life.

Identification of interests is more likely when each side is allowed to express themselves freely. Each should voice their interests but not belittle those of the other side. Acknowledgment of their interest as important in the negotiations will increase the chances for agreement. Negotiations that are based on the interests of both parties will be likely to satisfy both. While the final outcome may not fully satisfy the positions of either, the solution will deal with the underlying interests and beliefs of both. One side can hold firm to their principles while being flexible by considering an alternative solution.

OBJECTIVE CRITERIA

Finally, agreement should be based on an objective standard. Research should be done to determine what standards exist that could be applied to the disagreement. Such objective standards may include precedent, professional standards, scientific judgment, cost, efficiency, legal judgments, moral standards, equality, tradition, or reciprocity.

When applied to the scenario of the forensic scientist who did not feel that they should be held to a specific number of cases per month, data could be collected from other crime laboratories to determine the standard in the community. The data may show that while other laboratories do not require their analysts to report a certain number of cases per month, they are required to keep track of their time.

Objective criteria allows a principled basis for reaching an agreement that is less vulnerable to attack. Participants should both be open to applying appropriate standards to the problem. They should be willing to incorporate these standards into an agreement.

COMMUNICATION PROBLEMS

When discussions do not seem to be progressing toward a solution, it can be a result of several problems. The individuals may not be talking to each other but to a third party. If individuals are trying to persuade others to share their cause, negotiations will be difficult. A crime laboratory director should not discuss a problem with an employee in a group setting. Negotiation will be threatened, as the employee as well as the director will be trying to impress the others in the group. Instead, the director should ask the employee to discuss the problem after the meeting.

Another problem in communicating happens when one person is not listening to the other but thinking about what they will say when it is their turn. If they do listen, there is still a chance that they will misinterpret what is being said. In order to overcome communication problems, participants should practice active listening. First, really listen to what the other person is saying. Asking them to spell out exactly what they mean. If there is any uncertainty, ask them to repeat what they said in different terms.

To make sure that there is a clear understanding of how the employee views the situation, the director should listen until they understand the employee's perceptions and needs. At this point the director should acknowledge what they are saying. Generally this is done by rephrasing what the director understands them to say. It should be said in a positive manner. If it is not correct, the employee should be given a chance to correct the misperceptions.

When the employee's point of view is understood, the director can then speak of their own. The director's stand should not be criticized while they state their point of view. The director should also ensure that the employee understands their point of view. This can best be accomplished in an environment free of distractions and in a private forum.

BRAINSTORMING

Once the underlying interests of each party are understood, options can be explored that will mutually benefit both. Brainstorming is a commonly used technique for creative problem-solving. Brainstorming allows for many options to be raised without judgment or criticism.

Prior to beginning a brainstorming session, a small group of participants should be selected. Generally five to eight persons allow for individual participation and generate many ideas. The group should agree on what goal they expect to achieve with the session. Ideally, the session should be conducted in an informal, comfortable manner in a location separate from the routine. A facilitator should also be chosen to encourage participation while enforcing agreed-upon ground rules.

During the brainstorming session, participants should not be seated facing each other in an adversarial position. Rather, they should all face a board on which the problem is presented. The participants should agree upon ground rules. The most important rule for any brainstorming session is that no criticism be allowed, as it discourages presentation of ideas. Even wild ideas can provide the basis for a reasonable one from another participant.

During the session, each idea generated should be written on a board or newsprint that is clearly visible to all participants. This will allow others to build on ideas and generate additional ones. The goal is to develop as many ideas as possible and confront the problem from all angles. One suggestion to stimulate the imagination is to project slides of unrelated images to stimulate the imagination.

After all suggestions have been made, the most promising ideas should be marked for later consideration. These ideas may even be improved upon through discussions. A separate meeting may be useful to fully develop these ideas.

Brainstorming sessions can be used for generating ideas before a negotiating session with the other side; or, if the two parties are comfortable with their shared interests, they may be willing to undergo a brainstorming session to supplement negotiation sessions.

Solutions generated through brainstorming or other methods should take into account the interest of both parties. Shared interests should be identified if present, as they will make the negotiations easier. However, different interests can also be mutually beneficial. For example, during contract negotiations, a forensic scientist bargaining unit may feel that an increase in pension rates is more important than a large increase in pay. The administration may feel that they cannot support a large increase in pay but would be willing to supplement pensions that would not be paid until a future time. This agreement would be mutually beneficial to both parties.

IRRESOLVABLE DIFFERENCES

At times, parties may not be able to reach a mutually beneficial solution. When faced with the possibility of this occurrence, both sides should develop acceptable alternatives prior to negotiation. Knowing that alternatives exist will allow a party to walk away from a negotiation instead of accepting an agreement that they should have rejected. One alternative to an agreement would be to accept that an agreement cannot be reached and will amount to nothing more than leaving both parties in the same position they were in before negotiations.

When the other party will not negotiate on the principles of the problem but instead focus only on their position or in criticizing the director's position, Fisher and Ury (1991) recommend Negotiation Jujitsu. "When they assert their positions, do not reject them. When they attack your ideas, don't defend them. When they attack you, don't counterattack. Break the vicious cycle by refusing to react. Instead of pushing back, sidestep their attack and deflect it against the problem."

This approach allows redirection of their attacks on the director as an attack on the problem. The director's focus on the interests may cause the other party to shift to their focus as well.

Finally, if this still does not solve the problem, a third-party arbitrator can be brought in to assist with negotiations. This arbitrator can help to evaluate alternatives until all have been considered and revised to meet the interest of both parties.

BRINGING IT ALL TOGETHER WITH TEAM BUILDING

In order to make the crime laboratory an effective workplace, a crime laboratory director must ensure that the employees function as a team. The importance of teamwork has been documented throughout time. Clavell (1983) translates Sun Tzu from 500 BC to say, "You will not succeed unless your men have tenacity and unity of purpose, and above all, a spirit of sympathetic cooperation."

Successful teams share the same vision for the organization. They are willing to set aside their own successes for those of the team. This is evident in championship sports teams where one member passes off to another instead of taking the shot themselves. In a crime laboratory, a forensic scientist may withdraw their application for a training class so that a less experienced analyst may attend. Another analyst may pass on an opportunity that will gain recognition because they are aware that another analyst possesses the skills that will make the task more successful and benefit the laboratory more.

To build a successful team, a director needs to provide the vision and clear direction for the laboratory. They also need to provide the structure for their employees to operate independently toward the vision. By challenging their abilities through delegation, employees grow and learn. They must also be allowed to make mistakes without fear of reprimands.

Employees must initially be respectful of the different skills that each bring to the team and value those that are different from their own. This requires the director to employ and retain the right people. Employees need to develop cooperative communication skills as well as negotiation and conflict resolution skills.

Managers contribute to the team's effectiveness in many ways. Bennis and Nanus (1985) outline five key skills that leaders use in relating to others. First is the ability to accept people as they are, not as the manager would like them to be. Relationships are improved with the realization that all people are different and that all bring unique abilities and perspectives to a situation.

Second is to approach relationships and problems in terms of the present, not the past. Human nature makes it difficult for people to "forgive and forget." However, giving others a second chance will improve relationships. Also, approaching each day as an opportunity to improve one's own behaviors will make individuals more productive.

Third is to treat those who are close with the same courteous attention that is extended to strangers and casual acquaintances. As people are around often, their presence is taken for granted. When consideration is given to their thoughts and feelings, they are given permission to provide feedback regarding laboratory operations. Even informal communications provides an honest exchange where trust is built.

Fourth is to trust others. If a manager consistently views those around them as incompetent or untrustworthy, their trust will fade, affecting their relationship as well as the effectiveness of the workplace. On the other hand, if a manager trusts an employee to do the right thing, their manager's confidence in them will support their own belief in themselves and create a better workplace.

And finally, to do without constant approval and recognition from others. When a manager takes risks, they are not always popular decisions. The director must be willing to accept criticism regarding these decisions if the quality of the work is improved. The need for constant recognition can limit the decisions that a manager needs to make.

SUMMARY

The ultimate goal in human resource management is to not just oversee a group of employees, but to manage a team where the sum exceeds the individual talents of its members. In a group, individuals mindlessly go along with the thoughts and ideas of others. Teams build on these ideas, often challenging others. The respectful conflict that is created presents an opportunity for both individual growth and organizational improvements.

REFERENCES

Adapting to Your Boss. URL:
    http://www.dummies.com/Money/Career/Acquiring_career_skills/0-7645-5253-
    8_0005.html [1-17-02]

Ash, Mary Kay (1984) *On People Management.* Warner Books, New York.

Barrett, Katherine and Greene, Richard (2002) The Terminator. *Governing.* January 2002, 48.

Bennis, Warren (1989) *On Becoming a Leader.* Reading, Addison-Wesley, MS.

Bennis, Warren and Nanus, Burt (1985) *Leaders.* Harper and Row, New York.

Betof, Edward and Harwood, Frederic (1992) *Just Promoted.* McGraw-Hill, New York.

Blanchard, Kenneth and Hersey, Paul (1982) *Management of Organizational Behavior* (fifth edition). Prentice Hall, New Jersey.

Blanchard, Kenneth and Johnson, Spencer (1983) *The One Minute Manager.* Berkley Books, New York.

Blanchard, Kenneth and Peale, Norman Vincent (1988) *The Power of Ethical Management.* Fawcett Crest, New York.

Blanchard, Kenneth *et al.* (1985) *Leadership and the One Minute Manager.* William Morrow and Company, New York.

Carlson Learning Company (1994) *Personal Profile System.* Carlson Learning Company, Minneapolis, MN.

Carr, Clay and Fletcher, Mary (1990) *The Manager's Troubleshooter.* Prentice-Hall, Englewood Cliffs, NJ.

Clavell, James (1983) *The Art of War by Sun Tzu*, Delacorte Press, New York.

Coping with Burnout. URL:
    http://www.dummies.com/Money/Career/management_skills/0-7645-5253-8_0020.html
    [1-17-02]

Covey, Stephen R. (1990) *Principle Centered Leadership.* Simon & Shuster, New York.

Covey, Stephen R. (1989) *The Seven Habits of Highly Effective People.* Simon & Shuster, New York.

Dealing with Difficult People. URL:
    http://www.dummies.com/Money/Small_Business/Business_Etiquette/0-7645-5253-8_0014.html [1-17-02]

Delegating Effectively. URL:
    http://www.dummies.com/Money/Career/management_skills/1-5688-4858-7_0002.html
    [1-17-02]

Drucker, Peter (1964) *The Practice of Management.* HarperCollins, New York.

Drucker, Peter (1974) *Management: Tasks, Responsibilities, and Practices.* HarperCollins, New York.

Drucker, Peter (1986) *Managing for Results.* HarperCollins, New York.

Drucker, Peter (1990) *Managing the Non-Profit Organization.* HarperCollins, New York.

Firestien, Roger L. (1996) *Leading on the Creative Edge,* Piñon Press, Colorado Springs, CO.

Fisher, Roger, Ury, William and Patton, Bruce (1991) *Getting to Yes* (second edition). Penguin Books, New York.

Garfield, Charles (1986) *Peak Performers.* Avon Books, New York.

Godin, Seth (1995) *Wisdom, Inc.* HarperCollins, New York.

Gray, John (1992) *Men are from Mars, Women are from Venus.* HarperCollins, New York.

Hay Group (2001) *Top Teams: Why Some Work and Some Do Not.* URL:
    http://ww.haygroup.com

Hill, Pat *Illegal Hiring Questions.* URL:
    http://www.alllaw.com/articles/employment/article14.asp [2-20-02]

Hiring. URL:
    http://www.lectlaw.com/files/emp24.htm [2-20-02]

Hirsh, Sandra and Kummerow, Jean (1989) *Lifetypes*. Warner Books, New York.

Johnson, Spencer (1998) *Who Moved My Cheese*. G. P. Putnam's Sons, New York.

Kindall, Cindy *et al*. *An Online Guide for Dealing with Difficult People*. URL:
    http://www.mimas.csuchico.edu/~brinkman [1-17-02]

Laws and Resources. URL:
    http://www.creativeservices.com/laws.htm [2-20-02]

Lichtenberg, Ronna (1998) *Work Would be Great if it Weren't for the People*. Hyperion,
    New York.

Manz, Charles C. (1999) *The Leadership Wisdom of Jesus*. Berret-Koehler Publishers, New
    York.

Maintaining Workplace Confidentiality. URL:
    http://www.dummies.com/Money/small_business/business_etiquette/0-7645-5282-
    1_0013.html [1-17-02]

Making Better Decisions. URL:
    http://www.dummies.com/Money/Career/management_skills/0-7645-5253-8_0017.html
    [1-17-02]

Maxwell, John C. (2000) *Failing Forward*. Thomas Nelson Publishers, Nashville, TN.

Michaelson, Gerald A. (2001) *Sun Tzu, The Art of War for Managers*. Adams Media Corpora-
    tion, Avon, MA.

Myers, Isabel Briggs; McCaulley, Mary H. (1987) *Manual for the Myers-Briggs Type Indicator:
    A Guide to the Development and Use of the MBTI*. Consulting Psychologists Press, Palo
    Alto, CA.

Oakley, Ed and Krug, Doug (1991) *Enlightened Leadership*. Fireside, New York.

Ohio Civil Rights Commission (1996) *Questioning Applicants for Employment and Member-
    ship in Labor Organizations*. Columbus, OH.

Peters, Tom (1988) *Thriving on Chaos*. Knopf, New York.

Peters, Tom and Waterman, Robert, Jr (1982) *In Search of Excellence*. Harper and Row, New
    York.

Quinn, Robert E. (1988) *Beyond Rational Management*. Jossey-Bass Publishers, San
    Francisco.

Quinn, Robert E., Faerman, Sue, Thompson, Michael, McGrath, Michael (1990) *Becoming a
    Master Manager*. John Wiley and Sons, New York.

Roberts, Wess (1985) *Leadership Secrets of Attila the Hun*. Warner Books, New York.

Scott-Morgan, Peter (1994) *The Unwritten Rules of the Game*. McGraw-Hill, New York.

Senge, Peter M. (1990) *The Fifth Discipline: the art and practice of the learning organiza-tion.* Currency Doubleday, New York.

Sewell, James D. (2000) Identifying and Mitigating Workplace Stress Among Forensic Labo-ratory Managers. *Forensic Science Communications.* 2(2). April. URL: http://www.fbi.gov/hq/lab/fsc/backissu/april2000/sewell.htm [1-17-02]

Smith, Manuel J. (1975) *When I Say No, I Feel Guilty*. Bantam Books, New York.

Stone, Douglas, Patton, Bruce and Heen, Sheila (1999) *Difficult Conversations*. Viking Penguin, New York.

Succeeding as a Team Leader. URL: http://www.dummies.com/Money/Career/management_skills/0-7645-5253-8_0019.html [1-17-02]

Temme, Jim (1996) *Team Power*. Skillpath Publications, Mission, KS.

Tzu, Sun (1983) *The Art of War.* Clavell, James (ed.). Dell Publishing, New York.

Waitley, Denis (1995) *Empires of the Mind.* William Morrow and Company, New York.

Whetten, David and Cameron, Kim (1995) *Developing Management Skills* (third edition). HarperCollins College Publishers, New York.

Yate, Martin (1994) *Hiring the Best.* Bob Adams Inc., Holbrook, MA.

Ziglar, Zig (1986) *Top Performance.* Fleming H. Revell Co., Old Tappan, NJ.

Ziglar, Zig (1997) *Over the Top.* Thomas Nelson Inc., Nashville, TN.

CHAPTER 3

ETHICS

An ethical person ought to do more than required and less than allowed.
(Michael Josephson)

No man is allowed to be a judge in his own cause, because his interest would certainly bias his judgment, and, not improbably, corrupt his integrity.
(James Madison)

INTRODUCTION

The crime laboratory has a unique position in the criminal justice system. It is both hero and villain; highly exalted and severely criticized; savior and scapegoat. Forensic analysis is becoming increasingly more important in criminal and civil prosecutions. The burden to prove that the analysis has been performed properly weighs heavy on forensic scientists each time that they issue a report and provide expert testimony. No longer are they merely playing a supporting role in investigations. Law enforcement officers, prosecutors, and the public all expect miraculous feats from the crime laboratory that will result in evidence of guilt for every crime. They are disappointed when ambiguous findings are reported.

The forensic scientists of tomorrow have grown up watching television fiction and documentaries that highlight the extraordinary cases. They have an impression that all cases are solvable through unconventional scientific analysis. When they gain employment, they quickly learn that this is not the case. In addition to having to perform monotonous routine analysis daily, new analysts also learn that they are expected to analyze a lot of cases. However, the belief of those outside of the crime laboratory has not changed. There remains pressure from stakeholders to perform miracles in minutes. When analysts yield to the pressure, they are vulnerable to unethical behavior.

Employees in public service are unarguably held to a higher standard. When an applicant is offered a position in a public crime laboratory, they must be aware of the obligations of the position that they are accepting. They will be working for the public and receiving compensation for their service through public funding. The public has the right to expect their "servants" to behave in a manner respectful of that position. DeLattre (1989) states that "Not only is this a fair demand; granting authority without expecting public servants to live up to it would be unfair to everyone they are expected to serve."

When forensic scientists engage in unethical acts, supporters and critics alike search for answers. Supporters seek opportunities for improvement such as accreditation, whereas critics search for scapegoats and preach that all forensic scientists are just "cops in lab coats." Most individuals do not intentionally commit unethical acts but commit them as a result of poor decision-making. It is the responsibility of the crime laboratory director to reinforce the value of ethical decision-making in all aspects of a forensic scientist's daily routine.

WHY UNETHICAL ACTS OCCUR

Ethics is more than just a standard of conduct that mandates how individuals should behave. In addition to recognizing what is the right thing to do, individuals must also have the conviction and courage to do the right thing. Often unethical acts result when an individual does not possess the strength to take the action that they recognize as being just. They may attempt to justify their action in many ways, but in their hearts, they know that they should have chosen a different solution.

There is no single reason why individuals engage in unethical behavior. Much of an individual's behavioral traits begin early in life. In their early development, children are taught by their parents to be good people. They are told not to lie or steal. However, as they progress through life, they may observe contradictory behavior by the same parents who told them otherwise. If they don't observe penalties for unethical behavior, they may not feel that they will receive punishment if they engage in wrongdoing themselves later in life. As analysts, they may give in to pressure applied by the police or prosecutor to overstate their findings to impress a jury and achieve a conviction.

If an individual has been taught throughout their life that unethical acts are acceptable, it is arguable that they can be retrained to behave ethically. Rather than attempting to change someone with blatant unethical tendencies, a crime laboratory director should carefully screen applicants based on their ethical behavior. This can be accomplished in the hiring process either through prior acts exposed in the polygraph or other background investigation, or through careful questioning. For example, the crime laboratory director should ask applicants to tell about a time when they were faced with an ethical dilemma and how they resolved it.

In a survey of crime laboratory directors that was presented at the 1998 Symposium on Crime Laboratory Development, it was revealed that the number one integrity-related need facing crime laboratories was the need for more personnel. Whether a crime laboratory is part of a government agency or a private entity, it will always face a lack of resources. Government crime laboratories compete for scarce funding with other agencies as well as within their own. Even private crime laboratories that rely on income resulting from casework are unable to freely purchase equipment and hire personnel. Therefore, this stressor will always be a factor in forensic laboratories. As criminalists are asked to conduct analyses within these constraints, they may give in to the temptation to perform unethical acts. For example, a criminalist may be expected to conduct a given number of tests per month. If so inclined by their character, they may choose to cut corners to accomplish this quota rather than to face the consequences of completing a lesser number of cases. If they see that rewards are based strictly on quantity of cases worked and not quality, this may serve as another incentive to cut corners.

There are a number of underlying reasons that may drive a usual ethical individual to engage in unethical conduct. Whether as a result of experiences learned through life or a momentary bad decision, the act can result in career-ending attention for the analyst and embarrassment for the laboratory. Crime laboratory directors must be aware of the circumstances under which unethical decisions can be made. They must also train their employees regarding these circumstances along with the consequences of unethical decisions.

GOOD INTENTIONS

Increasingly, crime laboratories are establishing new rules and policies either as a result of accreditation requirements or internal quality processes. Criminalists are required to conduct time-consuming checks and elaborate documentation to validate their analysis. Criminalists may view these policies as a hindrance to the timely completion of casework. Complicating this is the pressure that they feel to produce a valuable product to assist in an investigation. As a result, they are tempted to cut corners in order to complete cases more quickly. They view this as helping their stakeholders and the public by getting a "bad guy" off the streets as soon as possible. While their intentions may be good, they are actually harming themselves and the laboratory. If their analysis is flawed, the suspect could be released regardless of their guilt or innocence.

Crime laboratory directors must be willing to intercede for analysts when they feel pressured by outside forces such as investigators or prosecutors. They must also be willing to correct analysts when they do not follow procedures, even when these same outside forces laud their acts. Crime laboratory directors must be cautious not to reward individuals based solely on the number of cases completed or the timeliness of the completion. In addition, the quality of the analysis and non-biased reporting should be emphasized.

Analysts often feel resentment toward attorneys and experts representing an opposing view. In the past, it was not common practice to share the scientific results of testing with defense attorneys and experts. Those forensic scientists that were taught this point of view feel that it is right to not share. They may feel that the evidence was not destroyed and if the opposing side feels that the testing was not done correctly, they can pay to have it re-examined. However, among many, the opinion has shifted to one of open information. These individuals feel that if the analysis is performed in a quality manner, there is no reason to conceal information. In many instances, the decision to disclose information is not just an ethical decision but a legal one. If a forensic scientist is performing testing that will be introduced by the prosecution, the "Discovery" process entitles that the defense has access to all information.

IGNORANCE OF LAWS, CODES, POLICIES, AND PROCEDURES

Because there are always new policies and procedures that are established, policy manuals have grown larger. A crime laboratory has procedure manuals, quality assurance manuals, administrative manuals from several layers of bureaucracy, regulatory agency guidelines, and many more. It is conceivable that individuals are not aware of all of an agency's policies or legal requirements. Often new employees are handed a stack of documents on their first day at a crime laboratory. They may not be questioned about the content until they do not follow one of the policies within. It is important that a supervisor ensures that employees understand the content of the manuals.

Nothing is more frustrating to a supervisor than for an employee to complain that they did not know something that was in the quality assurance manual. Not all people are inclined to learn from reading a manual, nor do they have time to review manuals often. In order to maximize an employee's knowledge of the policies, a crime laboratory director must reiterate the policies of the laboratory whenever possible to the laboratory staff. This may be accomplished by discussing one of the most critical of the policies at each regularly held staff meeting.

RECOGNITION

The desire to be recognized can be a dangerous motivator. An individual whose inherent needs dictate a need for recognition above all else, may be willing to cut corners to get work done more quickly, or be willing to overstate their results in order to get a conviction if they believe that they will be recognized for the "achievement."

To some extent all humans need to be credited for their work and accomplishments. A crime laboratory director should recognize employees whenever possible either through a simple "good job" or with a formal award. However, care should be taken to ensure that the analyst followed policies while performing the recognized deed.

FRIENDSHIP

Individuals with a strong sense of friends and family may be tempted to participate in unethical behavior to help out a friend. Strict confidentiality is a policy of all crime laboratories. The release of information could compromise an investigation. Yet an analyst with a strong need to be accepted may be willing to violate this policy. They may not feel that discussing a case with a "trusted" one will result in any damage; however, they risk that the confidante will also discuss it with others. At some point, the information becomes public and the harm is done.

Friendship with members of the media is particularly problematic. When a journalist becomes aware of information that can be broadcast, they will feel an ethical responsibility to do so. Forensic scientists should be particularly cautious of journalists who seek to develop relationships with them through intentional means. While most journalists are ethical, as with other professions, there will be those who will seek to deceive in order to further their career.

An illegal act that occasionally occurs in crime laboratories is the theft of drugs or money from cases either for their own use or a friend's use. This act can be minimized by not hiring individuals with history of drug abuse or those who associate with drug abusers. In order to dissuade forensic scientists from turning to drugs as a source of stress relief, the crime laboratory administration should encourage or even provide positive outlets for the analysts. Finally, the crime laboratory director and staff should be alert for signs of drug usage and the crime laboratory should have quality assurance processes to deter and detect such illegal activity. These processes may involve confirming bulk weights of drugs after analysis and random reanalysis of samples.

PERSONAL GAIN

New forensic scientists learn quickly that they do not do the job for the money. However, there are financial responsibilities that must be faced in life. Forensic scientists get married, buy homes, educate children and plan for the future, as do people in all walks of life. Many feel that supplemental income is necessary to fulfill their financial obligations without resorting to unethical conduct. Others, though, may choose illegal or unethical routes to obtaining additional resources.

While a common illegal act includes taking drugs or money from a case, a rare example would be to accept a bribe to call a test inconclusive or to make a match where one does not exist. More commonly, an analyst may have secondary employment that affects their work in a crime laboratory. For example, document examiners often perform private examinations in civil matters. Should they perform this work while on agency time, this deducts from the service they should be providing the citizens of their jurisdiction.

Additionally, if they feel that they will receive monetary compensation in the form of a raise or cash award based on production, they will focus on quantity above quality. To discourage this behavior, crime laboratory administration must be cautious not to promote or reward individuals based solely on the number of cases completed. As individuals focus on that for which they are rewarded, they may put this above all else, including quality.

ACTS OF STUPIDITY

Despite training to the contrary and simply "knowing better," individuals will perform unethical acts. Stupidity may strike at any time during duty hours or outside of the laboratory. For example, a forensic scientist trusted with performing alcohol quantitation may be arrested for drunk driving. When questioned about the act, an individual will generally claim that "they weren't thinking."

While it is difficult to control acts of stupidity, a crime laboratory director can reinforce the need for professional conduct both on and off duty. New forensic scientists may have difficulty accepting that they will be held accountable for their actions whether at the laboratory or not. They do not realize that their professional reputation as well as the laboratory's reputation depends on their vigilant good conduct. This expectation must be made clear when hiring new employees.

Often when acts of stupidity are committed off-duty, it is a result of excessive alcohol consumption. Crime laboratory employees who exhibit addictive tendencies should be counseled regarding the risk that they incur not only to their career but to their health and personal relationships. If the laboratory has access to an Employee Assistance Program, voluntary participation can be encouraged. If the employee's action requires discipline, their mandatory participation in such a program may be required as an element of the disciplinary process.

ACTS OF RETRIBUTION

Crime laboratory directors make decisions every day that their employees disagree with. If an employee believes that their employer is exploiting them, they may seek retribution and as a result be motivated to perform unethical acts. These acts could include actively engaging in a "work slowdown" or spending a considerable time at work doing non-work-related activities. The attitude may develop as a result of not getting an increase in salary, a promotion, or simply recognition for their efforts.

A crime laboratory director can help prevent attitudes of retribution by recognizing the efforts of employees. When faced with a difficult decision, a crime laboratory director can seek input from the laboratory staff. If their decision is unpopular and may appear threatening to the staff, the director may choose to explain the criteria they used to reach the process. This may assist the employees in understanding why the decision was made.

GOING ALONG

Criminalists work beside each other for 40 hours a week and often see themselves as "comrades in arms." When they observe one of their co-workers performing an illegal or unethical act, they are faced with an ethical dilemma. They can confront the co-worker, inform management, talk to other co-workers about the act, do nothing, or even disclose the information to the media. How they react will depend on their training. Crime laboratory directors must encourage analysts to come forward with observations of unethical behavior. When forensic scientists understand how the acts of one person can affect the reputation of the entire laboratory, they are motivated to inform management.

ETHICAL DECISION-MAKING

Values are the core beliefs that guide individual decision-making. Often an individual's values conflict, and decisions are made based on how they rank their values. The values that are consistently used to base decisions on are the ones that make up the individual's character. While individuals may hold personal values that differ from others, consensually held principles are universal. Since these principles are universally accepted, there is little disagreement regarding their use to determine ethical conduct.

The Josephson Institute of Ethics refers to six core ethical values; trustworthiness, respect, responsibility, fairness, caring, and citizenship. They teach that these are "The Six Pillars of Character" and should be used to guide ethical decisions.

Blanchard and Peale (1988) present five principles of ethical power for individuals and organizations. They claim that practicing these principles provides an individual with the strength to make ethical decisions.

The first principle is *purpose*. On an individual level it refers to the purpose of an individual's life. If an individual follows a purposeful life, they have a clear conscience and are able to look at themselves in the mirror without regret. On an organizational level, it reflects that ethical decision-making is valued and encouraged from the administration. Further, the leaders of the organization practice ethical behavior and their ethics policy is not just words on paper. Crime laboratory managers must set a good example for their criminalists to follow. Criminalists who observe a crime laboratory director lying to their supervisor are more likely to do it themselves as they interpret an unethical behavior as acceptable.

The second principle is *pride*. If a person feels pride in their actions, they don't need the acceptance of others. They won't be tempted to engage in unethical acts in order to gain acceptance. The pride that individuals have in themselves carries to their organization. Crime laboratory directors should promote pride in their employees through recognition of ethical actions.

The third principle is *patience*. Practicing patience leads one to accept that immediate decisions do not mean immediate success. Patience will allow individuals to pass on an unethical decision in favor of an ethical one down the road. Patience also allows individuals to believe that ethical decisions will bring about success in the long run for both themselves and the laboratory. A balance is reached between obtaining results and how results are achieved. Often criminalists feel pressure to analyze a large number of cases. A lack of patience may lead them to shortcut analyses instead of applying other processes that would allow cases to be expedited without compromising the testing.

The fourth principle is *persistence*. The individual maintains their ethical behavior regardless of convenience. In an organization, the leadership must behave consistently to their ethics policy. The organization recognizes ethical behavior but at the same time holds individuals accountable for unethical acts. A crime laboratory director should take immediate action against analysts who cut corners as a symbol that ethical behavior is considered primary to all behavior.

The final principle is *perspective*. An individual will reflect upon their actions and feelings to reinforce their ethical behavior. In organizations, the strategic planning process allows for reflection of the organization's direction. The planning should include consideration of the ethical nature of the organization. In crime laboratories, mission statements generally reflect on the quality of the analysis provided. Strategic plans should include ways to continually improve the quality of the analysis through ethical decision-making.

A manager can help ensure ethical behavior by responding when misconduct is reported. They should reward ethical behavior and punish unethical behavior. If they ignore a situation, they essentially condone the behavior. They should also behave in an ethical fashion themselves. Most crime laboratory directors feel that they are ethical, and their employees will observe and follow their high moral example. Yet it is often not enough to just set an example; it is important to provide instruction to employees on ethical decision-making.

TEACHING ETHICS TO FORENSIC SCIENTISTS

It is important to remember that inherently unethical people cannot be trained to be ethical. The first step to ensuring ethical decision-making in employees is to employ only those individuals capable of doing so by including integrity-related questions in the hiring process. Further, it is not sufficient to simply employ ethical employees; they must receive ongoing training to ensure that they continue to make proper decisions.

Professional speaker, Gordon Graham, theorizes that proper conduct is often achieved through experience. The more times that individuals experience a situation, the more likely they are to perform it correctly. This is referred to as recognition-primed decision-making. When managers want to ensure their employees act properly in given situations, they should provide them with opportunities to experience those situations. Graham outlines experiences in regards to frequency and risk as presented in Figure 3.1. Regardless of the risk associated with an event, individuals will make appropriate decisions regarding high-frequency tasks (Quadrants 2 and 4). High-frequency tasks for drug analysts include the analysis of routine cocaine or marijuana cases. They are presented with the situation on a daily basis and are comfortable with the proper decision-making required for these cases. However, when presented with a request to analyze a rarely seen controlled substance, the risk of making a poor decision increases.

	Quadrant 1: High risk Low frequency	Quadrant 2: High risk High frequency
Risk	Quadrant 3: Low risk Low frequency	Quadrant 4: Low risk High frequency
	Frequency	

Figure 3.1
Risk/frequency diagram.

Events are also rated in terms of risk. Risk can be defined in terms of safety or integrity. Safety risks involve endangering self and others and may result in injury or death. Integrity risks can result in embarrassment to self and agency, discipline, release of guilty individuals, incarceration of innocent individuals, law suits, criminal charges to self, and retribution to plaintiffs bringing suit against self and employer. An event may involve a small amount of risk such as opening a case or answering a phone. Many events experienced by forensic scientists pose medium to great risk to integrity as well as safety.

Graham (2001) proposes that training should be ongoing, especially with low-frequency tasks (Quadrants 1 and 3). Providing repetitious training on situations that are rarely encountered will increase an analyst's experience regarding those situations. When they are encountered, the analyst will be better prepared to make the correct decision.

Particular attention should be paid to training regarding high risk/low-frequency tasks (Quadrant 1) as improper decision-making in these rarely encountered situations can have disastrous consequences.

All decisions have some ethical aspect to them and should be presented in all training sessions. Even when training regarding safety issues, ethical elements such as one's responsibility to protect others should be discussed. Constant encounters with the ethical aspects of a decision will prepare the analyst to make ethical decisions in even low-frequency tasks.

MODELS OF ETHICAL DECISION-MAKING

Preparing individuals to make proper ethical decisions can be facilitated by giving them the proper tools to use and providing them with experiences in which to use the tools. Various decision-making models have been proposed to help individuals to consider all aspects of a decision. Once the model has been selected, various scenarios that may be encountered should be presented and discussed regularly in group discussions. New forensic scientists have the opportunity to learn from the experiences of others. One rule that should be in place for these training exercises is that no judgments or punishment will be made regarding the experiences shared. In this way, individuals will be encouraged to share experiences.

Categorical imperative

Immanuel Kant promotes that individuals should act in a manner that could be adopted by everyone. This imperative is duty-based in that people have an absolute obligation to behave according to the "Rule of Universality" regardless of the consequences. While Kant's ethical model provides clear direction regarding good and evil, it does not allow for resolution of conflicting values.

Utilitarianism

Kant's strict theory of absolutism is often moderated to include consideration of the consequences. The Utilitarianism Principle of ethical conduct devised by Jeremy Bentham and John Stuart Mill is based on decisions that provide the greatest good for the greatest number of people. Often this principle is used in public policy-making. However, utilitarianism lends itself to manipulation by allowing individuals to choose self-serving paths and definitions as to what constitutes the "greater good."

The Josephson Institute ethical decision-making model

The Josephson Institute incorporates the classical theories in designing their model of decision-making. They dictate that:

1. All decisions must take into account and reflect a concern for the interests and well-being of all stakeholders.
2. Ethical values and principles always take precedence over non-ethical ones.
3. It is ethically proper to violate an ethical principle only when it is clearly necessary to advance another true ethical principle, which, according to the decision-maker's conscience, will produce the greatest balance of good in the long run.

ETHICAL DILEMMAS

Ethical dilemmas occur when ethical values conflict. Dilemmas require that an individual reach a decision that ranks one value higher than another. Often this is difficult and individuals approach the decision in various and inconsistent ways.

ETHICS CHECK

When considering the ethical aspects of a decision, Blanchard and Peale (1988) present a useful approach in *The Power of Ethical Management*. They present the "Ethics Check" and propose that when an individual is faced with an ethical dilemma, they should ask themselves three questions: Is it legal?; Is it balanced?; How will it make me feel about myself?

Is it legal?

Significant weight should be given to the legality of the decision. If it violates a criminal or civil law, it is not only unethical but also illegal and should be avoided. Many governments have ethics laws that outline acceptable and unacceptable behavior for government employees. In addition to criminal or civil laws, an individual must consider whether their decision complies with existing codes of conduct. These codes may come from the employing agency or a professional organization.

Of particular use to a forensic scientist is the American Academy of Forensic Scientists Code of Conduct (Appendix A). This provides practical objectives of excellence to which forensic scientists can aspire. It is necessary to remind employees of these guidelines by posting them in the laboratory as well as holding ongoing discussions regarding their importance and the implications of violating them. Other codes of ethics and professional guidelines include those of the American Society of Public Administrators (Appendix B) and the American Society of Crime Laboratory Directors (Appendices C and D).

A laboratory should also consider incorporating its own ethics policy that addresses issues specific to a crime laboratory such as cutting corners on analyses or testifying falsely in court. All laboratory employees should then be made familiar with the policies and the benefits of following them, as well as the consequences of violating them. They should also be provided with ongoing training throughout their career regarding these ethical policies.

Is it balanced?

If it is legal, then the individual should ask if it is balanced and fair. If the decision will cause one party to benefit greatly over another, it could reflect negatively upon the decision-maker. For example, if a criminalist words a report to "match" a suspect based solely on a preliminary examination, they are providing unbalanced and misleading information to the criminal justice system. This situation also reflects upon the actions of the other criminalists in the laboratory, as well as the management of the laboratory.

How will it make me feel about myself?

The final Ethics Check question is, "How will it make me feel about myself?" This question focuses on an individual's emotions and own sense of mortality. Other supportive questions are: Will it make me proud? Would I feel good if my decision was published in the newspaper? And would I feel good if my family knew about it? This allows an individual to search their conscience regarding their own feelings of right and wrong. While a decision may be legal and balanced, it may still cause distress to the individual.

ETHICAL GUIDE

The Josephson Institute presents a similar "Ethical Guide" that proposes that ethical decisions be considered in light of the Golden Rule (Are others being treated as the decision-maker would like to be treated?), Publicity (Would the reasoning used and decision reached be embarrassing if it appeared on the front page of the paper?), and Kid-on-your-shoulder (Would the decision-maker be comfortable with children watching?).

A PRACTICAL APPROACH TO DECISION-MAKING

As with other problem-solving exercises, individuals should consider a general approach to ethical dilemmas. The proposed approach includes clarification, data collection and evaluation, decision, implementation, and monitoring evaluation.

Clarification

The problem should be clearly understood prior to devising a solution. If the true problem is not identified, the solution may be inadequate or complicate the problem. In addition to the problem, the ethical issues surrounding the problem should be identified. The issues should include identification of the conflicting ethical values and the stakeholders who will be affected by the decision. Will anyone be harmed or will any rights be violated when a decision is reached?

Data collection and evaluation

When evaluating the situation, it is necessary to ensure that all necessary information has been collected. When obtaining the information, the decision-maker should be cautious to ensure that the information is objective. Biased information may result in a poor decision.

Decision

Once the information has been collected, the decision-maker should determine the criteria upon which they will base their decision. This may include laws, organizational and professional codes of conduct or agency policies.

When considering their decision, they should make a list of options based upon ethical guides such as those proposed by Blanchard and Peale or the Josephson Institute. It may also be helpful to discuss the alternatives with a trusted adviser, especially if the decision-maker feels that they are allowing their own biases to affect their decision.

Implementation

Once a decision is reached, it should be acted upon. If necessary, the decision-maker should develop a plan to implement the decision. It is also useful to document the decision and criteria used in reaching the decision. This will not only assist in making future decisions, but if the decision pertained to personnel matters, it will likely be reviewed by others.

Monitoring/evaluation

After the decision has been implemented, it should be monitored and evaluated for effectiveness. If the results are different than anticipated, the decision should be reconsidered in light of new information learned.

SCENARIOS

A group discussion of practical scenarios will assist the forensic scientists in determining how to begin to make ethical decisions. The following ethical dilemmas were compiled by the National Institute of Ethics and presented at the 1998 FBI Symposium for Crime Laboratory Development. They provide suggestions for ethical discussions among employees.

Dilemma 1

As a criminalist working for a government crime laboratory, you have received five items of evidence to examine in conjunction with a homicide investigation. You have completed your examinations of all five items and are about to complete a written report. The report would reveal that items 1, 2, and 3 implicate the defendant in this case. Items 4 and 5 do not associate this defendant with the crime and in fact suggest involvement by others. You reveal these results over the phone to the prosecuting attorney. She says to you, "Send me a report with only the results to your examinations of items 1, 2, and 3."

How do you respond?

Dilemma 2

You are a senior scientist in a forensic science laboratory and have completed your examinations and issued a report of your findings to the submitting agency. You have received a court order to release the items you examined to a second criminalist for re-examination by the opposing side. The prosecutor does not trust this second criminalist and requests that you accompany the evidence and observe the examinations as they are being conducted to insure that they are performed properly.

How do you respond to this request?

Dilemma 3

A secondary examination is conducted on evidence for which you performed the initial analysis. A few questions come up concerning your initial examination techniques. The second criminalist asks you to clarify a few details about your previous examination.

Do you talk to her? Do you answer her questions?

Dilemma 4

You are aware of a criminalist who on many occasions has "stretched the truth." This has been occurring for a number of years in the form of extending expertise in areas of no training, "puffing up" qualifications and outright perjury on the witness stand. You have documentation of these events in the form of transcripts and case studies.

What do you do? Talk to the criminalist; contact the laboratory director; bring formal charges to the professional associations; file criminal perjury charges; pass the word on to others but do nothing more; or do nothing?

Dilemma 5

It is your laboratory's policy not to accept evidence without proper seal. However, a urine sample with scotch tape across the lid was inadvertently accepted for determination of alcohol content.

Do you analyze the urine?

Dilemma 6

You suspect a criminalist of cutting corners on analysis. You have attempted to talk to the criminalist as well as the supervisor, but you do not feel that satisfactory corrective action has been taken against your co-worker.

What do you do?

Dilemma 7

During a trial in which you both performed analysis, you are approached by a defense attorney concerning your analysis. You talk to her about your techniques. Do you share your concerns about your co-worker's analysis?

Dilemma 8

You are a criminalist in a small town and eat breakfast with the local police, prosecutor and judge every morning. A brutal homicide of a seven-year-old girl is committed in your usually peaceful town. The inexperienced police collect the evidence at the crime scene. When the evidence arrives at the laboratory you discover that the victim's clothing has been stored unsealed in the trunk of the police cruiser over the weekend. You have been requested to perform trace evidence analysis on this evidence to link it to the trunk of a suspect's car. No other evidence is available on this case.

What do you do?

Dilemma 9

You work in the drug analysis section of a crime laboratory. The supervisor reviews the number of cases that each analyst works in a month and awards the analyst who works the most cases with an extra day of vacation. Your mother has been ill with an extended illness and you have consumed all your sick and vacation days caring for her. You are sure after seeing marijuana every day of your career that you do not need to perform microscopic and color tests which are required by laboratory policy to identify marijuana.

Do you cut corners in order to get that extra day of vacation to spend with your dying mother?

Dilemma 10

You are a criminalist working in the drug identification unit. You receive a phone call from an undercover officer concerning the drug case on which you are working. The officer tells you that this is a very important case and she knows that the weight of the substance is very close to bulk amount. She emphasizes that it would *really* be nice if the weight was over bulk amount so that the defendant could get a harsher sentence. You interpret her discussion as a request that you add weight to the sample to make it over bulk amount.

What do you do?

ETHICAL DILEMMAS FACING CRIME LABORATORY DIRECTORS

Crime laboratory directors face the same ethical responsibilities as forensic scientists. In addition to these, they are faced with unique managerial decisions. Managers set examples of integrity with these decisions. Everyone learns from the actions of others and are especially influenced by the actions of their supervisors. Therefore, managers should set high standards for themselves if they expect them from others. This applies both to their professional and personal lives. It is hypocritical for a crime laboratory director to condemn an applicant for driving while intoxicated when they themselves are guilty of the same thing. This behavior is not hidden from others in the laboratory and will cause the director to lose the confidence of their employees.

Managers are responsible for their organization's integrity. Gordon Graham (2001) discusses "five pillars of success" that agencies should follow in order to minimize embarrassing and costly situations resulting from unethical decisions. The five pillars are people, policy, training, supervision, and discipline.

PEOPLE

The people who are hired should be willing and able to comply with the ethical aspects of our agencies. Crime laboratory directors have an ethical responsibility to ensure new forensic scientists are aware that they will be held to a higher standard of integrity both on and off the job. If it is revealed that they do not have the integrity required, it is management's obligation to the agency and the profession to provide training if possible and seek dismissal if training is not possible. Also, it is the crime laboratory director's ethical responsibility to both the employee as well as the agency to provide honest and fair performance evaluations throughout their career. The employee can take steps to correct deficiencies before they become career-ending.

POLICY

Management has the responsibility of implementing and maintaining policies that will maximize ethical conduct. This entails identifying high-risk tasks that occur infrequently and constructing policies to address these situations. It also entails ensuring that the policies comply with legal requirements and are understood by the employees. Often these policies are not written down until someone commits an act that facilitates the policy's introduction. Crime laboratory directors should search for situations that may have been experienced by other crime laboratories and institute policies before they have an opportunity to occur in their own agency.

Crime laboratories should implement quality assurance policies that will deter unethical actions. Technical and administrative reviews of casework as well as annual audits of operational procedures can detect both intentional and accidental errors. Policies requiring review of expert testimony will provide a means of ensuring that analysts are not overstating their credentials or conclusions.

TRAINING

To ensure ethical conduct, management must provide employees with training regarding situations in which they will be expected to make ethical decisions. Training should be provided not only at the beginning of their career but should continue throughout it. Training is especially necessary for high-risk situations that occur infrequently. For liability purposes, the training as well as the knowledge obtained should be documented.

While it is the crime laboratory director's responsibility to train analysts regarding policies, the ultimate responsibility for compliance still belongs to the employee. Initial training can be provided and ongoing training conducted and documented, but still a forensic scientist can make an unethical decision. However, the director can be free of guilt as well as liability that they provided the individual with the tools necessary to make the proper decision.

SUPERVISION

It is imperative that managers enforce organizational policies fairly and consistently. Ambiguous signals are sent to employees when a crime laboratory director enforces some of the policies some of the time with some of the employees. Employees are left with unclear guidelines on what is expected from them. They are more likely to make unethical decisions because they didn't clearly understand it to be wrong. Also, a crime laboratory director should be willing to audit the laboratory's operation and the work of the forensic scientists as often as necessary to ensure proper conduct. While ASCLD/LAB® accreditation requires annual audits; more frequent ones may be dictated if there is an indication of wrongdoing.

DISCIPLINE

Finally, managers have an ethical obligation to fairly and consistently initiate discipline when a policy has been violated. As with supervision, if discipline is dispensed in an unfair manner, employees do not have clear guidelines on what is expected. Also, the consequences of wrongdoing should not be considered when determining discipline. If two forensic scientists commit the same act, both should receive the same consideration even if one results in a much more severe outcome.

PREVENTION

Godin (1995) surveyed business leaders to ascertain which virtue was most important for employees. Nearly 50 percent of the respondents chose ethics as the number one virtue valued in employees. Crime laboratories will no doubt agree with this assessment. Recruiting and hiring employees with a high degree of integrity can minimize unethical behavior. However, unethical acts will continue to occur regardless of the individuals and the training provided.

Godin suggests that unethical acts thrive in secrecy, and individuals are likely to act more ethically when their actions are public. Gregory and Miller (1998) support this argument in the science community. They argue that as the public becomes more knowledgeable regarding scientific principles, "discoveries" will be more closely scrutinized and "bad science" uncovered. The same argument can be made for the forensic sciences where conclusions based on invalid testing will be questioned and disclosed.

Barry Scheck and Peter Neufeld, noted attorneys and vocal critics of many forensic science practices, propose suggestions to minimize "forensic fraud" and "junk science" (2001). Among their proposals are that crime laboratories should operate independently from law enforcement agencies, the scientific basis for forensic testing should be publicly re-examined in light of current legal standards for scientific acceptability, and crime laboratory accreditation should be mandatory to ensure that quality assurance processes are followed.

Whether or not these proposals will be implemented or whether they will be the panacea for ethical conduct remains to be seen. Over the past 20 years, the forensic science community has allowed greater accessibility to its operations. Often the accessibility was mandated because of questionable actions that became public knowledge. Other times it was due to a change in the attitudes held by crime laboratory leaders. The criticism raised as a result of the accessibility has unquestionably raised the quality of the forensic services as a whole. The challenge for the forensic science community is to put aside its pride and objectively consider the suggestions made by both the public and the laboratory's critics.

SUMMARY

Crime laboratory directors can minimize the occurrence of unethical acts by carefully screening applicants as well as by providing continual ethics training. An additional preventive measure includes the institution of quality assurance processes that deter and detect illegal and unethical actions. However, these acts will never be entirely eliminated. For the sake of personal and organization reputations, crime laboratory administration and staff alike are responsible for identifying, reporting, and responding to unethical and illegal actions.

REFERENCES

American Academy of Forensic Sciences, *Code of Ethics and Conduct.* Colorado Springs, CO.

American Society of Crime Laboratory Directors, *Guidelines for Ethical Management.*

American Society of Public Administrators, *Code of Ethics.* URL: http://www.aspanet.org/ethics/coe.html [3-7-02]

Barnett, Peter D. (2001) *Ethics in Forensic Science.* CRC Press, Boca Raton, FL,

Bashinski, Jan S. (1997) *Ethical Issues in Forensic Science Management.* Presented at 1997 American Academy of Forensic Sciences Annual Meeting.

Blanchard, Kenneth and Peale, Norman Vincent (1988) *The Power of Ethical Management.* Fawcett Crest, New York.

Bok, Sissela (1989) *Lying: Moral Choices in Public and Private Life.* Vintage Books, New York.

Bromwich, Michael R. (1997) *Testimony before the United States House Committee on the Judiciary, Subcommittee on Crime.* May 13.

DeLattre, Edwin (1989) Ethics in Public Service: Higher Standards and Double Standards. *Criminal Justice Ethics.* Summer/Winter.

Godin, Seth (1995) *Wisdom, Inc.* HarperCollins, New York.

Graham, Gordon J. (2001) *Law Enforcement 2001.* Presented at 2001 FBI/ASCLD Symposium on Crime Laboratory Development.

Gregory, Jane and Miller, Steve (1998) *Science in Public.* Perseus Publishing, Cambridge, MA.

Josephson Institute of Ethics, *Making Ethical Decisions.* URL: http://www.josephsoninstitute.org/MED [3-7-02]

Machiavelli, Niccolo (1966) *The Prince.* London, Penguin Books.

Macklin, Ruth (1997) Ethics and Value Bias in the Forensic Sciences. *Journal of Forensic Sciences.* 42(6). 1203–1206.

Mills, Don H. (1997) Comments from the Perspective of the AAFS Ethics Committtee Chairman. *Journal of Forensic Sciences.* 42(6). 1207–1208.

Norby, Jon J. (1997) A Member of the Roy Rogers Riders Club is Expected to Follow the Rules Faithfully. *Journal of Forensic Sciences.* 42(6). 1195–1197.

Rosner, Richard (1997) Foundations of Ethical Practice in the Forensic Sciences. *Journal of Forensic Sciences.* 42(6). 1191–1194.

Southwestern Law Enforcement Institute (1996) *Ethics Train-The-Trainer Manual.*

Scheck, Barry and Neufeld, Peter (2001) *Actual Innocence.* Signet, New York.

Steinberg, Sheldon S. and Austen, David T. (1990) *Government, Ethics, and Managers.* Quorum Books, New York.

Trautman, Neal E. (1998) *Crime Lab Integrity.* Presented at 1998 FBI/ASCLD Sypmosium on Crime Laboratory Development.

Waitley, Denis (1995) *Empires of the Mind.* William Morrow and Company, New York.

Weinstock, Robert (1997) Ethical Practice in the Forensic Sciences. *Journal of Forensic Sciences.* 42(6). 1189–1190.

Weinstock, R., Leong, G. B. and Silva, J. A. (2000) Ethics. In: Seigel, J. (ed.) *Encyclopedia of Forensic Science.* Academic Press, London. 706–712.

CHAPTER 4

QUALITY IN CRIME LABORATORIES

Jo Ann Given

Fast is fine, but accuracy is everything.

(Wyatt Earp)

INTRODUCTION

Quality is defined by Juran (1999) as "freedom from deficiencies – freedom from errors that require doing work over again (rework) or that result in field failure, customer dissatisfaction, customer claims, and so on."[1] While such a definition is quite suitable for traditional fields such as engineering and industry, in a crime laboratory there is often no opportunity of "doing the work over again." Also, someone is usually "dissatisfied" with the results of the examination, and customer claims are settled in a criminal court. Quality in a crime laboratory is better described as obtaining as much information as possible from the available evidence, doing it as accurately as possible, and reporting results and conclusions objectively and accurately. The ultimate judge of the quality of work in a forensic laboratory is the court in which the examiner presents his testimony. Many judges and most jurors, however, have no way of evaluating the testimony that is presented to them. It is therefore the responsibility of the individuals working in a forensic laboratory and the management of the laboratory to ensure that the highest standards are maintained.

In the 1990s several events occurred that made it clear that quality processes within crime laboratories were not only essential but would be subject to public review. For the general public, the O. J. Simpson trial put forensic sciences in the spotlight and showed what appeared to be glaring errors in forensic work. Another less dramatic, but vitally important case, illustrates how matters of quality control can influence national medial coverage. In the state of West Virginia it was revealed in 1993 that an examiner was found to have falsified evidence using traditional serology and DNA technology so as to support the prosecution. In both of these situations a strong quality assurance program might well have prevented the unfortunate actions or brought them to light before they became national media happenings.

Another major event was the 1993 United States Supreme Court decision in

1 Juran, J. M. (1999). In *Juran's Quality Handbook* (fifth edition), ed. J. M. Juran. McGraw-Hill, New York. 2.2.

2 *Daubert v Merrell Dow Pharmaceuticals, Inc.* 509 US 579 (1993).

3 *Frye v United States,* 293 F 1013 DC Cir. 1923.

the case of *Daubert v. Merrill Dow Pharmaceutical.*[2] Previously the *Frye*[3] standard required only that for scientific testimony to be admitted it had to be generally accepted by the scientific community. *Daubert* sets forth several criteria that judges may use to determine if scientific testimony is relevant and reliable:

- Does the testing technique have a known and or potential rate of error?
- Is the technique generally accepted within the appropriate scientific community?
- Has the technique been peer reviewed?
- Has the scientific theory been tested or is it testable?
- Do standards exist for controlling the operation of the technique?

Until recently there were few colleges or universities that offered degrees in forensic science. An individual would obtain a chemistry or biology degree and if they entered a forensic laboratory, would become a drug chemist, serologist or criminalist. Many questioned documents examiners, fingerprint specialists, and firearms examiners began their careers in police departments or the military. Training was "on the job," and the quality of the teaching varied according to the expertise of the examiner who was teaching. There were no national guidelines that determined what would be the minimum standards for examiners or when an individual had "completed their training."

Managers of forensic laboratories acknowledged the importance of ensuring the quality of work produced in their facilities and in the 1980s put in place several measures to create strong, viable quality assurance programs. The quality systems that were established begin with a positive, supportive attitude from everyone in the laboratory from management to the cleaning staff. Many laboratories hired individuals as quality managers whose responsibilities, either full- or part-time, is to constantly review and maintain quality system. A Quality Manual, a document that articulates management's commitment to quality and the objectives of the quality system, has become a standard feature in crime laboratories. This document serves as a reference and starting point for the system that includes procedures manuals, a safety manual, training manuals, and any other documents related to the quality system.

In the same time-frame the forensic science community as a whole began to acknowledge that outside recognition of the quality of work by the laboratories and individual examiners was essential. Several processes and procedures were developed and put into place to allow the evaluation of laboratories against established standards and evaluation of individual examiners against standards in their field of expertise:

- Accreditation is the process by which an accreditation body formally recognizes that a laboratory is competent to carry out specific tasks.
- Certification is the process by which an organization recognizes the qualifications of an individual to practice a forensic discipline.
- Competency testing (as used in the United States) is the evaluation of a person's ability to perform work in any functional area prior to the performance of independent casework.
- Proficiency testing is used to evaluate the continued capability of analysts, technical support personnel and/or the quality performance of a laboratory.

ACCREDITATION

Accrediting bodies measure a laboratory or system of laboratories against a set of standards by sending a team to do an audit or inspection of the laboratory. If the laboratory or system is determined to meet the standards, the laboratory is recognized as able to carry out specific tasks. The accreditation is not a guarantee that every examination done by the laboratory will be complete and accurate; it is a statement that the laboratory, as a whole, is capable of doing complete and accurate work.

Most accreditation programs have several requirements in common:

- An on-site visit by a team of inspectors or auditors.
- The laboratory must have some kind of quality document such as a Quality Manual.
- The laboratory must have written procedures for any tests that are done in the laboratory, and must be able to document that those procedures are followed.
- Staff members must be qualified for their positions and receive some type of ongoing training.
- Examiners and others who are involved in the examination of evidence must undergo proficiency testing.
- Newly hired or trained examiners must undergo some type of competency test to indicate their mastery of their new duties.
- Instrumentation and equipment must be adequate and within calibration standards.
- Case reports must be adequately reviewed before release.
- The evidence must be safely handled and stored at all times and proper security must be maintained.

CASE REVIEW

Ongoing case review is a part of all accreditation programs. There are generally two types of review that are conducted in crime laboratories – administrative and technical. Administrative review is conducted on all reports in an effort to

ensure that the report is correct, consistent and complete. ASCLD/LAB®
defines administrative review as "a procedure used to check for consistency with
laboratory policy and for editorial correctness."[4] The individual doing the
administrative review will check items such as case numbers and spelling, and
ensure that all necessary paperwork is included in the case file. Depending on
the laboratory's standard procedures, this review can be conducted by the
author of the report or a member of the laboratory's administrative, supervisory
or management staff. Technical review of case reports is sometimes called peer
review, although the individual conducting the review does not have to be a
"peer" of the author of the report. Technical review is conducted by an individual who has "sufficient knowledge of the discipline to verify compliance with the
laboratory's technical procedures and that the conclusions reached are
supported with the examination documentation".[5] The technical reviewer does
not have to be an active examiner in the field; they are often supervisors who are
no longer doing casework but have had past experience in the discipline for
which they are doing technical review. The technical review includes a review of
all case documentation, including reports, notes, and data obtained during the
examination. Some laboratories and accreditation systems require that two
different individuals do the administrative review and technical review; others
allow one individual to do both reviews simultaneously.

COMPETENCY TESTS

In the US, competency tests are those given to an individual to evaluate their
ability to perform work in a specific area prior to beginning independent
casework. These tests should ensure that the individual has a good understanding of the field in which they will be performing casework and may include
written and oral tests, analysis of test samples and a moot court. For examiners
who do casework in more than one discipline several competency tests may be
necessary. Competency tests are also necessary for experienced examiners who
are newly hired into a laboratory.

ACCREDITING BODIES

ASCLD/LAB® (www.ascld_lab.org)

When the American Society of Crime Laboratory Directors (ASCLD) was
founded in 1973 one of the purposes of the organization was, and remains, to
"encourage and maintain the highest standards of practice in the field of crime
laboratory services . . ."[6] One of the first ASCLD committees was the Committee
on Laboratory Evaluation and Standards. Beginning in the late 1970s, this
Committee worked to develop a program which could be used to evaluate the

4 American Society of
Crime Laboratory
Directors/Laboratory
Accreditation Board
Manual, 2001 Version. 75.

5 American Society of
Crime Laboratory
Directors/Laboratory
Accreditation Board
Manual, 2001 Version. 43.

6 Bylaws of the American
Society of Crime Labora-
tory Directors, Inc.

quality of the work in forensic laboratories. The committee members also hoped to develop a program that would assist in the continuing improvement of the quality of overall laboratory operations. By June 1981 the committee had been renamed the ASCLD Committee on Laboratory Accreditation and an initial program for accreditation had been presented to the ASCLD membership. In February 1982 the laboratories of the Illinois State Police underwent the first inspection, and in May of that year they became the first accredited laboratories. In September 1982 the three laboratories of the Arizona Department of Public Safety were accredited. By 1993 the Committee became an independent organization – the American Society of Crime Laboratory Directors/Laboratory Accreditation Board (ASCLD/LAB®). This was the first accreditation program developed specifically for forensic laboratories. In the first five years 54 laboratories were accredited and in 1990 the South Australia State Forensic Science Laboratory in Adelaide was the first laboratory outside of the US accredited by ASCLD/LAB®. In October 1994 an agreement was signed with National Association of Testing Authorities – Australia (NATA) for joint inspections and accreditation of laboratories in Australia. In the following years laboratories in Canada, New Zealand, Singapore and Hong Kong were accredited. By January 2002, 217 forensic laboratories were accredited by ASCLD/LAB®. The directors of all accredited laboratories are members of the Delegate Assembly. A Board of Directors and an Executive Director do the daily management of ASCLD/LAB®. The Board of Directors consists of seven members of the Delegate Assembly, one member representing law enforcement and prosecuting attorneys and one public member. There is one ex-officio member representing ASCLD.

The objectives of ASCLD/LAB® are stated in the Manual:

- To improve the quality of laboratory services provided to the criminal justice system.
- To develop and maintain criteria which can be used by a laboratory to assess its level of performance and to strengthen its operation.
- To provide an independent, impartial, and objective system by which laboratories can benefit from a total operational review.
- To offer to the general public and to users of laboratory services a means of identifying those laboratories which have demonstrated that they meet established standards.

The ASCLD/LAB® program is a strictly voluntary program in which any public or private crime laboratory may participate to demonstrate that its management operations, personnel, procedures and instruments, physical plant and security, and personnel safety procedures meet certain standards. Incorporated into the program are requirements for proficiency testing, basic and continuing education requirements, and quality system requirements to assist the laboratory in an ongoing quality assurance program.

7 American Society of Crime Laboratory Directors/Laboratory Accreditation Board Manual, 2001 Version. 2.

8 ibid.

The ASCLD/LAB® program is divided into three sections, each covering a number of elements in the program – Management and Operations, Personnel Standards, and Physical Plant Standards. Each section contains a number of principles. A principle is "a basic rule, assumption or quality; a fixed or predetermined policy or mode of action."[7] Standards are written for each principle; these are "statements which describe acceptable levels of performance, excellence or attainment in that particular activity."[8] For each standard a criterion is given which is used to evaluate whether the laboratory activity meets the standards. These criteria are questions which can be answered as Yes, No, or Not applicable. Discussion sections provide more details and explanations of some of the criteria.

As an inspection team reviews all parts of a laboratory's operations and interviews staff members, they grade the laboratory based on the criteria. Each criterion is rated as essential, important or desirable and can be rated Yes, No or Not applicable. A laboratory must be graded as "Yes" for 100 percent of the essential criteria, at least 75 percent of the important criteria and 50 percent of the desirable criteria. Essential criteria are used to measure standards that directly affect the work product of the laboratory or the integrity of the evidence. Important criteria relate to standards that are key indicators of the quality of the laboratory but may not directly affect the work product or the integrity of the evidence. Desirable criteria relate to standards which enhance the professionalism of the laboratory but have little effect on the work product or the evidence.

The ASCLD/LAB® inspection process begins with a laboratory performing a self-inspection using the ASCLD/LAB® Manual and submitting an application to the Executive Director. An inspection team, consisting of a team leader and one or more additional inspectors will visit the laboratory. The team leader may be one of several contract employees or a volunteer who has been specially trained as a team leader. The additional inspectors are volunteers with expertise in laboratory quality assurance or a specific forensic discipline. The number of inspectors is based on the size of the laboratory and types of evidence examined in the laboratory. The team's visit may be as short as two days or last for several weeks during which each phase of the laboratory's processes and procedures are reviewed. Case files will be examined for each examiner; management, examiners and other staff members will be interviewed; training records reviewed; and quality system documents reviewed. Following the inspection, the team captain prepares a draft report. The report is then reviewed by an Audit Committee appointed by the Board. The audited report is returned to the director of the laboratory who can then begin remediation of any non-compliance issues or appeal decisions to the Board. Following any necessary remediation a final report is prepared for the laboratory and ASCLD/LAB® Board. The final decision to grant accreditation is made by the Board. Accreditation is granted for a five-year period.

Ongoing monitoring of accredited laboratories is an essential part of all good accreditation programs. ASCLD/LAB® accomplishes this by yearly self-audits and continued proficiency tests of examiners. Each year accredited laboratories are required to submit to the Executive Director an "Annual Accreditation Review" which requires that the laboratory management do a complete self-inspection and grade the laboratory based on the ASCLD/LAB® criteria. Any non-compliances must be reported, as well as errors in any proficiency tests. The continued proficiency testing of individual examiners is the other component of the monitoring process. Each examiner must complete an annual proficiency test in each discipline in which they do examinations. The proficiency test must come from an ASCLD/LAB® approved provider, if one is available, and results must be reported back to the provider. The results are reviewed by members of a Proficiency Review Committee (PRC) made up of experts in each discipline. These individuals review the results of each proficiency test and report incorrect answers and the laboratory's response to the Board of Directors.

NAME (www.thename.org)

Medical Examiners' Offices are often co-located with forensic laboratories and may choose to undergo accreditation by the National Association of Medical Examiners (NAME). NAME, the national professional organization of physician medical examiners, medical death investigators, and death investigation system administrators was founded in 1966. The NAME Accreditation Program is a peer review system based on standards developed to improve the quality of the medicolegal investigation of death in the US. Inspections are carried out by a board certified forensic pathologist, usually an individual affiliated with an accredited facility. The Accreditation Standards are a series of questions divided into two phases. Phase I questions are not essential and a deficiency will not directly alter the quality of work or endanger the welfare of the public. The Phase II questions are essential requirements and deficiencies may seriously impact the work or adversely affect the health and safety of the public or agency staff. In order to obtain full accreditation an office must meet all of the Phase II requirements. The Chair of the NAME Standards, Inspection and Accreditation Committee confers accreditation for a period of five years after which the facility must undergo reinspection. As of January, 2002, 41 jurisdictions have NAME-accredited facilities.

ABFT (www.abft.org)

The American Board of Forensic Toxicology (ABFT) was formed in 1975 as a joint program between the American Academy of Forensic Science, Society of Forensic Toxicologists, California Association of Toxicologists, Canadian Society of Forensic Science and Southwestern Association of Toxicologists. In 1996 ABFT began an accreditation program for laboratories that practice post-mortem forensic toxicology or human performance toxicology. Many of these laboratories are a part of crime laboratories. The program is somewhat analogous to the ASCLD/LAB® program with a series of questions that are designated as "essential," "important" or "desirable." On-site inspections are done by two or three inspectors who are ABFT Diplomates and last for two or three days. Accreditation is granted only when all essential questions are answered Yes, as well as at least 80 percent of the important questions and 50 percent of the desirable questions. Prior to application, a laboratory must successfully participate in at least one alcohol and one non-alcohol (or drug) proficiency-testing program. Any false negatives or other deficiencies must be documented as well as corrective actions taken as a vital part of the program. The Board of the ABFT initially grants accreditation for one year with an extension given for the second year subject to a satisfactory self-inspection and completion of appropriate proficiency tests. Following the second year a laboratory must reapply for accreditation. As of January, 2002, ABFT has accredited ten toxicology laboratories.

NFSTC (www.nfstc.org)

The National Forensic Science Technology Center (NFSTC) was established by ASCLD in 1994 to help laboratories to achieve the highest quality of operations. In 2000 NFSTC began to offer ISO 17025 compliant accreditation to forensic laboratories in the US that did not qualify for ASCLD/LAB® accreditation such as environmental laboratories and horse-racing laboratories. Since then it has expanded to include accreditation of crime laboratories to ISO Standard 17025 using the Standards Council of Canada forensic specific documentation. As of January 2002 NFSTC has accredited one laboratory system with eight laboratories.

NATA (www.nata.asn.au)

The National Association of Testing Authorities, Australia (NATA) was established in 1947; it is the oldest comprehensive laboratory accreditation provider. NATA offers accreditation of a wide variety of laboratories conducting tests, calibrations and measurements in a wide spectrum of technical fields; forensic science is just one of these areas. All laboratories accredited by NATA must comply with ISO 17025; an extensive Application Document "provides an explanation of the application of ISO/IEC 17025 for forensic science laboratories and also a description of the NATA accreditation procedures in this field."[9] In October 1994 NATA and ASCLD/LAB® signed an agreement for joint inspections and accreditation of Australian crime laboratories. All teams included members from both NATA and ASCLD/LAB® and crime laboratories received accreditation from both organizations. By 2000 the number of qualified technical inspectors in Australia had grown large enough to allow Australian laboratories to apply only to NATA for accreditation. The process begins with an on-site assessment by a team composed of at least one NATA staff officer and one or more technical assessors. The technical assessors are volunteers selected for their specialized knowledge. The assessment includes a review of case records of all examiners, interviews with staff, and a review of procedures. The NATA staff officer reviews the quality system and acts as lead assessor. The written report of the assessment is review by the Forensic Science Accreditation Advisory Committee consisting of forensic science experts from a variety of states and types of laboratories. Accreditation is granted by NATA's Board in the appropriate fields to include controlled substances, toxicology, forensic chemistry/criminalistics (fire and explosives, glass), forensic biology (serology, blood splash pattern examination, DNA, hair), firearms, document examination, fingerprints, crime scene investigation and parentage testing. Reassessments are normally carried out every two years but may occur more frequently if there is a significant change in staffing or when a change in the scope of accreditation is requested. The NATA program includes requirements for annual proficiency testing and review of those tests by the Proficiency Review Committees established by the Forensic Science Accreditation Advisory Committee.

9 National Association of Testing Authorities, Australia, ISO/IEC 17025 Application Document:2000 Version 1, Section 1. 4.

SCC (www.scc.ca)

In 1994 the Canadian Society of Forensic Science established a committee to study accreditation processes available to Canadian forensic science laboratories. This committee worked with the Standards Council of Canada (SCC), and in 1999 CAN-P-1578, "Guidelines for the Accreditation of Forensic Testing Laboratories," was published. The program meets ISO requirements and is operated by the SCC through the Program for Accreditation of Laboratories (PALCAN). An on-site assessment is done by a PALCAN-qualified Team Leader and one Technical Assessor for each discipline. The Technical Assessor will be a subject matter expert. A report is prepared and the applicant laboratory given the opportunity to reply and correct any non-compliances. Accreditation is granted by the Chair of SCC and members of the Task Group Laboratories (laboratories doing similar work to that of the laboratory under consideration) for a period of four years. A reassessment is conducted one year after accreditation is granted and biennial visits occur after the first year. A short surveillance questionnaire is completed in the years between visits to confirm that the quality management system remains in operation and to indicate major changes in the laboratory. In addition to the general CAN-P-1578 for forensic laboratories there are specific requirements for toxicology, chemistry and trace evidence, biology (which includes DNA), and equine drug testing – each of which include requirements for proficiency testing.

EUROPE

Within Europe few of the forensic science laboratories are accredited by their national accrediting organizations. It is the policy of the European Network of Forensic Science Institutes (ENSFI) that member laboratories should be moving toward accreditation, but there is no set time-frame. None of the national accrediting organizations have separate programs for forensic laboratories such as those in the US, Canada and Australia. The Laboratories of the Forensic Science Service in England are accredited by the United Kingdom Accreditation Service (UKAS) to ISO 17025 and by the British Standards Institute to the ISO 9001 standards.

INTERNATIONAL PROGRAMS

There are numerous international organizations that serve to link accreditation processes throughout the world. Some of these organizations produce the standards, while others serve as "umbrella" organizations bringing together groups with mutual concerns and interests.

ISO (www.iso.ch)

The International Organization for Standardization (ISO) which was established in 1947 is a non-governmental, worldwide federation of national standards bodies from over 140 countries. ISO does not do accreditations, its mission is to support the development and acceptance of international standards, to facilitate international trade, and develop international cooperation in intellectual, scientific, technological and economic fields. In order to do this, ISO, along with the International Electrochemical Commission (IEC), prepares standards that can be in the form of a "requirement" or a "guide." A requirement standard is mandatory and is written with the term "shall" in the text. A guideline standard is an advisory document written using the term "should." The ISO standards are "generic"; they do not apply to a specific product or organization.

When the need for a new standard is recognized or changes need to be considered for a present standard or guide, a committee is appointed from among the members of ISO to develop or revise standards. The first ISO/IEC Guide 25, *General requirements for the competence of calibration and testing laboratories,* was published in 1978 and the second in 1982; these covered only the technical aspects of a laboratory's operations. The third Guide 25, published in 1990, included the requirement for a quality management system. During this time-frame all types of organizations were beginning to incorporate quality management systems to comply with the International Standard ISO 9000 for quality management systems. This lead to ISO/IEC International Standard 17025 – *General requirements for the competence of testing and calibration laboratories* which incorporates the quality system requirements of ISO 9000 that are applicable to testing and calibrations laboratories. Since the types of laboratories vary, as well as the types of testing they do, ISO 17025 includes guidelines for "applications" for specific fields. These are documents that provide explanations or elaboration of the general requirements of the standards in ISO 17025. Some national organizations that accredit forensic laboratories, such as NATA and SCC, have written applications documents for use in crime laboratories; these documents include specific requirements for forensic laboratories including security requirements and more specific requirements in areas such as DNA.

The adoption of Guide 25 and ISO 17025 by accrediting bodies around the world has led to a uniform approach to determining laboratory competence. International agreements, called mutual recognition agreements (MRA), are developed between countries by evaluating each other's accrediting systems. These MRAs form the basis of agreements between countries for the acceptance of test data. Forensic laboratories are not presently directly involved in such agreements but these may some day be the basis of agreements between laboratories as international data bases are developed in fingerprints, DNA, areas of trace evidence, and other fields.

Two other ISO documents are directly relevant to forensic sciences. Guide 58 *Calibration and testing laboratory accreditation systems – General requirements for operation and recognition* which applies to organizations doing accreditation of laboratories, and Guide 43, *Proficiency testing by interlaboratory comparisons* for organizations preparing proficiency tests, accrediting bodies, and laboratories.

Membership in ISO is limited to one member organization per country; for the US the representative is the American National Standards Institute (ANSI).

ILAC (www.ilac.org)

The International Laboratory Accreditation Cooperation (ILAC) is an international association of accreditation bodies, national coordination bodies, regional accreditation bodies, and "stakeholders" working to define standards and coordinate practices so as to establish consistency in accreditation. Stakeholders include associations of laboratories or practitioners and regulatory authorities. Consistency in accreditations is essential to facilitate international trade. The ILAC Mutual Recognition Arrangement serves as the basis for a multilateral recognition agreement between ILAC members who will recognize the accreditations of other members leading to the international acceptance of test data and enhanced international trade. In February 2001 ILAC published a document for forensic laboratory accreditation. NATA and SCC are members of ILAC, the NFSTC became an Associate Member in 2001.

NACLA (www.nacla.org)

The National Cooperation for Laboratory Accreditation was established in 1997 in the United States as a partnership between public and private sectors to provide a uniform approach for accrediting organizations and accredited laboratories to meet international standards. Most counties have a single accrediting body that accredits all laboratories and can act as a single voice for a country in accrediting matters. Since the US has many accrediting organizations, many of which accredit laboratories in a single field (such as forensics), NACLA provides an opportunity for these organizations, and the laboratories they accredit, to present a more unified international voice. Much of the initial support came from the National Institute of Standards and Technology (NIST) which was directed by the National Technology Transfer and Advancement Act of 1995 to "provide leadership in coordinating standards and conformity assessment activity within federal, state and local government agencies and the private sector."[10] Members of NACLA include laboratory-accrediting organizations, laboratories, industry groups, and others interested in laboratory accreditation. Members of NACLA can apply for NACLA recognition when they are operating according to Guide 58, accrediting to 17025 and are fully operational. This recognition is based on an evaluation that includes an assessment by a NACLA evaluation team and leads to recognition that the accrediting body is compliant with Guide 58. Both ASCLD/LAB® and NFSTC are members of NACLA.

10 Public Law 104-113, signed March 7, 1996.

CERTIFICATION

Certification, as the term is used in the United States, is the recognition by a certifying body that an individual has the knowledge, skills, and ability to practice a specific forensic specialty. Certification may be granted by organizations affiliated with specific forensic disciplines or more broad-based organizations that certify individuals in a variety of fields. With the help of the American Academy of Forensic Science and NIJ, the Forensic Specialties Accreditation Board (FSAB) has been established. In an attempt to offer a method for determining the rigor of certifications offered by certification groups, this Board has developed guidelines for the accreditation of forensic specialty certification boards. The Board is establishing guidelines for a certification process that include:

- review and verification of the applicant's education and experience as well as other licences, certification or registration;
- assessment of competency by an examination of the knowledge, skills, and abilities in the relevant discipline. Part of the examination must be written;
- assessment may include review of proficiency tests, case audits, audit of court testimony, case presentations, and/or appraisals;
- the assessment must cover ethical and professional standards and the applicant process must include some type of inquiry into the applicant's adherence to ethical and professional standards;
- a recertification process that considers continuing competency, continuing education, work experience and ethical standards.

In the US there are several certifying organizations, many that were established by professional organizations, that certify examiners in a variety of areas of expertise.

CERTIFYING BODIES

IAI (www.theiai.org)

The International Association established the first forensic certification program in 1977 for the field of latent fingerprints. The IAI now has six certification programs, each administered by a Board made up of experts in the field. The procedures for certification vary but each is approved by the IAI Board of Directors to ensure compliance with IAI goals and policies. Each of the programs has education requirements, a mandate that the applicant be of good character, a standard certification procedure, and a recertification procedure.

- *Latent Print Examiner* – requirements include a bachelor's degree, three years of experience (experience can be substituted for the degree), 80 hours of training, and one year in classification, filing and searching of inked prints, and two years' experience in the comparison and identification of latent print material. There is a written test, a practical test including pattern recognition of inked fingerprints and comparison of latent prints to inked prints, and either an oral board or presentation of a case for review.
- *Bloodstain Pattern Analysis* – requirements include 40 hours of specialized training, three years of work within the discipline, and 240 hours of related training or special-

ized training that must be approved by the Certification Board, or be certified as a Senior Crime Scene Technician by IAI. Certification is for three years.

- *Crime Scene Technician/Analyst* – this is a three-level program with progressively stricter requirements. At the Senior Crime Scene Analyst level the applicant must have six years of crime scene experience, have completed six crime scene courses and have published an article on crime scene investigation, have presented a paper to a professional organization, be an instructor in crime scene investigation or submit a court transcript. There is a written test at each level. Certification is for five years.

- *Footwear Examiner* – education requirements are a high school diploma and eight years of related experience, an associates degree and five years experience or a bachelor's degree with three year of experience as a Footwear Examiner. The applicant must have completed a training program and submit two letters of endorsement.

- *Forensic Artist* – this is a two-level program with the Level II requirements including 80 hours of training in the field of composite art at an approved school and 40 hours of related courses, five years of experience with a law enforcement agency; five successful composite drawings must be submitted, and a written, practical verbal exam completed.

- *Forensic Photography* – requirements include three years of experience in photography and/or digital imaging, 40 hours of photography courses, and written and practical tests.

ABC (www.criminalistics.com/ABC/)

In the late 1970s an NIJ grant sponsored the Criminalistics Certification Study Committee. Although this Committee did not develop a certification program, their work prompted the California Association of Criminalists (CAC) to develop an examination that led to a Certificate of Professional Competency which assessed the overall competence of applicants. Using the CAC work as a starting point, the American Board of Criminalistics (ABC) was incorporated in 1989 as a national certification program for criminalistics. General requirements for certification include a baccalaureate degree in a natural science or other appropriate field, and two years of experience in a forensic science. The ABC offers three types of certification:

- Diplomate of the ABC which requires successful completion of the General Knowledge Exam (GKE). This certification signifies that the analyst is qualified to supervise multidisciplinary examinations of physical evidence. This level of certification is appropriate for laboratory directors, supervisors and analysts in fields where no specialty examinations are available, for example, explosives, soil, etc.

- Fellow status requires successful completion of the GKE and the relevant specialty examination, at least two years' experience in the specialty area, and successful completion of a proficiency test. Specialty exams already exist in forensic biology, drug chemistry, fire debris analysis, and trace analysis, with tests in other areas under consideration.

■ Technical Specialist certification requires three years of experience, successful completion of a proficiency test, and successful completion of a specialty test. This certification is offered in forensic drug analysis and forensic molecular biology and signifies that the analyst is qualified to conduct examinations in the field tested.

All Fellows and Technical Specialists in ABC are required to take an annual proficiency test to maintain their certification. Certification is valid for five years and may be renewed by obtaining 50 recertification "points" during the five-year period. Points are awarded for continued involvement in forensic science through employment, membership in professional organizations, attendance at meetings, service to professional organizations, publishing, or retesting. As of January 2002 there were 548 Diplomates of ABC, 99 of whom hold one or more Fellow Certificates. There are seven Technical Specialists in Drug Analysis and six Technical Specialists in Molecular Biology.

ABFDE (www.abfde.org)

The American Board of Forensic Document Examiners, Inc. (ABFDE) was established in 1977 to provide a certification program for forensic document examiners. Forensic document examination was defined to include identification of handwriting, typewriting, the authenticity of signatures, examination of inks and papers, and photocopying processes. The American Academy of Forensic Sciences, the American Society of Questioned Documents Examiners (ASQDE) and the Canadian Society of Forensic Science sponsor the Board. It is composed of elected directors and a Professional Review Committee, made up of Board members. Certification by ABFDE is available only to permanent residents of the US, Canada and Mexico. An applicant must be of good moral character, reputation, and integrity and must possess a high ethical and professional standing. He/she must also have a baccalaureate degree and be working as a document examiner at the time of application. An applicant must have two years training in a forensic laboratory that is recognized by the Board and two years of full-time document work in a recognized laboratory. References from three qualified forensic document examiners are required. Applicants take comprehensive written, practical and oral examinations. Certificates of Qualification in Forensic Document Examination are valid for five years and can be renewed as long as the individual is involved in questioned document examination and earns 50 continuing education credits over a five-year period.

ABFT (www.abft.org)

The American Board of Forensic Toxicologists (ABFT), which accredits forensic toxicology laboratories, also sponsors a certification program for individuals working in forensic toxicology laboratories. Applicants for certification as a Forensic Toxicology Specialist must be permanent residents of the US or Canada, possess bachelor's degree in a natural science, and have three years of full-time professional experience; they must document appropriate professional activities in forensic toxicology and be actively employed in forensic toxicology. Applicants who pass a comprehensive written examination may be granted a certificate that is valid for five years. An applicant for Diplomate status in the American Board of Forensic Toxicology must have earned a doctorate of philosophy or doctor of science degree in one of the natural sciences, must have three years of professional experience, must document a record of appropriate professional activities in forensic toxicology, and be working in forensic toxicology. Applicants who successfully complete comprehensive written examinations on the broad principles of forensic science may be granted a certificate that is valid for five years.

AFTE (www.afte.org)

One of the newest certification programs in forensic science is that of the Association of Firearms and Toolmark Examiners (AFTE), which offer certification in three areas:

1. Firearm Evidence Examination and Identification.
2. Toolmark Evidence Examination and Identification.
3. Gunshot Residue Evidence Examination and Identification.

Each of these certifications requires that the applicant successfully complete a written examination and then a practical examination. Applicants must be a member of AFTE in good standing and after 2005 must have a baccalaureate degree in physical, or forensic science, criminalistics, criminal justice or a related field.

ACFE (www.acfe.com)

Application to the American College of Forensic Examiners (ACFE) is by invitation only. Diplomate status requirements include a baccalaureate degree, documentation showing a good foundation within the applicant's specialty area, five years of experience, and completion of four courses offered by the ACFE. Unlike the other certifications, ACFE does not require an examination in the applicant's field of specialization.

PERSONAL COMPETENCE

In the United Kingdom the approach toward affirming an individual's expertise has not been by certification but though recognition of personal competence. Supported by the Science, Technology and Mathematics Council, a program has been developed which allows the assessment of individual examiners in their workspace. The program consists of a compilation of high-level activities that together define the total activity under consideration. These activities are subdivided into subactivities that are subdivided into performance criteria. It is against these criteria that the examiner is assessed. By assessing what is done, not how it is done, the process can be used to assess an examiner in a large laboratory or in a single person laboratory. For example, for the task "Examine items and samples," one of the performance criteria used for assessment is "Select and use recovery methods that will optimize recovery." The assessor would be concerned that appropriate recovery methods were used and that the outcome defined by the performance criterion is achieved, but not how the outcome (in this case the recovery) was achieved. Assessors are experts in the field in which they are carrying out assessments and have been specially trained to conduct the assessments. The assessment could include observations by the assessor, statements by colleagues, and review of casework carried out by the examiner. The examiner would continue to collect material to demonstrate continued competence.[11]

11 Keith Hadley, presentation at American Academy of Forensic Sciences, February, 2002.

REGISTRATION OF FORENSIC PRACTITIONERS

A Council for the Registration of Forensic Practitioners (CRFP) has recently been established in the UK. The CRFP is a regulatory body that is establishing a register for competent forensic practitioners for use as a reference by anyone who desires professional information about an examiner. The registrant must:

- belong to a professional group;
- subscribe to high professional values;
- have taken all necessary steps to keep up to date ;
- possess the confidence to have their competence assessed by a peer or professional tribunal in cases of serious questions regarding their fitness.

Registration is based on evidence of competent performance on current casework that for most potential registrants means work carried out in the six months prior to registration. The applicant for registration provides a summary of their qualifications and experience and a declaration of their character. Two professional referees then assess and comment on the applicant's evidence of

12 ibid.

professional performance. The register is presently open to forensic scientists, scene examiners and fingerprint examiners.[12]

PROFICIENCY TESTS

All of the accreditation programs and most certification programs in forensic science require participation in proficiency testing programs. Proficiency tests are used to evaluate an individual examiner or a group of individuals including technical support personnel who are doing a series of tests or the performance of the laboratory as a whole. Proficiency tests are a reliable method to demonstrate that a laboratory's technical procedures are valid and that an individual examiners are maintaining their competency.

Open tests are tests that the examiners and technical support personnel know are proficiency tests and are announced as such. When the examiner or technical support personnel are not aware that they are being tested, the tests are called "blind" proficiency tests. These samples are submitted as normal case samples to the individual being tested. Depending on the program, the supervisor and managers may not even be aware that blind samples are being tested. Proficiency tests that are prepared and conducted by the laboratory or laboratory system are called internal or interlaboratory tests. External proficiency tests are prepared by commercial agencies or laboratories external to the laboratory or system being tested. Most of the accreditation and certification programs require external tests be given, if they are available. If external proficiency tests are not available the use of intralaboratory tests should be considered – these are external tests prepared by a laboratory and then shipped to another laboratory for use as a proficiency test; several laboratories may be involved in a "round-robin" process.

Proficiency tests should be similar to casework encountered by the examiner, when possible. The process should be a positive one for the examiner, giving them confidence that they are doing their work well and identifying areas where additional training is needed. Managers should use each proficiency test as an evaluation of their laboratory as a whole. When an incorrect answer (one not agreeing with the answer given by the provider) is given for a proficiency test it is the responsibility of management and the quality assurance team to determine the cause and take corrective action. Numerous issues must be examined from the test itself to the testing procedures and equipment to the reporting process:

- *Test* – was the test properly prepared and presented? Was the sample protected during shipping to ensure that the sample sent from the provider was identical to what was tested in the laboratory? Is there any chance the sample could have been mishandled in the laboratory before going to the examiner?

- *Testing procedure* – was the procedure appropriate for the sample, was it done correctly, was the equipment used correctly, were results interpreted correctly?
- *Reporting process* – were there simple errors in typing or transposed numbers that led to an incorrect answer?
- *Examiner* – did the examiner make an error in testing, does he or she have the knowledge to do the correct test and interpret the results?

When the root cause is determined, the focus must switch to corrective actions:

- If the problem was with the test, how can that be corrected or another proficiency test given?
- Does a process or procedure need to be modified or eliminated and replaced?
- Does a piece of equipment need recalibration or repair?
- Does an examiner need more training, should they be removed from casework?
- Has a similar situation occurred in casework, do some cases have to be re-examined, prosecutors and or investigators notified?

Corrective actions should include steps to ensure that the situation does not reoccur.

QUALITY SAMPLES

For publicly funded crime laboratories in the US, the National Forensic Science Technology Center can provide "Quality Samples." Funded by the National Institute of Justice (NIJ), the NFSTC distributes these samples with a certificate

Table 4.1

Proficiency test providers.

Provider	What they provide tests on
Collaborative Testing Services, Inc.	Controlled substances, serology, DNA, firearms, toolmarks, imprint/impression evidence, fibers, latent prints, paint, glass, flammables, questioned documents, bloodstain pattern
Cellmark Diagnostics, Inc.	DNA
College of American Pathologists	DNA, toxicology program, urine toxicology program, forensic urine drug testing program
Serological Research Institute	DNA, serology
Quality Forensics, Inc.	Ignitable liquids, DNA, drug chemistry, toxicology, latent prints, trace evidence
CAT Proficiency Testing Program	Toxicology
FAA Forensic Toxicology Program	Postmortem forensic toxicology

of analysis. A laboratory may use these samples as the laboratory management feels appropriate. They cannot be used as proficiency tests to meet the requirements of ASCLD/LAB® but can be used internally to provide samples for training of new examiners, internal proficiency tests, remedial tests or for validation of procedures. Quality samples have included flammables, toxicology samples, controlled substances and hair samples.

STANDARDS

In order for accreditation systems, certification systems, and even proficiency tests to be useful measures of the competency of laboratories and individual examiners, there need to be standards or standard procedures for tests. These standards are written procedures or methods that are accepted by a recognized group as the method for performing routine or repetitive tasks. Most standards in forensic science are "consensus standards" – the majority of group establishing the standard has agreed that the standard is appropriate. In an effort to establish standards for forensic science the FBI, DEA, and NIJ have established the Scientific Working Groups (SWGs) and Technical Working Groups (TWGs) to produce consensus standards. Members of the groups are subject matter experts and include forensic examiners, laboratory managers, academics, researchers, law enforcement officers, legal practitioners, and representatives of other appropriate groups. Many of the guidelines published in the SWGs and TWGs can be found in *Forensic Science Communications,* an on-line journal produced by the FBI. Most of the standards are "voluntary standards"; there are no laws or regulations requiring their use in forensic laboratories.

STANDARDS-PRODUCING BODIES

ASTM (www.astm.org)

The American Standards Testing Materials, now ASTM International, is one of the largest voluntary standards development organizations in the world. ASTM Committee E-30 on forensic science has developed approximately 35 consensus standards in different forensic science disciplines. The fire debris analysis standards are the most widely recognized. One of the main concerns many forensic scientists have with ASTM standards is that all members of ASTM committees have equal votes on the ASTM standards. Many of these committee members have no forensic background and consequently possess limited understanding of the various issues that may impinge upon evidence in a criminal case – from extremely small, contaminated samples to short analysis time-frames. In response to this concern, ASTM Committee E-30 has begun to adopt some of the procedures and processes that have been proposed by the

TWGs and SWGs. Support for the work product of the SWGs and TWGs by ASTM will encourage international review and acceptance of these processes and procedures.

SWGDAM (www.fbiva.fbiacademy.edu)

The Scientific Working Group on DNA Analysis Methods (SWGDAM) was established in 1988 with the support of the FBI to allow forensic DNA examiners to exchange analytical methods and protocols. SWGDAM has developed guidelines for quality assurance, proficiency testing, databases, and consensus statements on DNA technologies and techniques. The work of SWGDAM was the basis for much of the material in the *Quality Assurance Standards for Forensic DNA Testing Laboratories* issued in 1998 by the FBI and the *Quality Assurance Standards for Convicted Offender DNA Databasing Laboratories*. These standards were combined to form the *Quality Assurance Audit for Forensic DNA and Convicted Offender DNA Databasing Laboratories*[13] which is used by ASCLD/LAB® and other organizations when auditing DNA laboratories.

SWGMAT (www.fbiva.fbiacademy.edu)

Scientific Working Group on Materials Examination (SWGMAT) was formed in 1995 by the merger of the earlier Technical Working Group on Fibers (TWGFIBE) and the Technical Working Group on Paint (TWGPAINT). SWGMAT has subgroups working in the areas of paint, glass, soil, fibers and other polymeric materials to provide examination guidelines, round-robin studies, and establishment of QA/QC information. Among the guidelines they have published are *Trace Evidence Quality Assurance Guidelines*,[14] *Trace Evidence Recovery Guidelines*,[15] *Forensic Fiber Examination Guidelines*[16] and *Forensic Paint Analysis and Comparison Guidelines*.[17]

SWGDRUG (www.swgdrug.org)

The Scientific Working Group for the Analysis of Seized Drugs (SWGDRUG) was the first of the working groups initially established as an international group. Representatives from around the world were present in 1997 at the first meeting, sponsored by the Drug Enforcement Administration. The United States Office of National Drug Control Policy (ONDCP) funds this SWG. The objectives of SWGDRUG are:

- To specify requirements for forensic drug practitioners' knowledge, skills and abilities.
- To promote professional development for forensic drug practitioners.
- To provide a means of information exchange with the forensic science community.
- To promote the highest ethical standards of practitioners in all areas of forensic drug analysis.

13 *Forensic Science Communications*, January 2001. 3(1).

14 *Forensic Science Communications*, January 2000. 2(1).

15 *Forensic Science Communications*, October 1999. 1(3).

16 *Forensic Science Communications*, April 1999. 1(1).

17 *Forensic Science Communications*, July 1999. 1(2).

- To provide minimum standards for drug examinations and reporting.
- To establish quality assurance requirements.
- To seek international acceptance for SWGDRUG standards.

The SWG has published a booklet of recommendations for education and training, quality assurance guidelines in forensic drug analysis, and recommended minimum standards for forensic drug identification.[18] Work continues on sampling procedures, analysis procedures, validation and verification schemes, and guidance for ethical standards and standards and assessment of professional competence.

SWGDOC (www.fbiva.fbiacademy.edu)

The Scientific Working Group for Document Examination was established by the FBI in 1998 with representatives from law enforcement at all levels, private practice, the legal profession and academia. By 1999 SWGDOC had issued draft guidelines and recommendations for several document examination technologies and procedures. Standards and guidelines on handwriting as well subjects such as indentations, printing processes and other areas will be developed by SWGDOC members.

TWGFEX (http://ncfs.ucf.edu)

The Technical working group for Fire and Explosives (TWGFEX) was established in 1997 by the National Center for Forensic Science (NCFS) with the support of NIJ to serve as an advisory panel in matters related to fire and explosives. The goal of the TWG is to develop protocols and guides for the collection and analysis of fire and explosive debris, quality assurance guides for fire and explosive professional and job descriptions for practitioner positions. The Technical Working Group on Fire/Arson Scene Investigation (TWGFASI) developed from that group and has prepared the *Fire and Arson Scene Evidence: A Guide for Public Safety Personnel*.[19] The Technical Working Group for Bombing Scene Investigation (TWGBSI), another subgroup of TWGFEX, has produced *A Guide for Explosion and Bombing Scene Investigation*.[20]

SWGDE (www.fbiva.fbiacademy.edu)

The Scientific Working Group on Digital Evidence (SWGDE) was established in 1998 through a collaborative effort of the Federal Crime Laboratory Directors. As participants in the International Organization on Computer Evidence (IOCE) the members are working to establish standards for the exchange of digital evidence between nations. SWGDE, with the assistance of the National Center for Forensic Science, is developing cross-disciplinary guidelines and standards for the recovery, presentation and examination of all types of digital

18 United States Department of Justice Drug Enforcement Administration, 2001.

19 United States Department of Justice, Office of Justice Programs, June 2000, NCJ 181584.

20 United States Department of Justice, Office of Justice Programs, June 2000, NCJ 181869.

evidence, including computer evidence, digital audio, and digital video. Standards have been proposed for international definitions and standards relating to evidence collection, storage, examination and transfer of digital evidence. SWGDE members have participated in the development of many NIJ guides including *Electronic Crime Scene Investigations: A Guide for First Responders,*[21] *How to Plan, Design, Construct, Staff and Equip a Computer Forensic Unit* (draft) and *Digital Evidence in the Courtroom* (draft).

[21] United States Department of Justice, Office of Justice Programs, July 2001, NCJ 187736.

SWGFAST (www.fbiva.fbiacademy.edu)

The Scientific Working Group on Friction Ridge Analysis, Study and Technology (SWGFAST) first met in 1995. The objectives include: providing minimum standards for the knowledge, skills, and abilities of latent fingerprint analysis, to share analytical methods and protocols, encourage and evaluate research in the field, establish QA and QC guidelines for friction ridge analysis, cooperate with national and international organizations in the preparation of standards, and to inform the community of their work. The guidelines prepared by SWGFAST – *Minimum Qualifications for Latent Print Examiner Trainees, Training to Competency for Latent Print Examiners, and Quality Assurance Guidelines for Latent Print Examiners* – have all been published in the *Journal of Forensic Identification*[22]

[22] *Journal of Forensic Identification.* 51. 229-296

SWGGUN (www.fbiva.fbiacademy.edu)

The FBI sponsors the Scientific Working Group for Firearms and Toolmarks (SWGGUN). The purpose of SWGGUN is to provide consensus guidelines for the firearms and toolmarks discipline and to disseminate these guidelines, studies, and other findings that may be of benefit to the forensic community. Quality Assurance Guidelines were published in December of 1999; future guidelines will be published in the *Forensic Science Communications* on-line journal.

SWGIT (www.fbiva.fbiacademy.edu)

The Scientific Working Group on Digital Imaging (SWGIT) was established in 1997 by the FBI to facilitate the use of imaging technology and systems within the criminal justice system. Members of SWGIT have produced *Definitions and Guidelines for the Use of Imaging Technologies in the Criminal Justice System.*[23] The guidelines include evidence handling, quality assurance, and training, qualification and proficiency of examiners.

[23] *Forensic Science Communications*, October, 1999. 1(3).

TWGCSI (www.ojp.usdoj.gov)

The Technical Working Group on Crime Scene Investigation, created in 1998 by NIJ, was a multidisciplinary group tasked with preparing a document that could be used to as a guide by large or small agencies for the processing of a

24 United States Department of Justice, Office of Justice Programs, January 2000, NCJ 178280.

variety of crime scenes. In January, 2000, their first work product, *Crime Scene Investigation, a Guide for Law Enforcement*[24] was published.

TWGED (www.ojp.usdoj.gov)

The Technical Working Group on Education and Training in Forensic Science, sponsored by NIJ, was established in 2001. This TWG is developing guidelines for forensic education at all levels. Recommendations will start with candidate qualifications, professional orientation, expectations and prescreening of students, credentialing at all levels. They will be providing model curriculum for undergraduate and graduate students, and recommendations for continued education and training.

THE FUTURE

The work of the Scientific and Technical Working Groups that started with SWGDAM in 1988 will continue indefinitely. The creation of standard procedures for techniques currently in use throughout forensic science is becoming essential to meet the legal requirements placed upon the fields by new laws such as *Daubert*. When the work of forensic examiners is reviewed by others, either other examiners or individuals outside of the field, the existence and use of standard operating procedures will be one way to evaluate the results. As new techniques and procedures are introduced, the SWGs and TWGs will be one of the best means of sharing validation and validity studies which must be performed.

The accreditation of laboratories both in the US and internationally is expected to continue. Approximately half of the US crime laboratories are accredited as of 2002, and with the strong support of ENSFI the number in Europe is expected to rise. The establishment of international databases will make standardization and accreditation, as the means of measuring compliance with standards, more important.

ACKNOWLEDGMENT

The author would like to thank Mr. Ralph Keaton for information on the history of the American Society of Crime Laboratory Directors/Laboratory Accreditation Board; Dr. Graham Jones of the Medical Examiners Officer in Edmonton, Alberta, Canada for information on the Forensic Specialties Accreditation Board and Dr. Bob Bramley of the Forensic Science Services in Birmingham England for taking time to discuss the Registration of Forensic Practitioners and evaluation of personal competence in the United Kingdom.

Association/Organization	Acronym	URL
American Board of Forensic Toxicology	ABFT	www.abft.org
American Board of Criminalistics	ABC	www.criminalistics.com/ABC/
American Board of Forensic Documents Examiners	ABFDE	www.abfde.org
American College of Forensic Examiners	ACFE	www.acfe.com
American National Standards Institute	ANSI	www.ansi.org
American Society of Crime Laboratory Directors	ASCLD	www.ascld.org
American Society of Crime Laboratory Directors/Laboratory Accreditation Board	ASCLD/LAB	www.ascld_lab.org
Association of Firearms and Toolmarks Examiners	AFTE	www.afte.org
ASTM, International	ASTM	www.astm.org
California Association of Criminalists	CAC	www.cacnews.org
California Association of Toxicologists	CAT	www.cal-tox.org
Canadian Society of Forensic Science	CSFS	www.csfs.ca
Cellmark Diagnostics, Inc.		www.cellmark-labs.com
Collaborative Testing Services, Inc.	CTS	www.collaborativetesting.com
College of American Pathologists	CAP	www.cap.org
European Network of Forensic Science Institutes	ENSFI	www.ensfi.org
Federal Aviation Administration	FAA	www.faa.gov
Forensic Specialties Accreditation Board	FSAB	www.thefsab.org
International Association for Identification	IAI	www.theiai.org
International Laboratory Accreditation Cooperation	ILAC	www.ilac.org
International Organization for Standardization	ISO	www.iso.ch
National Association of Medical Examiners	NAME	www.thename.org
National Association of Testing Authorities, Australia	NATA	www.nata.asn.au
National Center for Forensic Science	NCFS	http://ncfs.ucf.edu
National Cooperation for Laboratory Accreditation	NACLA	www.nacla.org
National Forensic Science Technology Center	NFSTC	www.nfstc.org
National Institute of Justice	NIJ	www.ojp.usdoj.gov/nij
Quality Forensics, Inc.		www.qualityforensics.com
Scientific Working Group for the Analysis of Seized Drugs	SWGDRUG	www.swgdrug.org
Serological Research Institute	SERI	bwraxall@serological.com
Standards Council of Canada	SCC	www.scc.ca
SWG's sponsored by FBI		www.fbiva.fbiacademy.edu
TWG's sponsored by NIJ		www.ojp.usdoj.gov

Table 4.2

World Wide Web addresses for forensic, crime and crime laboratory organizations.

CHAPTER 5

STRATEGIC MANAGEMENT

The best way to predict the future is to create it.
(Peter Drucker)

The general who wins a battle makes many calculations in his temple before the battle
is fought.
(Sun Tzu)

INTRODUCTION

Organizations function with either a formal or informal mission. For crime laboratories, missions usually include the primary function of analyzing physical evidence in an objective and thorough manner. In addition to adhering to the mission, effective management of a laboratory or any organization requires a deep understanding of the organization's capabilities as well as the environment in which it must function. Crime laboratory directors must incorporate this information into their decision-making when outlining strategies for future operations of the laboratory. Clearly defining this information will help in developing a carefully considered strategic plan.

Strategic planning provides a roadmap for an organization. For crime laboratories, it is an exercise that can make the difference between being prepared for a new crime development and playing catch-up. It can also be the difference between haphazard and focused decision-making. A strategic plan provides a reference for management decisions. Universal adoption of a plan within the laboratory unifies the efforts of a crime laboratory's employees.

There are many different management programs that organizations follow in developing strategic plans. Often laboratories that operate as a segment of government are dictated to follow a different program with each election. Most management programs consider the same basic information. They all speak to the importance of defining an organization's mission, goals and objectives, and developing a plan for achieving the goals. They generally include customer and employee input while developing the plan. And they teach that the plan should be followed when making management decisions.

IMPORTANCE OF STRATEGIC PLANNING

Management through strategic planning provides a number of advantages. A plan defines desirable outcomes for the organization and in doing so provides direction to their activities and permits evaluation of the outcomes. It also provides a framework for management decisions regarding personnel, facilities, and other financial resources that support the desirable outcomes.

Strategic planning can be undertaken at many levels and for many reasons. An individual unit, such as a drug analysis unit in a government crime laboratory, may develop a plan for implementation of a new procedure. This plan is incorporated in the laboratory's operational plan adhering to the laboratory's mission. The crime laboratory's plan must then adhere to the parent agency's mission and goals. Ultimately, the agency must be responsive to the priorities and goals of an elected official.

Some governmental agencies require that their units develop a strategic plan. This plan may be used strictly for operational purposes or may be used for funding decisions. A decision-maker can determine which units best fulfill their policy priorities by evaluating plans submitted from several units. These units may be funded over others based on their strategic plans. Additional consideration may be given to funding units that were successful in meeting their strategic goals rather than those that were not.

While not all organizations are forced into a strategic planning exercise, several scenarios can occur, usually as a result of changes, that make it desirable to reconsider an organization's mission and goals. These "triggers" force an organization to evaluate its current practices and policies as it faces impending changes. Triggers for crime laboratories include growth or reduction to a laboratory and its services.

GROWTH OF SERVICES

The creation of a new organization demands that the strategic planning process be undertaken. It is best if a strategic plan is developed and implemented from the outset of a new operation. For private laboratories, the planning process is an integral part of establishing a business plan. It establishes the laboratory's purpose for existence as well as outlines their priorities and how they will derive income. A strategic plan for a new government laboratory helps provide direction for growth. It provides a step-by-step guide of what must be accomplished in order for the laboratory to effectively meet its goals and those of its parent agency.

As the population of cities, states, or nations increases, the demand for law enforcement services generally increases as well. A crime laboratory will likely see growth as a result of this population increase. The increase in the demand for services may be accompanied by an increase in revenue generated from the increased population. If this occurs there is a need to determine where the additional resources would be most effective. Staff and equipment funding could be justified through a strategic plan based on growth predictions. A review in operations is also required if no increase in revenue accompanies increased demand. Instead of considering increased revenue as a positive attribute, the lack of revenue would be a considered as a challenge through the planning process.

At times, crime laboratories have been merged either to reduce redundancy or improve efficiency. This may happen if two crime laboratories perform an overlapping service in the same geographical area. It may also occur if one laboratory has funding problems and cannot exist by itself. Mergers can cause difficulties among employees from both organizations if their priorities differ. It is important that a new unified strategy be developed that incorporates the needs of both organizations. This same reasoning applies within crime laboratories when sections are combined that were at one time autonomous. The individuals within the sections had goals and interests that were specific to a discipline. When new individuals are introduced, they must agree to new goals for the new section.

New crimes may also dictate re-examination of a crime laboratory's direction. An explosion in the use of a new controlled substance will require resources to be reallocated to implement analytical schemes for identification. A planning process should be undertaken to review this growing threat. The planning process should include an evaluation of whether additional resources can be located to address the need. If no resources are available, the process should include alternatives such as redirecting resources from a program in less need.

Also, legislative changes may require revision of priorities. For example, legislation is often instituted without consideration to the effect on crime laboratories. One such occurrence was when federal law and some states legislated that "crack" or cocaine base would carry a harsher penalty than that of cocaine powder or cocaine hydrochloride. This placed a burden on crime laboratories to differentiate between the two forms. Laboratories had to consider how they would efficiently accomplish this task without increased revenue. Many had to divert funds intended to assist in other disciplines to purchase new instrumentation for this purpose. Also, the federal oversight of DNA analysis caused laboratories to incorporate specific criteria in their analysis. A plan is useful to determine how to obtain and implement the resources necessary to comply with the regulations.

Laboratories also experience growth as technologies change. The availability of DNA analysis and the subsequent ability to identify an unknown DNA donor by comparison to a database caused a lot of laboratories to re-examine resource allocation. As DNA developed, most conventional serology was discontinued. Personnel had to be retrained and facilities modified. Through trend analysis and consideration of analytical effectiveness, many laboratories determined that an investment in this discipline would produce a greater impact on case solvability. This decision reduced funding from other, less specific areas of analysis, and in many laboratories drastically reduced or eliminated the hair analysis discipline.

Crime laboratories are often required to undertake new or expanded roles. State legislation mandated that DNA databases be established and maintained by the state crime laboratory in each state. This requirement forced many laboratories to undergo a planning process that considered where to obtain funding for typing DNA samples from convicted offenders to populate the database.

Crime laboratory reduction

As with all government and private organizations, crime laboratories will inevitably undergo a reduction in budget at some time. The reduction may be significant enough to affect operations. When this occurs, it is necessary for the laboratory to re-examine its current operation in order to determine what services may be cut. Input from stakeholders is an important aspect of this determination.

While changing technologies often require that new disciplines be incorporated, limited resources may dictate that an existing service be cut. A revised strategic plan should be developed not only to implement the new discipline, but also to manage the existing disciplines that may suffer reduction in budgets or even discontinuation. Stakeholder demand for these services may continue and it is important to determine how the laboratory will manage these demands. They should consider alternative options that enable stakeholders to continue to obtain the necessary analysis.

CHANGE IN LEADERSHIP

New leaders, either within or outside the crime laboratory, generally dictate a change in direction. New leaders have priorities that require laboratories to incorporate new policies. New laboratory directors may believe that accreditation is urgent, while a previous director may not have felt so strongly. For laboratories located within a police agency, sworn administrators change on a regular basis. Each new administrator incorporates law enforcement strategies that impact the laboratory. A strategic planning exercise that incorporates the traditions of the laboratory as well as the new goals establishes a common vision for all employees.

The change in priorities may be particularly noticeable with a change in elected officials at a federal level. Not only are the priorities of federal law enforcement agencies redirected but granting agencies receive funding to be directed to local or state crime laboratories for implementation of these new priorities. Following the September 11, 2001 attacks, President George W. Bush's priority for his administration changed to one of terrorism prevention. This type of change affects federal spending and grant-making priorities. Grant funding that was intended for one purpose quickly disappeared in order for funding to be available for a new priority.

CHANGE IN PERSONNEL

Even if there is not a change in leadership, constant turnover in the laboratory may cause lack of consensus among employees. A strategic planning exercise can help to coordinate the actions of the employees as well as revitalize their commitment to goals. A director may also wish to incorporate a new vision into the processes of the laboratory. It is not always necessary or practical to have all laboratory employees included in the strategic planning process. However, participation of key employees in the process provides ownership that will trickle to other employees.

The polar opposite of constant turnover is no turnover. When there is no change required, a laboratory may lose the motivation to change. This can lead to stagnation in the development of the laboratory. When change is forced upon a laboratory with this attitude, the employees will fight against the change. If a laboratory director realizes that this is the situation in their organization they should undertake a planning process to revitalize the laboratory and its staff.

OPERATIONAL REQUIREMENTS

Some crime laboratories are faced with political pressures to either develop a strategic plan or to implement changes that require development of a plan. A strategic plan is required for many federal laboratories to receive appropriations. The threat of not receiving funding is sufficient justification to undergo the process. Additionally, quality discrepancies, either real or perceived, have been a catalyst for many governments to require that a laboratory undergo accreditation. The accreditation process can be daunting and is more easily performed using a plan.

Federal grant requirements also require that crime laboratories operate in subscribed ways. DNA grants require that laboratories comply with the DNA Advisory Board standards. Recent grants require that states undergo a strategic planning process for incorporation of a technology within a state. Generally, this requires that unrelated laboratories agree upon a strategy for the state. When laboratory directors agree to the strategy, it can be submitted to a state granting agency where distribution of the funding is determined. It can also be used as evidence to legislators that crime laboratories consider the importance of their role in ensuring the effective use of public funds to maximize the desired outcomes.

MISSION STATEMENTS

Prior to establishing a strategic plan, it is important that the mission of the organization be clearly defined. This is usually accomplished by developing a mission statement. A mission statement builds on a leader's vision for an organization by outlining how it will function in light of that vision. An organization's mission statement should be short yet encompass their reason for existing.

Development of a mission statement can include all members of a small laboratory or representatives of several employee segments in a large laboratory. It is important the employees share in the development of the mission statement. With their participation in the process, they accept the final product as well as the obligation to conform to it.

Management decisions should always be considered in light of the mission statement as it provides a uniform, objective basis for decision-making. When a director's decisions consistently support the crime laboratory's mission, employees will also make recommendations and decisions using this criterion. Employees can be confident that their decisions will be supported by management because they are based on a mutually agreed-to standard.

DEVELOPING A STRATEGIC PLAN

The goal of a strategic plan is to give detail to a leader's vision and garner the commitment of stakeholders. A plan can be developed at any time but is particularly useful when the laboratory is facing changes. A strategic plan is more than just a change in priorities that occur as a result of change. It considers the mission of the organization as well as the strengths and weaknesses inherent to it. A strategic plan also considers the environment in which the organization must operate as well as the opportunities and threats that face the organization. Finally, after consideration of these factors, a strategic plan should address what is to be accomplished, by whom, and by when.

While all organizations have requirements placed on them by their stakeholders, each is different with respect to its capabilities and environment. All government and private crime laboratories must operate with limited resources under extensive internal and external regulations. Laboratories have a limited number of employees and equipment. The physical capabilities restrict the amount and type of analysis that a crime laboratory can offer. In addition, quality and legal regulations require specific processes to be followed in support of the analysts' conclusions.

While crime laboratories share these general similarities, the specific capabilities and restrictions vary. Legal regulations in one jurisdiction may require a crime laboratory to analyze drug cases within days, while in another jurisdiction there may be no such requirement. Additionally, a private laboratory can generally hire additional personnel in a much shorter time and much easier process than can a government laboratory.

Crime laboratory directors must be aware of both these similarities and differences. A director can receive valuable information by researching what other laboratories do in certain situations. However, they must also be aware of their own environment before deciding whether a particular strategy will work for them.

The preferable way to develop a strategic plan is to undergo a formalized strategic planning process. The first step in the process is to organize a strategic management group that will develop the plan. This group should be composed of key stakeholders that have an interest in the crime laboratory's operation and service. Obvious among these are the criminalists as well as the crime laboratory's leadership. However, they may also include police officers and prosecutors. The group could even be expanded to include victims' aid groups and defense attorneys. However, the group should not be so large as to hinder decision-making. Certain stakeholders may be invited to participate only in select discussions depending upon their interest or contribution's value. Input from other stakeholders may come from surveys or other opinion-gathering devices.

It is often valuable to have an experienced consultant act as a facilitator to the group. A manager may wish to participate in the group in order to convey their vision to the group. There will likely be reservations about speaking freely with the manager present. Also, participants in the group may feel overly constrained if the manager is directing the discussion instead of being only a participant. The facilitator will help in setting ground rules that include non-judgmental discussions to encourage free-flowing discussions.

Once members are selected, the first task is to ensure that all understand the historical context of how the laboratory has been affected and has reacted to past events and trends. It is important that the members agree to the organizational identity and purpose as well as the perception of others toward the laboratory. It is important to have a realistic understanding of the organization within which the crime laboratory operates. This can be accomplished in a number of ways, using a survey of stakeholders including officers, prosecutors, defense attorneys, judges.

The strengths and weaknesses of the crime laboratory must be documented as they provide the mechanism for a successful plan. In order for a strategic plan to be achievable, it must build on the strengths and overcome the weaknesses of the organization. A particular crime laboratory's strengths may include knowledgeable personnel and adequate instrumentation, whereas their weaknesses include inadequate facilities and funding. One can see how the strengths and weaknesses must be considered in order to achieve a goal. If a plan to implement a new process were developed, it would have to include a mechanism to improve facilities and funding.

In addition to the events that the organization has faced in the past, the group must consider the current trends and events that will influence the future. These trends will present opportunities that can be seized as well as threats to the success of the laboratory's plan. An achievable plan should consider the opportunities and threats that the laboratory will face in the future. If the laboratory wished to increase funding for its DNA program, the opportunity of obtaining funds through new grant opportunities should be investigated. Also, the threat that a downturn in the economy may threaten laboratory revenue should also be considered when looking at the institution of a new program.

A goal can then be developed based upon the group's discussion of strengths, weaknesses, opportunities, and threats. This goal becomes a target for the strategic plan to achieve, and should be stated clearly and address measurable objectives. For example, building on the knowledgeable staff and adequate instrumentation, the laboratory develops the goal of expanding its toxicology program. In order to overcome the inadequate facilities and funding, the plan includes soliciting funding support through the administration by outlining past successes. If they are unsuccessful with this, they have also included an objective of contacting other law enforcement agencies, prosecutors, and Mothers Against Drunk Driving to request their support for expansion of the program. The objectives are concrete and their completion can be easily documented.

A goal may also come first. A new laboratory director may have a program that they wish to incorporate into the laboratory's operation. The group's purpose would then be to evaluate various alternatives that could be utilized to implement the program and select the optimal alternative. Also, if a laboratory director has become aware of several trends that will influence the future of the laboratory, there may be several programs to consider. It is necessary for the group to evaluate and prioritize the programs with regard to the strengths, weaknesses, opportunities, and threats.

When the group has established a goal, a strategy can then be devised to achieve that goal. The strategy must include consideration of issues that will add to or hinder achievement. Issues to be considered include the desire of individuals to avoid change, equity issues for personnel affected, and how productivity may be affected. Also important in the development of a strategy is assessment of the resources and support available to achieve the plan. If support is minimal, education of key stakeholders will be necessary to increase their interest in the success of the plan. Stakeholder education may also succeed in garnering necessary resources.

A plan is never final. Often unexpected situations arise that dictate revisiting the plan. A plan that is devised to implement a single program may not require revision. However, a continuous operational plan should be reviewed at least annually as the environment in which a laboratory operates changes.

OBSTACLES TO ACHIEVING CONSENSUS

When developing a strategic plan, there are some obstacles that can be encountered. First, it is often difficult to obtain consensus on objectives. When a number of trends must be addressed, there may be a number of objectives that are developed. The participants may not agree on the priority of these objectives. For crime laboratory strategic plans, some participants may feel that the need for more funding in controlled analysis is more urgent than the need for funding in DNA analysis. In these instances it is important for the group to negotiate alternatives and carefully consider options in order to reach a consensus. Close examination of the alignment of the objectives to the laboratory's mission as well as the priorities of stakeholders may resolve the disagreement.

When the leader of an organization promotes an objective, it must be included in the plan. However, unless there is general support of the idea, there will be resistance to implementing the objective, and difficulties will result. In cases such as this, it is important to insure that the concerns of all are heard and addressed.

It may be that political constraints hinder an organization from addressing a problem situation. For example, it may be the wish of an elected official for the program to exist no matter how ineffective it may be. In this case, strategic management would consist of planning around the ineffectiveness or devising a plan to increase effectiveness.

In some cases there may not be enough information regarding a situation to adequately determine the strategy to address it. Problems may be over-simplified and the strategy selected may not consider all the parameters surrounding it. In these cases, additional information from stakeholders should be sought in order to design a successful strategy.

A SCENARIO

A new director has just been named to lead a state crime laboratory system. She has several programs that she believes would greatly enhance the services provided to the community. However, she has been hired from outside of the agency and does not have a good understanding of the laboratory system, its available resources, or its support mechanism.

The director decides to implement a process of strategic management to achieve her program goals. Her first step is to select key stakeholders to participate in the process. She selects a long-time supervisor, a new supervisor recently promoted from the bench, a bargaining unit representative from both the criminalist and clerical unions, a detective, and a prosecutor who often utilizes the laboratory to participate in the taskforce.

Prior to the first meeting she and the selected participants devise a survey to be distributed to the laboratory's stakeholders. These stakeholders include external law enforcement officers, prosecutors, and judges. Internal stakeholders, supervisors, criminalists, and support staff are also requested to respond anonymously to the survey. The survey is presented in Figure 5.1.

The director considers how she will participate in the process. Because she wishes to incorporate programs into the laboratory's operation, the director decides that she will participate as a group member. She further decides to contract with a facilitator to educate the taskforce on strategic planning and to organize the taskforce's discussions. She finds that business administration graduate students at the local university are willing to participate for no cost.

The director sees this exercise as the beginning of a continual process. The strategic plan will be reviewed biannually in order to ensure that progress is being made on the projects. While a facilitator has been contracted for the initial plan, the director will lead future taskforces as she continues to use a strategic approach to crime laboratory management.

Prior to the first meeting of the taskforce, surveys are collected by the facilitator. The facilitator averages the responses received from the specific questions for overall, internal, and external responses. The facilitator summarizes the trends and events that were reported in the surveys. Additionally, the strengths and weaknesses are summarized from the general questions. Members are asked to review the summaries and prepare additional comments to be discussed at their first meeting. During the first meeting of the taskforce, the facilitator leads the taskforce's discussions concerning the current situation of the crime laboratory as reported in the survey feedback. They discuss the events and trends that are shaping the future. Included in this discussion are the programs that the director wishes to implement.

They also discuss the strengths and weaknesses of the laboratory. Attention is

What is your occupation? _____

Which laboratory do you utilize? _____

Please rate on a scale from 1 to 10 your perceptions about the State crime laboratory. A "10" indicates complete satisfaction and a "1" indicates complete dissatisfaction. Please indicate NA for categories for which you have no knowledge. Please provide explanations for responses less than 5.

Turnaround time of casework:	1 2 3 4 5 6 7 8 9 10
Analytical capability of laboratory:	1 2 3 4 5 6 7 8 9 10
Testimony skills of analysts:	1 2 3 4 5 6 7 8 9 10
Responsiveness of laboratory personnel:	1 2 3 4 5 6 7 8 9 10
Physical condition of laboratory:	1 2 3 4 5 6 7 8 9 10
Other:	1 2 3 4 5 6 7 8 9 10

Laboratory employees only:

Treatment of employees:	1 2 3 4 5 6 7 8 9 10
Support from administration:	1 2 3 4 5 6 7 8 9 10
Other:	1 2 3 4 5 6 7 8 9 10

Please list events and trends that you feel the laboratory should address now or in the future.

Please list the laboratory's strengths.

Please list the laboratory's weaknesses.

Your participation in this process is appreciated.

Figure 5.1
Survey.

also given to the environment that will shape the future and whether certain situations propose opportunities for success or threaten success. The taskforce then generates actions (objectives) to react to the trends and incorporate the programs based on the strengths and weaknesses with consideration to the opportunities and threats. The strategic plan includes who will be responsible for performing the tasks, as well as when the task is to be completed.

One trend selected for action was the increased number of clandestine laboratories in the state. The taskforce agrees that the drug analysis section is composed of well-trained chemists who are willing to assist with response to the crime scenes (strengths). However, the section does not have sufficient personnel to respond to crime scenes and continue to maintain current turnaround. Additionally, they lack the training necessary to decommission clandestine laboratories. Nor do they have the supplies and instrumentation necessary to perform the testing of precursors. Finally, there is currently no established procedure for compensating criminalists who are required to be on-call (weaknesses).

Upon discussion of overcoming the weaknesses, it is discovered that training for clandestine laboratory chemists is regularly offered by qualified organizations, and federal grants are available for training and instrument purchases (opportunities). The lack of personnel and opposition of the criminalist bargaining unit present threats to the success of the implementation of a clandestine laboratory response team. Additionally, federal grants are not assured.

The survey received from the prosecutors and law enforcement revealed strong support. The taskforce determined that in order to accomplish its plan, support had to be garnered from this community and reported to the granting agencies. In order to overcome the opposition of the bargaining unit, a Memorandum of Understanding was drawn up allowing the "on-call" criminalists to receive an additional vacation day per month. Because the bargaining unit representative was a member of the taskforce, this agreement was easily reached.

ORGANIZATIONAL MANAGEMENT PROGRAMS

Since W. Edward Demings developed Total Quality Improvement (TQM) after World War II and assisted the Japanese reinvent their industrial enterprises and government, improvement programs have been designed and promoted as *the* way of ensuring efficiency and effectiveness for an organization. Generally these programs were initially developed for commercial enterprises as a way of increasing profits through management focus on specific areas of operation such as customer satisfaction, team-building, and measurement. Public agencies followed in adopting these programs and adapting them to meet the often rigid structures in which they operate.

As a part of a governmental agency, crime laboratories are often required to incorporate a specific management program embraced by an elected or appointed leader. Each new leader brings with them a new program that they feel will improve the effectiveness and efficiency of the organization. The constant change in programs results in a feeling of futility to the organization's mid-level managers who must relive the exercise every few years.

Often modifications are necessary in order to implement many quality improvement programs to public sector agencies. For a variety of reasons, programs intended for use by the private sector cannot be directly implemented by government organizations. Many of the programs, including TQM, focus on measuring the quality of products. Product quality can easily be evaluated through objective physical measurements but evaluation of services is subjective and based on many factors. Because government agencies, including crime laboratories, overwhelmingly provide services, evaluation of these programs is often difficult. Surveys of police officers and prosecutors can reveal areas where improvement is needed but they rely on the subjective nature of the survey. If a prosecutor recently lost a case, he may rate the testimony of a criminalist lower than if he won the case. A police officer who did not receive a test result that supported his case may do the same. Also, survey results can be biased by a highly publicized event that is not indicative of the entire operation. The actions of one individual in the laboratory could negatively reflect on the actions of the entire laboratory staff.

Often quality improvement program are customer-focused. They focus on ensuring that the customer is more than satisfied with the product that they receive. The government customer is more difficult to define. While a crime laboratory's immediate customer may be the officer who submitted the cases or the prosecutor who is trying the case, there are many others who are also customers. The victim, suspect, defense attorney, and judge all have a stake in the quality of the forensic testing. Ultimately, the general public pays the taxes that support the laboratory, thereby making them the "paying" customer. At times the needs of direct recipients of the forensic services may contradict those of the paying customers. While all agree that high-quality and thorough analyses are desirable, the general public does not want to pay the extra taxes that would be needed to make all instruments and technologies readily available for every case.

TOTAL QUALITY MANAGEMENT

The most recognized management improvement program also proves to be the most difficult to apply to public sector agencies. For example, TQM endorses a focus on inputs rather than outcomes. Traditionally governmental agencies were concerned about maximizing inputs, e.g. increasing their budget, but increasingly they have instituted programs that focus on results, which counters some of TQM's tenets.

TQM also minimizes the focus on individual performance. It calls for elimination of employee evaluations as well as merit incentives as they may foster resentment among the employees. The concept of eliminating evaluations contradicts the current practices of most governmental agencies as well as many laboratory accreditation programs that include performance appraisals as an element of the quality process.

Swiss (1992) recognizes the limitations of implementing TQM in public administration and instead offers a "Reformed TQM." While de-emphasizing some elements, Swiss's Reformed TQM promotes orthodox TQM's "feedback from clients, its emphasis on tracking performance, and its principles of continuous improvement and participation of the workers."

BALANCED SCORECARD

The Balanced Scorecard management program provides another tool for improving organizations based on measurement of specific areas and promotes translating an organization's mission and strategy into measurable objectives. It views performance from four perspectives: financial, customer, internal processes, and learning and growth. As with other improvement programs, public sector agencies apply this program to communicate the effectiveness and efficiency of the agency.

BALDRIGE INTEGRATED MANAGEMENT SYSTEM

The Baldrige Framework for improvement focuses on customer-driven quality led by management, based on facts and focused on results. The participation and development of employees and incorporation of strategic planning is also used to achieve organizational successes.

The Baldridge Framework serves as a basis for the Malcolm Baldridge National Quality Award. The award program is authorized in federal legislation and recognizes the quality improvement principles promoted by Malcolm Baldridge, who served as United States Secretary of Commerce from 1981 to 1987. The award recognizes organizations for their quality and performance excellence as it relates to customer satisfaction and retention; financial and marketplace performance; human resource performance and development; supplier performance and development; product and service performance; productivity, operational effectiveness, and responsiveness; and public responsibility and good citizenship.

ORGANIZATIONAL EXCELLENCE

Peters and Waterman (1982) conducted a study of continually innovative big companies in order to ascertain shared attributes for what they defined as "excellence." These attributes are often embraced by other organization improvement programs as criteria toward which an organization should strive, and they are as follows:

1. A bias for action.
2. Close to the customer.
3. Autonomy and entrepreneurship.
4. Productivity through people.
5. Hands on, value driven.
6. Stick to the knitting.
7. Simple form, lean staff.
8. Simultaneous loose–tight properties.

Both public and private organizations share the need to be innovative in response to trends. When leaders of public agencies embrace these attributes they can help their organization adapt as necessary to the ever-changing political climate.

A BIAS FOR ACTION

Peters and Waterman found that innovative companies often act quickly to solve problems by pulling together the appropriate individuals who work to develop a solution and then implement it. If, upon evaluation, the solution is not effective, another solution is proposed and implemented. Crime laboratories can easily adapt this same innovative approach to most problems. However, if the problem involves analytical processes, care must be taken to ensure that solutions include appropriate validation.

CLOSE TO THE CUSTOMER

Essential to excellent organizational performance is relying on feedback derived from customers. For public crime laboratories, law enforcement agencies serve as the major customer. The laboratory can be responsive to their customers by seeking input regarding their needs and their opinions regarding laboratory operations.

AUTONOMY AND ENTREPRENEURSHIP

Innovative companies empower their employees to solve customer problems as well as to be creative when solving process problems. Crime laboratories should allow forensic scientists to take responsibility for responding to requests for service. Any laboratory director who has ever been told by a customer service representative that they "don't have authority to do that" or "I have to ask my supervisor" should realize why this is important for the efficiency of the laboratory. If all requests for expedited service or special requests have to go through a supervisor, the efficiency of the laboratory as well as the confidence of the officer in the abilities of the forensic scientist suffers.

PRODUCTIVITY THROUGH PEOPLE

Peters and Waterman found that the management of "excellent" companies respect their employees. They appreciate that the employees are not just tools to complete necessary tasks but add to the quality and productivity of the organization with their ideas. As in all organizations, the crime laboratory employees are essential to the effective operation of the agency. Laboratories that do not foster a team approach to operations but contribute to a we/they management/labor philosophy, risk adversarial environments and loss of effectiveness.

HANDS ON, VALUE DRIVEN

Excellent companies reflect the clear value system outlined by their top executives not only through a value "statement" but also because the executive honors the system in their everyday behavior. This behavior is observed and reflected by all employees of the organization. In a crime laboratory, it is not enough that the leader says that quality is more important than quantity; they must also support it in their daily decision-making, including the evaluation of the analysts.

STICK TO THE KNITTING

Most successful businesses excel by building on what they do best. While expansion related to their primary operation may increase effectiveness, expansion into disassociated territory leads to losses in effectiveness. This is not to say that private or public laboratories should not incorporate new disciplines, but they should be wary of expansions that may include duties for which they have no existing knowledge. Even when building on existing skills, planning should be undertaken to maximize chances for success.

SIMPLE FORM, LEAN STAFF

Peters and Waterman found that even the very large companies operate with a small number of top managers in order to maximize efficiency. In a crime laboratory system, care should be taken that the management structure is not "top heavy" with administrators. When this occurs there is often confusion regarding to which supervisor an employee reports and can result in inefficiency.

SIMULTANEOUS LOOSE–TIGHT PROPERTIES

Many excellent companies conform to both centralized and decentralized ideals. Often the responsibility for improvements falls to the line worker, but all workers are expected to conform to the company's core values. This same attribute can be adopted by crime laboratories.

SUMMARY

Crime laboratories should be managed using objective standards applied consistently to decision-making. The plan that is adopted by a laboratory should be based upon a leader's vision for the organization and embraced by its staff. A successful plan considers how the organization can best leverage its strengths to face future challenges. Also it addresses how weaknesses can threaten an organization's success and how they can be minimized. The strategic planning process should allow a crime laboratory to continuously improve towards its goal of excellence.

Often crime laboratories implement management improvement programs either through their own initiatives or those of an upper-level administrator. While it is difficult to adapt most of these programs to public sector agencies, quality processes are nonetheless important to incorporate. Generally agreed-upon components in all the quality improvement programs include a customer focus, employee participation, and continuous improvement of processes. Whether through formal or informal means, the adoption of these elements in daily crime laboratory operations will ultimately improve both employee pride and stakeholder satisfaction.

REFERENCES

The Baldridge Framework. URL:
  http://mqi.com/mbnqa.htm [8-6-01]

Barbour, George P, Jr (1984) Taking Action to Promote Excellence. *Public Management.* April
  1984. 9–11.

Brice, G. Rex. (1991) Quality Management Theories and Their Applications. *Quality.* January
  1991. 15–18.

Firestien, Roger L. (1996) *Leading on the Creative Edge.* Piñon Press, Colorado Springs, CO.

Hyde, A. C. and Jordon, Jennifer (1992) The Proverbs of TQM: Recharting the Path to
  Quality Improvement in the Public Sector. Presented at ASPA National Conference –
  Chicago, 1992.

Kaplan, Robert S. and Norton, David P. (1996) *The Balanced Scorecard.* Harvard Business
  School Press, Boston, MA.

Murch, Randall (1999) New Ecology of Quality Assurance. *Forensic Science Communication.*
  1(1). April 1999. URL:
  http://www.fbi.gov/hq/lab/backissu/april1999/murch.htm [1-17-02]

Nutt, Paul C and Backoff, Robert W. (1992) *Strategic Management of Public and Third
  Sector Organizations.* Jossey-Bass Publishers, San Francisco.

Peters, Thomas J. and Waterman, Robert H. Jr (1982) *In Search of Excellence.* Harper and
  Row, New York.

Sipel, George (1984) Putting *In Search of Excellence* to Work in Local Government. *Public
  Management.* April 1984. 2–5.

Swiss, James E. (1992) Adapting Total Quality Management (TQM) to Government. *Public
  Administration Review.* 52(4). 356–362.

Vaill, Peter B. (1982) The Purposing of High-Performing Systems. *Organizational Dynamics.*
  Autumn, 1982. 23–39.

Walters, Jonathan (1992) The Cult of Total Quality. *Governing.* May 1992. 38–42.

CHAPTER 6

PROJECT MANAGEMENT

Never mistake motion for action.
(Ernest Hemingway)

Any new venture goes through the following stages: enthusiasm, complication,
 disillusionment, search for the guilty, punishment of the innocent, and decoration
of those who did nothing.
(Unknown)

INTRODUCTION

Projects differ from ongoing tasks in that they have a beginning and an end. Projects should have established goals, costs, schedules and quality objectives. In a crime laboratory, projects can last a few minutes (completing a marijuana identification case) to several years (building a new laboratory). In either case, there are steps that must be taken and considerations that must be applied in order to assure the successful completion of the project.

Often projects allow an organization to address needed changes. A project may be initiated to respond to a change in priorities in a laboratory or a new law may require that a new procedure be put into place. When changes occur, a project may be undertaken to purchase an instrument or validate and implement a procedure.

In order for successful completion, projects must be properly managed. Projects are not initiated by themselves and are not completed by themselves. Project management requires skills that are exhibited by effective managers. Among these are communication, negotiation, problem-solving and leadership skills. Additionally, the general management skills of planning, organizing, and executing projects are required. Finally, knowledge of the technical issues involved in the project is necessary for successful completion. If the laboratory director does not have a good understanding of how DNA tests are conducted, they will not be able to consider all the issues that are involved in instituting a new procedure.

The crime laboratory director is responsible for ensuring that projects are completed by the most efficient means and results in an optimum outcome. If the laboratory director does not take on the responsibility personally, they must delegate the responsibility to an individual who they trust will be able to fulfill the objectives of the project in a timely manner consistent with the manner to which the director envisions.

ESTABLISHING PROJECT NEED

When something is not working, it is not enough to only know that it is not working: the root causes of why it is not working must be understood in order to thoroughly change the situation. In a crime laboratory it may appear as if the problem is low morale among the employees. When looking into the problem, it may be discovered that due to the large backlog, analysts are frustrated. Therefore, one of the solutions to improving morale is to implement a program to obtain instrumentation that will help reduce the backlog. Obviously this simplifies a complex problem but it illustrates that the initially identified problem may only be a symptom of the underlying problem.

In order to fully identify the problem, Sylvia *et al.* (1997) discuss several techniques to be employed, including surveys, group interviews, and other supplemental procedures. Surveys can be time-consuming and expensive to develop, distribute, and evaluate, but they do provide a means to obtain a representative sampling of staff and stakeholder opinions regarding the situation. If questions are worded correctly, they provide a means to identify the problem and its extent.

GROUP INTERVIEWS

Group interviews can be arranged quickly and inexpensively. As each set of stakeholder has a different view of the problem, each group should be interviewed separately. The analysts in the laboratory have an entirely different perspective regarding a problem than does the laboratory management or the law enforcement officers it serves. When conducting group interviews, there are limitations to be aware of, including what Sylvia *et al.* (1997) call The Squeaky Wheel Syndrome, The Despot/Suppression Syndrome, and Unstructured Input.

All meetings have participants who are more vocal than others. When all do not participate, it is difficult to determine if others in the group share their opinions. It is premature to identify a problem based only on the opinion of one squeaky wheel. An equally premature problem identification can occur when, while the entire group agrees, their opinions of a problem are in sharp contrast to another group of stakeholders. This is particularly true when there is mistrust among management and staff, and relationships between the groups are troubled. A laboratory staff may feel that management is trying to "get" them and management feels that the staff is consciously participating in a work slowdown.

If group interviews are conducted with an outside consultant, there exists the possibility that the supervisor may have met with the staff beforehand consciously or unconsciously encouraging them to keep the problems within the unit or to focus their comments to one specific problem. During the consultants' meeting, the staff may not express opinions different from those of the supervisor and the true problem may not be discovered. On the other hand, the supervisor may feel that they do not want to lead the discussion and feel suppressed in expressing their own and possibly different view of the problem. All members should be encouraged and given the opportunity to express their opinions. It may be necessary for each group to meet separately with the consultant in order that a free exchange of ideas is not suppressed.

Group interviews can also turn into a general gripe session of all problems, big or small. This unstructured discussion may not address the problem at hand and effectively derail the problem identification agenda. While some general discussion may reveal some insight into the problem at hand, it should not be allowed to get out of hand.

PARTICIPANT–OBSERVER APPROACH

In addition to group interviews, it may be valuable to observe the operations of the organization. While interviews can give a preliminary idea as to the nature of the problem, direct observation can confirm its existence. A laboratory director may wish to spend time with a new supervisor who is having trouble with due dates. They may be able to observe inefficient behaviors and offer suggestions for improvements. While this approach can be initially intimidating for the staff, if done correctly they will be become relaxed and assist by identifying obstacles to improvement.

INTERACTIVE MANAGERIAL AUDIT

Reviewing the policies and procedures of the organization can further identify a problem. This type of audit demands that the auditor be familiar with acceptable management operations. This is often undertaken during an accreditation inspection. Often problems are identified by inspectors who have considerable experience observing crime laboratory operations in other laboratories. They can identify problems that the crime laboratory management was unaware of.

PROJECT INITIATION

Prior to undertaking a significant project, the laboratory must establish the need for the project and ensure that the administration understands and supports the time and funding necessary to achieve completion. A clear understanding of why the project is necessary must be established. Among the issues to be considered are the identification of the stakeholders for the project and their needs that the project should fill, the cost of the project, the length of time for completion, and what steps will be taken to successfully complete the project.

Projects are initiated either because the project initiator feels that the project will be beneficial or because someone else feels it will be beneficial. When a project is identified, the goal of the project must be clarified. For example, while the purchase of an additional gas chromatograph/mass spectrometer is an objective that must be conveyed to a funding authority, the goal is to reduce turnaround time and accuracy of controlled substance analysis.

This goal should be introduced to the funding authority to ensure that funding exists for the project. Government laboratories operate under strict budgetary structures and realize that they compete with other sections within their organization for funding. Without approval from the organization's executive officer, the proposed project will not receive funding.

While an organization's leader may believe in the project and support its goals, the organization itself may not have the funding necessary to undertake the project. The leader is faced with conflicting projects that tax scarce resources. A crime laboratory director must present the project in light of these conflicting projects. The need for the project must be presented with the overall goals of the organization in mind. For example, the laboratory director must show how the purchase of a new gas chromatograph/mass spectrometer contributes to the overall goals of the police department that they operate in. The decreased turnaround time of controlled substance analyses will allow the department to make timely arrests that can result in decreased criminal activity in a neighborhood.

The project should be presented in a clearly written document. If possible, a presentation should be made that will accompany the project. The document and presentation should outline the benefits as well as the costs. It should exhibit the support that has been obtained from internal and external stakeholders and include the strategy for acquiring support and funding from policymakers to fund the project. Finally, it should address the time required to complete significant stages of the project.

Often a project that was initiated from another individual is handed to the crime laboratory director. The project may come from an administrator or an employee. Neither may be completely familiar with the issues that surround implementation of the project, and the crime laboratory director must reframe the project to ensure that it adheres to the laboratory's primary goals.

When a project is handed "up" from an employee, the laboratory director may choose to delegate the project back to the employee. The project can be an opportunity for the director to teach the employee new skills and allow the employee to assume the responsibility for initiation of a project that will benefit the laboratory as well as themselves. Depending on the skill level of the particular employee, it may be necessary for the director to contribute a large amount of time to the employee as well as the project. The director may initially feel that they could do the project themselves quicker. But the director will benefit in the long run, as the employee will be able to take on more projects and relieve the director from some of these projects in the future.

When the project is handed "down" from an administrator, the laboratory director may choose to assume the role of project manager or may choose to delegate the project. Prior to initiating the project, the director should ensure that the administrator understands the resources necessary for completion. The laboratory director should also get input from the criminalists who will be affected by implementation of the project. Problems should be communicated to the administrator. Depending on the wishes of the administrator, these may not matter. The project may result from outside pressures of public concern and, regardless of how difficult the project will be to institute, it is up to the director to ensure compliance. When this occurs, the director should present the project in a positive light to the laboratory employees so that they might embrace the project and maximize its chances for a successful implementation.

Laboratory accreditation begins as a project. To achieve an accreditation certificate, there is a beginning and an end. There are specific costs involved for preparation and inspection. There are steps that are followed in preparing for inspection. However, after the accreditation certificate is earned, the processes put in place become part of the laboratory's ongoing operation.

Laboratory accreditation is not undertaken as a voluntary exercise by every laboratory that has achieved it. Unethical or illegal acts by criminalists or the appearance of impropriety or biased analyses has placed public pressure on some laboratories to achieve accreditation to exhibit the quality of its work product. When accreditation is forced upon a laboratory, the employees of the laboratory are even less willing to undertake the project. The laboratory director must embrace the process as a positive change and not allow the criminalists to believe that they are not behind the project. Lack of motivation by the project manager will surely lead to defeat of the project.

A laboratory director generally has several projects ongoing at any point in time. Larger projects can sap the human and financial resources available to a laboratory. Prior to beginning a project, consideration should be given to the other projects under way. Two large projects can feed off each other and decrease the quality of the final product of both.

A laboratory must have the resources to ensure neither project is adversely affected by the other. Laboratories face this predicament every day when balancing casework completion with other tasks such as updating procedural manuals. The criminalists are tasked to ensure that both are completed. They must be introduced to various time and project management skills to assist them with completion of both.

When initiating a significant project, there are several steps that should be accomplished to improve chances for success. Identifying stakeholders, formalizing authority, establishing rules, identifying tasks, and establishing a schedule ensures an organized approach to project management.

IDENTIFYING STAKEHOLDERS

The stakeholders in the project are those individuals who will benefit from its completion. There will be direct and indirect, and internal and external beneficiaries. They include those who will be financing the project, managing the project, benefiting financially from the project, and affected by the results of the project.

For the most part, crime laboratories are public institutions. Therefore the funding to undertake significant projects is derived from taxes and taxpayers. With consideration to this, the taxpayers are the ultimate stakeholders. They must realize benefits from any project undertaken by the agencies that they support. The public can demand that action be taken when they perceive that their money is wasted. Future budgets of the agency may be affected by this adverse attention. The elected official or appointed agency head who determined that the project had merit and approved its funding is also an important stakeholder. Elected officials must gain approval from voters and not be embarrassed by late completion or cost overruns. Appointed officials must report successes to enjoy personal successes as well.

For private laboratories, the project must gain the approval of owners or stockholders as well as the customers who use the laboratory's services. These groups have a stake in the financial well-being of the laboratory and its ability to respond to customer needs. If the project makes a positive impact and is accomplished in an efficient and effective manner, these groups will be satisfied.

The project manager will oversee the management of the project. They are responsible for ensuring that the project is completed on time and on budget. They are responsible for communication to stakeholders and retention of support. The project manager may be the laboratory director, a supervisor, or even a criminalist. The project manager should have the technical and organizational expertise and authority to ensure that the project is accomplished in an efficient and effective manner.

The project team should consist of individuals who must work to ensure that the project will be successfully completed. These individuals will set up the work schedule and the time-line of each task. They will meet on a regular basis to ensure the individual tasks are accomplished and meet the designated time-line and cost. The team will also include private vendors with which the laboratory partners. The vendors will be valuable in providing the expertise of past experiences. Vendors should have past experiences with the scope of the project and will be invaluable in discussing obstacles and short cuts faced in past projects. Finally, the team should consist of laboratory employees who will be directly affected by the project. If the project consists of building a new laboratory, the employees know what does not work in the current laboratory and what needs to be expanded or eliminated. If instituting a new program that requires the employees' time and energies to make it a success, their involvement provides insight into strengths and weaknesses from the employees' point of view.

While police officers, prosecutors, and elected officials are important in designing and supporting the project, their continuous input is not necessary. But if the project takes several months or years to complete, it is important to notify them of the progress of the project to ensure their ongoing support.

FORMALIZING PROJECT AUTHORITY

When a major project is undertaken, a variety of obstacles are inherent on the road to completion. If formal recognition of the project manager is made, the project manager is given the authority required to overcome the obstacles. A project charter may be drawn to provide this formal recognition. A project charter will name the project and state the goals of the project. This provides clear direction to both the project team and other internal and external stakeholders. The name of the project manager and a statement of support are also included. This recognition provides the project manager with the referent authority to accomplish the tasks that must be accomplished.

In organizations that are departmentalized, securing authority for the project manager may be particularly difficult. For example, laboratory directors within law enforcement agencies may take on the role as project manager for the implementation of a laboratory information management system. In order for the project to be successfully employed, the laboratory director will need the cooperation of the property control unit for adopting policies that complement the system, the computer operation section for ensuring the system will interact with other agency computers, and the physical facilities section to ensure that the laboratory has the necessary wiring or space to accommodate a computerized network. Recognized authority from the agency's leader – in this case, the Chief of Police – will assist the laboratory director in gaining the assistance of the other sections.

At times, the project manager may require the assistance of departments external to their department. For example, if the project entails building expansion or renovation, the crime laboratory's governing agency will likely not have the capabilities to undertake the task. The task is likely assigned to a physical facilities department located within another governmental agency. To secure their assistance, it may be necessary to obtain the formal recognition of an individual at an even higher level such as a mayor or a governor.

The formal recognition will also assist in maintaining control of personnel when other projects compete for the attention of the project team. Internal team members must be given the approval to concentrate their energies on completion of the project tasks instead of their routine duties. Conflicts can occur when criminalists who are assigned to a project team are also required to maintain their usual level of casework. The project manager must gain the cooperation of the criminalist's supervisor to ensure that the criminalist can fulfill their duties to the project.

Additionally, if a team member is interrupted to work on another "more important" task, this could threaten the timely completion of our project. The formalized support can help the project manager reinforce the upper level support for the project to the team member's supervisor. The conflicts faced by all team members may be lessened with the formalized support.

STATEMENT OF WORK

Once the project has been identified, support has been obtained, and team members appointed, the next step is outlining the tasks and assigning responsibility for the tasks as well as a mode of communicating progress. The tasks are usually outlined in a statement of work. A statement of work addresses the goals, the limitations, and success criteria for the project. All members of the project team agree upon its components prior to beginning the project. The document can be shared with the stakeholders and with their approval will serve as rules that govern the project.

A statement of work includes seven components including purpose, scope, deliverables, cost and schedule estimates, objectives, stakeholders, and chain of command.

The reason for the project is detailed in the purpose. This provides a foundation for why the project is necessary and what benefits will be derived from the project. The scope of the project includes the major activities of the project. By spelling out the activities at the beginning of the project, secondary tasks that may be added as the project progresses are avoided. Deliverables are measurable achievements that are necessary for completion of the project. A deliverable may be an intermediate step or the final product. An intermediate deliverable for installation of a LIMS may be running communication lines, and the final deliverable is installation of software onto laboratory computers.

The cost and time-lines of a project are of vital importance to ensure successful installation. For government agencies, cost overruns may result in the inability to complete the project. Therefore all cost factors must be anticipated and agreed upon at the project's onset. The project's schedule must also be agreed upon in order to ensure that the project is completed in a timely manner to fulfill the expectations of the stakeholders. Scope also influences the cost and schedule of the project. If additional tasks are added as the project progresses, the cost and schedules will likely be affected.

The objectives specify what will be accepted as successful completion. They should include quality standards that must be met as well as the completion of deliverables. The inclusion of stakeholders provides recognition by the project team that they are responsible to others. The stakeholders should receive regular communications regarding the progress of the project. The chain of command lists who has authority for specific decisions. The team will agree on the types of decisions that can be reached by individual members as well as those that require a decision by the project manager or external stakeholders.

Also involved in task identification is specifying who has responsibility for each specific task. A responsibility matrix can be agreed upon at the beginning of the project that will identify the key activities and stakeholders responsible for the activities. It will list the roles that they play in decision-making regarding the activity as well as the decisions that they are not authorized to make. In the long run it may prevent communication problems among the project team.

Finally, a communication plan must be agreed to that will address how and when stakeholders will be notified of the project's progress. This may include meetings of the project team as well as status reports to external stakeholders. The communication plan should consider what information stakeholders need and how often they need it. It should also consider the form in which the information is delivered and if any response is needed from the stakeholders.

It is also important to consider monitoring the implementation of the project. A monitor must be assigned to ensure that the project is on track. Monitoring must be done on a routine basis at periodic intervals. Depending on the length of the project, daily or weekly reviews may be appropriate. The reports on the implementation should be reported to the project manager or other stakeholders as appropriate.

Once the tasks have been specified and agreed upon, they need to be scheduled. The work breakdown schedule identifies all tasks and breaks down a large project into manageable components. The schedule provides a detailed outline of the project's scope as specified in the statement of work. It provides a mechanism for monitoring progress and determining cost and schedule estimates. It also helps team members identify how their task adds to the overall success of the project.

The work breakdown schedule begins with the major deliverables and considers each task that is required to produce it. There are several ways of creating a work breakdown schedule. One way to begin is through the use of a mind-map. Mind-mapping is a creative process that allows the project manager and team to brainstorm tasks and record them on paper. It is generally done prior to establishing an organized timetable of events. A sample mind-map is shown in Figure 6.1. The focus of the project is placed in the center of the page. Each key objective is placed on a branch extending from the center. Tasks related to the objective are placed on additional branches. A mind-map does not have to be organized and has no rules. As ideas are developed they can be documented in no specific order and in any manner that the developer desires.

Figure 6.1
Mind-map.

Following completion of the mind-map, a work breakdown schedule can be organized into a final project schedule that incorporates all the major activities. There are also many forms that can be used for a project schedule including milestone or Gantt charts. Both put the activities into their proper sequence considering if one task must be completed prior to beginning another or if tasks can be completed concurrently. The schedule should assign each task a start and finish date. When all tasks are graphed, the project manager can estimate the completion of the entire project. A milestone chart shows only where the key events of the project fall. The Gantt chart breaks down the events into tasks, assigns them to an individual and tracks beginning and ending dates for the task. A milestone chart developed from the mind-map is shown in Figure 6.2 and a Gantt chart in Figure 6.3.

Activity	Jan	Feb	Mar	Apr	May	June
Gain support	●					
Buy instrument	●	●	●	●		
Facility renovations		●	●	●		
Training			●	●		
Validate method				●	●	
Report wording						●
Begin reporting casework						●

Figure 6.2
Milestone chart.

PROJECT DELEGATION

The laboratory director may choose to delegate project management to another individual within the crime laboratory. When delegating a project, the laboratory director should consider the person to whom delegation is made. The person should have the time and interest for the project. Lack of either may produce a less than ideal outcome. The project could be completed late or of sub-standard quality. Additionally, the individual selected should possess the skills necessary to accomplish the tasks. The laboratory director may need to spend time developing the individual if they do not already possess knowledge. This time spent will allow the employee to grow in a new area as well as take pride in the accomplishment. When delegating a project, the laboratory director should provide clear guidelines on what resources are available to the

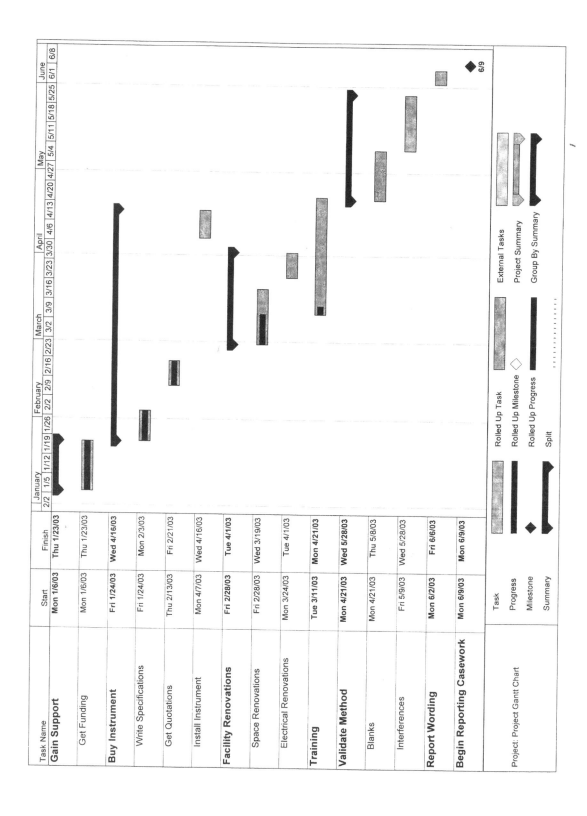

project manager. Instruction should be given regarding deadlines and what the end product should be, including quality standards.

Generally, the whole project should be delegated so that the employee will be able to think the project through and organize tasks as necessary. The laboratory director should express confidence in the project manager and allow them to creatively organize the project with periodic progress reports to the crime laboratory director. The laboratory director should ensure prior to beginning the project that the project manager understands what is expected from them and the project. Additionally, they should be clear on the level of responsibility and authority that they have in decision-making. If the laboratory director desires to be made aware of all expenses, the project manager should know that up front; not after several thousand dollars have been expended without the director's knowledge.

Throughout the project, the laboratory director should expect periodic progress reports as initially agreed upon. If the project manager is not forthcoming with the reports, the director should follow up quickly. The director should also monitor the intermediate stages and identify obstacles along the way for the project manager. The director should also be willing to identify additional resources as necessary.

When the project is completed, the laboratory director should give credit to the project manager for their leadership in the project. While the project may not be completed exactly as the laboratory director had envisioned, they should accept the final product but discuss with the project manager the lessons learned from the project.

Individual cases constitute projects for the forensic scientists who analyze them. In some cases only one analyst is responsible for the entire case. A simple marijuana case does not require that several analysts be involved in order to complete the case. In other disciplines, delegation is a routine process. In many toxicology laboratories, the laboratory director will sign the final report even though many analysts performed different analytical processes that contributed to the final conclusions. The chief toxicologist delegates the analytical tasks to the chemists under him. The individual analyst assumes the responsibility to perform their task with due diligence to quality concerns. It is ultimately the chief toxicologist's tasks to accept these individual contributions and complete the case (project).

Figure 6.3 (opposite)
Gantt chart.

EVALUATION OF PROGRAMS

Projects are undertaken to change a current situation. They may be necessary as a result of changing legislation, such as the need to identify a newly controlled substance. Projects may be necessary to change a currently unacceptable situation, such as building a new laboratory to accommodate a growing caseload. Whatever the reason for undertaking a new project, a deep understanding of the current situation must be held. Program evaluation is a useful method to determine the value of current programs as well as to judge the worth of proposed programs.

Evaluations look at the value of the program either in direct or indirect ways. Public programs are difficult to evaluate because their value to the community is subjective and therefore hard to measure. Each individual places a different value on a program based upon their own needs. For example, a DNA analysis for burglary investigation is extremely important for the victim of the burglary but may be of minimal importance to the victim of rape waiting for her DNA analysis to be completed.

Evaluations may be formal processes undertaken by an independent third party as is the case in accreditation inspections or audits. They may also be initiated by the organization itself to determine what improvements are necessary to the overall operation.

Programs are most effectively evaluated in their planning stage. Evaluations done early in the planning process can help the decision-makers determine whether a proposed program is necessary or will have the desired impact. If an agency must choose between two or more programs, an evaluation that measures the efficiency and effectiveness of all proposed programs will allow decision-makers to select between alternative proposals. After program implementation, an evaluation of the new program provides stakeholders with justification for the program by highlighting how it is achieving the desired goal.

Ideally, the impact of programs should be evaluated on a continuous basis to identify when effectiveness and efficiency decline and if new approaches are called for. A crime laboratory has ongoing policies regarding case management. For example, prior to the mid-1990s, many laboratories had a policy against differentiating between cocaine hydrochloride and cocaine base due to the time and resources necessary to perform the testing. Around that time, changes were made in many state as well as federal sentencing guidelines as a reaction to increased abuse of cocaine base (crack). These changes made the possession or sell of cocaine base a more severe penalty than that for possession or sell of cocaine hydrochloride. The crime laboratories' policies suddenly did not meet the requirements of their stakeholders, the law enforcement officers and courts. While crime laboratories may not have performed a formal evaluation, informal evaluations determined that changes were necessary to address the needs of their stakeholders. Projects were undertaken to determine all alternatives, select the optimum alternative, and implement the selected program.

PROGRAM ASSESSMENTS

In comparing programs, various assessments may be considered. Efficiency assessments, or cost-benefit analyses compare the relationship between the costs of the projects and the outcomes of the project expressed in monetary terms. Cost–benefit analysis is primarily concerned with efficiency; how well a program is managed. Often cost–benefit analysis is required for budgetary purposes. Many legislative agencies require that an evaluation of programs be submitted to ensure continued appropriations. This is especially true for federal programs. However, when performed as a strictly quantitative exercise, the assessment does not take into account public or political interests. These are subjective and impossible to measure using quantitative means.

Cost–benefit analysis may assist in determining the least costly of two programs. Sylvia *et al.* (1997) state, "Cost–benefit analysis is a powerful tool for choosing between alternatives. All else being equal, decision makers may choose the alternative that costs the least. Unfortunately, in government all else is rarely equal, so decision makers must closely scrutinize the assumptions that underlie the application of cost–benefit analysis." Because humans do the analysis, they have internal biases that often are intentionally or unintentionally included in program assessments. The criteria used for assessment may even be slanted.

When considering the value of a cost–benefit analysis, a manager should consider several things. First, it is important that all the costs and the benefits of the program can be identified and quantified in similar units. The costs of contracting with an external laboratory to perform DNA testing may seem fairly direct. However, a crime laboratory director must also consider the indirect costs of personnel time to review the contracting laboratory's quality assurance programs, personnel cost for packaging and shipping samples as well as cost for the packaging materials and shipping that ensures a secure chain of custody. The benefits of subcontracting are also difficult to determine. The value of obtaining results faster and possibly identifying a suspect is impossible to determine.

Cost–benefit analysis does not consider the impact of the program; how effective the program is at delivering the desired results. Programs therefore may also be evaluated using impact assessments or cost-effectiveness analysis. These analyses compare the relationship between the costs of the projects and the outcomes expressed in cost per unit of outcome achieved. For example, when performing a cost-effectiveness study of DNA analysis, a laboratory director may consider the cost required to obtain each match to a convicted offender rather than simply the cost to analyze one case. This is because the true effectiveness of DNA analysis is realized when a non-subject case is solved through matches with database samples. Many legislatures are now requiring this type of analysis for budgetary processes as it provides a deeper understanding of how effectively a population is served by the program; is the funding being used in a worthwhile manner.

When performing an impact or cost-effectiveness evaluation, it is important to determine what the desired effect of the program will be in measurable terms. Two programs that produce the same impact can be compared as to their cost, or two programs that cost the same can be compared as to their impact. If programs to reduce the backlog of drug cases are being considered, the cost of the programs as well as their effect on the backlog should be evaluated. One program may require $100,000 to purchase an additional gas chromatograph/mass spectrometer and reduce the case backlog by 75 percent. Another, such as streamlining existing procedures without affecting quality, will have a minimal cost yet still produce a reduction of 25 percent in the backlog. The crime laboratory director may want to immediately implement the second suggestion while working on achieving the first.

There are often external factors that can influence a program's apparent success or failure. This is particularly true when performing impact evaluations. For example, a crime laboratory may institute a program of hiring more analysts and purchasing additional instrumentation to address its backlog of drug analysis cases. While the backlog may decrease, any reduction in drug submissions must also be considered as an external factor before declaring the new program solely responsible for the reduction.

EVALUATION PROCESS

For one of several reasons, a crime laboratory director or their administration may determine that a change is necessary. This may be due to a development of a social condition, new legislation, desire for recognition, or negative attention by the media. Regardless of the reason for undertaking an evaluation process, the evaluation will provide a systematic approach to precisely identify the problem that a new program will address as well as the alternative that will provide the optimum resolution for the problem.

Initially, a needs assessment should be undertaken to identify the problem, as well as its scope. This can be done through surveying key persons with interviews or questionnaires or reviewing agency records. If a laboratory believes that there may be a need to institute a new service, a survey instrument may be sent to agencies that use the laboratory to determine their need for the service. Additional methods for assessing the need for a project include the "squeaky wheel" where consideration is given to the number of agencies requesting service. Finally, through trend analysis the agency may predict and prepare for future trends in their jurisdiction by looking at economic or crime trends in other jurisdictions.

The needs assessment may provide a qualitative or quantitative approach to the problem. Initially, the assessment may determine that there is a need that should be addressed (qualitative). In order to determine the extent of the problem as well as the amount of resources necessary to correct the problem, a quantitative assessment must be made. This may require more expansive surveys to more stakeholders.

Evaluations of new and existing programs each have particular concerns. When evaluating proposed programs, it is often difficult to translate the proposed goals into measurable objectives. As the program has not been developed it is difficult to be fully aware of its exact day-to-day operation. Also, while the desired impact can be hypothesized, its realized impact may be slightly different. Therefore, the specific procedures for assessing the program's effectiveness and efficiency may vary after implementation. For example, a crime laboratory theorizes that a new instrument will increase the number of cases analyzed as well as the number of conclusive results produced. However, upon installing the instrument, it is discovered to require more extensive sample preparation. Because this unanticipated development significantly impacts the number of cases that can be analyzed, this objective is no longer valid.

Existing programs were established under specific conditions. Knowing this history provides better understanding of the criteria on which to measure success. Additionally, evolution of various conditions can assist in justifying the need to change or maintain a program. These conditions include a change in perception of the stakeholders such as the general public or agency administrator. Laboratories often adopt specific policies for case screening to quicken their turnaround of casework. While the reduction in turnaround time is one measure of success, the laboratory will suffer if their screening policy causes criticism from the law enforcement agencies that they service. If the criticism is severe enough, it may force the laboratory to reevaluate the new policy.

Often, existing programs require modification instead of discontinuation. If the conditions have changed, an existing program may experience an increase in effectiveness through a change in objectives and outcomes. New criteria can be identified by which to measure the effectiveness of the program change. When DNA analysis became widespread, many laboratories questioned the usefulness of hair comparisons. Many eliminated the hair comparison programs altogether. Other laboratories modified the hair comparison in that the analysts no longer performed extended comparisons but instead did quick evaluations to ascertain if DNA was called for.

After the project has been completed, a simple evaluation will consider if the individual steps were completed on time, the project was within cost estimates, if it met the specifications, and if it fulfilled the needs of the stakeholders.

Sylvia *et al.* (1997) present a ten-point checklist for evaluating programs. These points provide laboratory directors with ideas on how to set up an appropriate evaluation of a program to accurately designate and measure performance objectives.

Is the program experimental or ongoing?

The value of experimental or new programs is difficult to predict. The evaluation required to influence decision-makers that the program is worthwhile is costly and time-consuming. The evaluation that a crime laboratory must undertake to prove that a new trace evidence technique is worthwhile is extensive. The cost of the program, including instrument and maintenance, training, value to the criminal justice community, personnel time, costs to other disciplines, and facility renovations, are just part of the issues to be included in the evaluation. Some are objective and can be measured directly, such as the cost of the instrumentation. However, the value to the community is extremely subjective and requires data collection through surveys, interviews, or other devices.

By contrast, ongoing programs are generally supported by decision-makers. Evaluations of ongoing programs may be undertaken to determine if the program continues to meet the needs of the stakeholders or if improvements are needed. At times, program evaluations are triggered by criticism of the operation. Federal programs such as grant programs may be evaluated to ensure that they continue to meet the intent of legislation that initiated them. For crime laboratories, illegal or unethical acts of employees can force the review of a program. If the laboratory is not accredited, undergoing the accreditation process is often prescribed.

Who is the audience for evaluation?

The formality required of an evaluation is dependent upon the audience that will utilize its findings. When audits are undertaken by the organizational staff to evaluate the processes employed and will only be used internally, the evaluation process can be less formal. However, if an evaluation is precipitated through criticism of the operation and will be shared with external stakeholders, it is important that an independent auditor be contracted to perform the evaluation in a formal manner.

Are the designs, measures, and indicators appropriate for the needs of the audience?

The reason that the evaluation is being undertaken must be clear in order to determine what is to be measured. For example, outcome indicators such as surveys of stakeholder satisfaction can be utilized to determine if a crime laboratory is meeting its goals as an agency. A program audit on the other hand would determine if the laboratory is performing analytical procedures consistent with other laboratories or if they are following the agency's own guidelines.

Is an outcome evaluation or an impact evaluation desired?

If the question to be answered addresses only whether the appropriate level of service is being received, an outcome evaluation is called for. For example, if the crime laboratory offers a specific service for law enforcement and everyone accepts that that service is necessary, an outcome evaluation would be appropriate. An outcome evaluation would determine if the service is fulfilling the needs of the customers through surveys or interviews. It may be discovered that the service needs to be given additional resources to provide the services quicker. If there is not a consensus that the service is needed, an impact evaluation may be more appropriate. An impact evaluation would determine if the funds spent to maintain the service have the desired impact on the criminal justice system.

What is the purpose of the evaluation?

Internal annual audits are mandated in many accreditation programs. When these audits are performed strictly to comply with accreditation criteria, the laboratory may not perform the audit in-depth or may take the findings lightly. The laboratory does a disservice to itself if they do not consider the audit as an opportunity to improve the quality processes of the laboratory.

Do we seek decision-oriented data or are we building a theory about client population?

When reviewing a program, the criteria used and the decisions reached should reflect the needs of the stakeholders. Generally, crime laboratory audits collect data that will support operational decisions as opposed to building a theory regarding suspects or victims. If the data collected does not include the criteria necessary to reach a decision that will improve services to the criminal justice system, it is not worthwhile information for a decision-maker. It may be interesting to know the average age of suspects of controlled substance cases, but the information is not necessary for a crime laboratory to improve its services.

Will the information be used to decide whether or how much to cut program funding or how funding can best be allocated among various components of the program?

During times of cutbacks, agencies experience reduced budgets not because their programs are unnecessary but simply because the government's revenue is reduced. A previously performed audit that addresses the level of service available at a specific funding level will allow the agency to quickly respond to the cuts. For a crime laboratory, such an evaluation will allow the director to inform decision-makers how the reduction will affect the services provided. The decision-makers can then make an informed decision whether they are willing to accept this reduced level of service.

Realistically, can a design be developed that conforms to the standards of quality evaluations within the limits of available funding?

External evaluations can be expensive and literally exceed the value of the program. In evaluating the need for a $20,000 analytical scheme, it is unwise to spend $50,000 to determine if it is necessary. Evaluations then should be directed at collection of relevant data that will contribute to the question at hand.

What are we doing, how are we doing, and who will care if we tell them?

When designing an evaluation scheme, the overriding concerns should be to use objective data collected to evaluate the goals of the program to be used by decision-makers. When performing an evaluation of an evidence collection unit, information regarding the color of the walls in the room is extraneous and unnecessary to the director who is interested in ensuring that the submissions are being processed in a timely and courteous manner.

A PROJECT MANAGEMENT SCENARIO

Officers are complaining about the six-month turnaround time required for a drug analysis sample at a regional crime laboratory. Cases are being thrown out of court and the suspect in one case at the laboratory awaiting analysis has been arrested for murdering a convenience store clerk during a robbery. The police department has called attention to the fact that if the crime laboratory had analyzed the case in a timely manner, the suspect would be in prison and the murder would not have taken place. The scrutiny placed on the laboratory is intense and the public is demanding that something be done to decrease the turnaround time.

The laboratory director determines that a new policy must be devised, implemented, and announced quickly. He puts together a team of interested individuals to evaluate the problem, consider alternative solution ideas, select a solution, determine the cost and time that it will take to initiate the program of backlog reduction.

Members of the team include the laboratory director, the drug section supervisor, a union representative, a law enforcement officer, and a judge from one of the counties in which the cases are heard. The crime laboratory director announces in a press conference that the laboratory is extremely concerned about the backlog. He also announces that a team has been assembled to evaluate solutions to the problem. He states that the team will return with their recommendations in 30 days. This information reduces the pressure being placed upon the laboratory.

After the external members of the team are made aware of the current situation in the drug analysis section, they brainstorm possible solutions. The team comes up with a variety of ideas for backlog reduction. Many are very costly and their objectives for reducing backlog not reliable. If analysts analyzed small cases quickly, the number of cases would be reduced but the larger cases would sit for a longer period of time than they did originally. If one analyst was assigned larger cases and the others worked on smaller ones, there would be a large disparity in the workload of the analysts. Since part of their evaluation depends upon their working a specific number of cases per month, the analysts fear that if they were the one to work large cases, their evaluation would suffer.

The team meets with all the members of the drug section and shares their concepts for reduction of cases. This meeting provides the members of the section the opportunity to ask any questions and agree to the process.

The team approaches local granting agencies for funding to purchase the needed instrumentation. Being an elected official, the judge is helpful in levering funding approval for the instrument. Also, because the granting agency is aware of the laboratory's crisis through media coverage, they agree to the grant if the laboratory publicizes the fact that their agency is responsible for funding the needed instrumentation.

No longer needed, the law enforcement officer and judge are not present at the meeting planning the project tasks for purchasing the instrument and implementing the remainder of the plan at the crime laboratory. The team again meets with all the members of the drug section and together they agree upon the time-lines for completion of the specific project tasks.

When the program is finalized, the laboratory director announces to the public through a press conference of their plan for reducing the backlog. He invites all the members of the original team as well as all the drug analysts to attend. He gives credit to them for their hard work thus far and ongoing efforts to reduce the backlog. He especially recognizes the granting agency for their generous assistance. As the project progresses, he communicates with the press and the public by issuing press releases touting their successes. He invites the media to the laboratory when the instrument is received and in operation. He periodically releases graphs illustrating the decrease in number of cases backlogged as well as the increase in the number of cases reported in a month.

When the backlog is reduced to two weeks, the director makes one final announcement that the project was a success. While the project has come to an end, the policies that were adopted will remain and prevent the backlog from rising to the unacceptable level that it was at before.

SUMMARY

Project management should be approached in the same manner as the strategic planning process. However, unlike the strategic planning process, a project has a definite conclusion. The crime laboratory should first assess if there is a need for a project. If it has been determined that change is desirable, a project should be chosen that will meet the needs of the stakeholders. An organized plan should be undertaken to achieve successful implementation of the project in the necessary time-frame. After implementation, periodic assessment should be done to ensure that no modifications are necessary. Also, future evaluations will be an indicator that change is necessary and the change process should begin again.

REFERENCES

Fisher, Roger, Ury, William and Patton, Bruce (1991) *Getting to Yes* (second edition). Penguin Books, New York.

Greer, M. (1996) *The Project Manager's Partner: a step-by-step guide to project management*. HRD Press, Amherst, MA.

Konieczka, Richard (1998) *The 59-Second Mind Map*. Hara Publishing, Seattle, WA.

PMI Standards Committee (1996) *A Guide to the Project Management Body of Knowledge*. Project Management Institute, Newtown Square, PA.

Rossi, Peter H. and Freeman, Howard E. (1993) *Evaluation: a Systematic Approach* (fifth edition). Sage Publications, Newbury Park, CA.

Sylvia, Ronald, Sylvia, Kathleen and Gunn, Elizabeth (1997) *Program Planning and Evaluation for the Public Manager* (second edition). Waveland Press, Prospect Heights, IL.

CHAPTER 7

RESOURCE MANAGEMENT

You may blame the War Department for a great many things, but you cannot blame us for not asking for money. That is one fault to which we plead not guilty.

(Douglas MacArthur, 1935)

INTRODUCTION

In order for a crime laboratory to perform high-quality forensic analysis, it must have proper funding. The cost of operating a crime laboratory is very high. Although it varies, the cost of hiring and training a new analyst can exceed $100,000. To implement a new procedure may cost several hundred thousand and the cost of maintaining accreditation for a medium-sized laboratory, $100,000 per year. Therefore budget maintenance is one of the most important things for which a director is responsible. The decision to perform one type of analysis may very well mean that funding is not available to perform another type.

There are many different ways in which laboratories operate financially. They may have little control over their own budget or they may have 100 percent control. They may have no way of obtaining additional funds for a special project or they may have significant opportunities to obtain supplemental funds when needed.

PUBLIC BUDGETING

As most crime laboratories receive funds from tax dollars, it is worth considering how budgeting for public agencies operates. In the United States, public budgets are proposed by a government's executive branch. The legislative branch then works with and against the executive branch to finalize the budgetary legislation. The budget considers the revenue that will be derived from tax dollars and how best to allocate the scarce resources to fulfill the priorities of the government. Political scientist, V.O. Key, Jr. (1992) identifies the basic budgeting problem as, "On what basis shall it be decided to allocate X dollars to activity A instead of activity B?"

A public budget is designed by politicians and therefore is a subjective instrument that reflects their priorities. As each politician is responsible to their constituents, the desires of the constituents have a great deal to do with the makeup of the budget. The budget priorities in rural states will be different from those that are mostly urban. And as the political beliefs are different between Democrats and Republicans, the budgets derived from Republican executives will differ from those of Democratic executives. Politicians designate their priorities by specifying the level of funding for particular programs and agencies.

The budget ensures that programs will be reviewed and evaluated every budget cycle. This gives the legislature leverage over agencies that they expect to fulfill their wishes. When funding is provided to an agency with specific instructions regarding its use, the agency is expected to use it for the intended purpose. If they do not, the agency will be expected to explain why it wasn't used for that purpose. If no specific instruction was given, the agency is still expected to operate within the given budget and to fulfill the mission of their agency.

Crime laboratories that operate independently within a state or federal government must be more active advocates for their agencies. The more influential an agency is with legislators, the easier they are able to acquire operating or expansion funding. Public agencies would like to believe that programs are funded on their merits, the efficiency with which they operate, and the value that their operation has on the citizenry. It is more likely that agencies are funded only in part by their merits but also by the influence that they have. If a laboratory is able to convince the legislature by their words or deeds or the words or deeds of the citizenry that they produce a valuable service, they will be more successful in getting the funding that they desire.

Aaron Wildavsky (1992) notes that in order to maximize funding to federal agencies they must cultivate an active clientele and develop confidence among governmental officials. Though not all crime laboratories operate on a federal level, all can benefit from understanding this premise. Crime laboratory directors must mobilize their clientele (stakeholders) to act as advocates. When stakeholders understand how they benefit from the laboratory's services, they will speak on behalf of crime laboratories. Their independent voice can help influence legislators and other decision-makers regarding the importance of the crime laboratory and the need to fund it at an appropriate level.

When a crime laboratory chooses to mobilize their stakeholders, they must inform them how the funding will assist in providing the needed services. For example, if a crime laboratory requires funding to initiate a DNA analysis program, they must inform the law enforcement agencies that they serve how it will allow them to get a faster turnaround time on cases that they must now send to a state or private laboratory with a very long turnaround time.

Crime laboratories that operate as units of a larger agency can also motivate other internal stakeholders to speak on their behalf. When making funding decisions, a crime laboratory's request alone may receive no special notice. However, if the Narcotics Unit also requests funding for the laboratory so that drug analysis cases can be analyzed in a quicker fashion, the decision-maker is more likely to appropriate funds to the crime laboratory.

It is also wise to expand the types of advocates that promote the laboratory's interests. In addition to the law enforcement agencies, others within the criminal justice system can be approached. These include prosecutors and even defense attorney associations whose clients may be released sooner when DNA analysis reveals that they were not the donors of biological evidence. When a new program directly affects the prosecution of drunk-driving cases, agencies such as Mothers Against Drunk Drivers can be approached for their support as well. Other community activist groups may also be valuable advocates for the crime laboratory, depending on the program.

The confidence of the decision-makers is a valuable tool in obtaining funding. Government agencies are expected to be responsive to the public's needs while being conscious of costs. If crime laboratories receive their operating funds from state or federal appropriations, the elected officials who sit on the committee will consider how their constituents were aided by the agency. If the official has confidence that their constituents are receiving fair and prompt service, the funding process may be expedited.

When confidence is lost, the funding process becomes more difficult. It is easier to stay in good standing by being honest with decision-makers than trying to regain confidence after it is lost. When the public turns against an agency due to a breach of integrity, the agency faces a difficult time in obtaining funding for new projects. The public as well as the legislators generally prefer that funding be directed toward correcting problems than instituting another program that can be doomed by poor management.

MANAGING A BUDGET

Once an agency has been allocated funds with which to operate, they must manage their agency accordingly by considering what tasks can be accomplished with those funds to support the agency's mission. If the budget is not sufficient to complete all their tasks, it may be necessary to determine which tasks must be eliminated in order to operate with the allotted funds.

STRATEGIC PLANNING

When managing a budget, it is important to perform strategic planning to ensure awareness of the laboratory's objectives. When strategic planning is performed as a group effort and everyone, from the analysts to the administration, is aware of the plan, a consensus can be reached on what is important to everyone. This agreement can then be used as justification for fiscal decisions. For example, during the strategic planning process, if it were agreed upon that the laboratory's primary goal would be to reduce the backlog of DNA cases, available funding would be directed toward that goal first. Depending on the remaining funds available, other objectives agreed upon in the planning process may receive less funding than requested based on their agreed-upon priority listing.

PROGRAM EVALUATION

The evaluation of programs is important to determine their usefulness to the goals of the crime laboratory. When evaluating a public agency program, efficiency, effectiveness, and equity should be addressed.

Efficiency is commonly performed using cost–benefit analysis. This is done more easily when the benefits of a program can be quantified in a monetary sense. For example, a crime laboratory that charges for analysis may determine which analyses to offer based upon the cost of performing the analysis versus the income to be derived from the service. The analyses that do not require a significant amount of personnel time, instrumentation or supplies, and in addition are highly sought after by their customers, will likely be funded. However, if the cost of performing the testing is great and there is little call for the analysis, it will most likely not be funded.

A lot of programs cannot be quantified using cost–benefit analysis. Their outcomes may not easily lend themselves to quantification. In that case, the effectiveness of the program must be considered. Effectiveness analysis evaluates the cost of the program versus the subjective benefit yielded by the program in helping the organization reach their goals. For example, DNA testing indisputably costs a lot of money to perform; however, it has the potential for identification of a particular individual to the exclusion of all others. This makes it a highly effective program in the eyes of many. However, glass analysis usually provides only class identification, and therefore many may view it as a much less effective program.

The final consideration in program evaluation is equity. Public agencies must always be aware of fairness issues. If a program unfairly targets one group of individuals over another, it should be re-evaluated to eliminate inequities. In crime laboratories, equity issues regarding programs are less common than in parent law enforcement agencies that may have social programs in place. One area where equity issues may arise in crime laboratories is regarding the proper administration of electronic databases. The laws governing DNA and fingerprint databases must be strictly followed to protect privacy. Many civil libertarians have concerns over the inclusion of suspect standards after they have been excluded as suspects for a specific crime. For example, an individual may provide a DNA sample that subsequently clears them of suspicion in the crime. Many question whether it is appropriate to add this DNA profile to a DNA database. The equity issues surrounding this entry must be considered prior to implementing policy.

CRIME LABORATORY FUNDING

Funding in crime laboratories located within larger organizations differ somewhat from those laboratories that operate independently. Laboratories within larger organizations such as police agencies may not control their own budget but receive funds as available. They have less opportunity to plan for future purchases because they compete with other sections of the agency for funding. When faced with a funding decision between cruisers and scientific instrumentation, often the instrumentation receives second priority. However, crime laboratories operating in this manner also have an emergency source of funds when unexpected needs arise. The parent agency has a larger budget and can appropriate funds from other units if necessary.

Crime laboratories that operate within law enforcement agencies also have access to funds derived from programs available only to these agencies. For example, funds derived from seizures of money and personal property related to criminal offenses can be a source of supplemental income for law enforcement agencies and the crime laboratories located within them.

Crime laboratories located within parent agencies often have less flexibility with fiscal decisions. Strict guidelines set at an agency level must be complied with. Decisions regarding purchases and administrative processes are delayed, as they must come from an executive many levels removed from the laboratory. If the laboratory collects fees for services performed for outside agencies, the fees may not directly benefit the laboratory but may instead go to a general fund benefiting the entire law enforcement agency or even the entire government such as a city or county.

Crime laboratories that operate independently may not have emergency funding available but they usually have more control over revenues collected and how the revenue is spent. For example, they may choose to charge fees or increase fees in order to obtain funds to implement a new program. Or, they may decide to reappropriate funds to increase the availability of training in lieu of instrument purchases.

PROCUREMENT

The purpose of procurement as stated by Reed and Swain (1997) is "to obtain the most appropriate and highest quality good or service possible for the least cost." When permission is received to purchase instrumentation, purchases must generally follow specific guidelines. This is particularly true for governmental agencies. Often a particular level of government has a procurement office that is responsible for ensuring that purchases comply with the guidelines.

The National Association of State Purchasing Officials is a professional organization representing purchasing professionals. The NASPO (1997) advocates purchasing programs "where public business is open to competition; where vendors are treated fairly; where contracts are administered impartially; where value, quality and economy are basic and equally important aims; and where the process is open for public scrutiny." Centralized procurement offices are intended to ensure that the government both gives and receives fair treatment. Through a centralized approach to purchasing, where one agency is responsible for all the purchasing, a greater volume of purchases can mean a lower price for all. Procurement guidelines are intended to benefit the government by creating competition between the companies wishing to supply a good or service to the government. This allows the government to acquire the necessary goods at the least expensive price. Centralized purchasing is especially useful for office supplies, furniture, and other goods or services that can be used by all sections of the government.

A centralized procurement office is also able to institute policies of equal treatment for all vendors. Many governments have guidelines that are intended to give small businesses, women, minorities, disabled individuals, and veterans an equal opportunity to compete for the government's business. Other governments give preference to companies that are located within the same city or state.

Centralized purchasing can be frustrating when a laboratory requires specialized supplies or instrumentation. Often the purchases do not fit easily within the guidelines. Guidelines may require that several quotes be obtained; if a specific item is available from only one manufacturer, this is not possible. The lack of an easy fit delays the purchase.

The National Association of State Purchasing Officials (Bartle and La Course Korosec 2001) states that "the best of both worlds is easily possible – central management and delegation of procurement authority under a thoughtful set of delegation standards, with adequate training and authoritative monitoring." The challenge to government is to establish standards, training and monitoring guidelines for decentralization. Increased dollar limit on purchases not requiring formal bids that go through central procurement office and increase use of purchasing cards are important in decentralizing purchasing authority.

In addition to purchasing supplies and instrumentation, a crime laboratory may need to contract for a specific service. A contract is beneficial for services for which internal skills are not available or for when they can be performed less expensively or more quickly. Many laboratories have contracted with private laboratories to perform DNA testing of convicted offender samples. This allowed for quick population of the DNA databases and a larger library against which to search unsolved cases. Most of the testing was also performed less expensively than could be done in-house.

Contractors may be reimbursed based upon their performance. This is especially beneficial when contracting with a company for computer technology. The contract must contain language that specifies the exact performance expected. The contractor is paid not for their actions but for the results produced from their actions. A crime laboratory that contracts for a laboratory information system should include performance specifications such as the ability to produce certain management reports into the contract. This gives the laboratory a legally binding contract that, if not complied with, allows for legal action.

The quality of the contract services is also an important consideration. Many quality assurance programs require that subcontractors adhere to quality standards. Laboratory directors must implement strict guidelines for contractors to follow and monitor compliance with the guidelines throughout the length of the contract. Contractor compliance can also be monitored through terms and conditions specified in a legally binding contract.

While the lowest price of a good or service is important, many purchasing offices are switching to "best value" purchasing. Best value purchasing also considers life cycle costs, performance history of vendors, quality, proposed technical performance, timeliness of delivery, assessment of risk, and availability and cost of supplies and technical support. For crime laboratories, this may mean consideration of the product as well as the support that has traditionally been available. Information that can help with assessment is available from other laboratories that have had experiences with this manufacturer.

When assessing bids for goods or services, a laboratory director must consider the value of the price, assurances of timely delivery, quality or performance standard for the product or service, and qualifications of the producer as well as their record of performance. This is especially true for items not monitored by a centralized procurement office.

OPERATING WITH LIMITED FUNDS

Crime laboratories, like other governmental agencies, are always challenged by a lack of resources. Scarce resources can result in a number of challenges. The inability to hire and train analysts, the inability to purchase and maintain instruments, and the inability to maintain and improve facilities can hinder a laboratory's ability to perform adequate analysis on casework. At times, all crime laboratories will have to manage in a period of reduced resources. The usual reason for this is a decline in taxes collected that results in reduced funding to governmental agencies. However, other causes may include the elimination of funding for programs no longer deemed necessary by the criminal justice community. This is especially significant if the laboratory operates on a "fee for service" basis. Federal laboratories may be particularly vulnerable to reductions in funding due to political reasons. If the legislature wishes to punish an organization for what they view to be illegal or unethical practices, a reduction in funding may reflect their displeasure.

When faced with the possibility of funding reductions, a crime laboratory must decide how to confront the situation. Some laboratories may be in a situation where they can resist the reduction, others may only be able to reduce the impact of it. Depending on which direction is chosen, various tactics may be chosen to carry out the decision.

In a period of a poor economy when the laboratory is facing reduced funding, a director may seek to maximize funding by improving liaisons with the decision-makers. One way of doing this is to have a laboratory open house to showcase the valuable services performed by the laboratory. A public open house with media attention will provide the laboratory with the opportunity to mobilize the public to become advocates on their behalf. It can also serve to motivate the law enforcement agencies and the criminal justice system for whom the laboratory works to speak as advocates as well.

If a crime laboratory is unsuccessful in gaining additional operating funds through general funds, they may seek grants to supplement resources. Crime laboratory grants are commonly known to be available from state and federal criminal justice agencies such as the National Institute of Justice. However, many private foundations exist that provide grant funding for specific projects. Corporations may also be a source of funding or may be willing to donate equipment for specific projects.

Laboratories that operate on a "fee for service" basis may seek to increase the cost for services. Laboratories that traditionally have not charged for services may consider doing so if not specifically prohibited to do so through their charter. If this direction is chosen, there is likely to be resistance among the criminal justice community that the crime laboratory serves. The threat of imposed or increased fees may be sufficient motivation for the law enforcement agencies to speak as advocates for the laboratory.

If there are no additional funds available through alternative sources, the laboratory may target areas where efficiency can be improved. It may be possible to reduce costs without cutting services through the purchase of less expensive supplies or other cost-saving measures. It may also be possible to improve efficiency through increasing the productivity of analysts. If not already in place, the automation of analyses greatly improves laboratory efficiency and should be investigated. Input from analysts may provide some information on where improvements are possible. However, an analyst may feel that they are operating at their peak, and being required to do more will affect the quality of the work product. If this is the assertion, the director may choose to evaluate the situation either through personal observation or the observations of an independent consultant.

If all efficiency improvements have been taken and there continue to be budgetary concerns, the laboratory may choose to discontinue a service. As with the threat of increased fees, the threat of service reduction may also be a successful tactic to maintain funding by motivating stakeholders to speak on the laboratory's behalf. If a popular program is discontinued, the backlash from law enforcement agencies may be sufficient to reinstate the funding necessary to continue analysis. For example, when faced with cutbacks in funding, a crime laboratory may choose to discontinue the expedited turnaround of drug analyses cases. The lack of a laboratory analysis will affect the timely resolution of these cases and result in complaints from the court system. These complaints can be publicized in the media to show how the cutbacks are affecting the community and serve as motivation to restore funding. This tactic can be risky in that the criticism directed at the laboratory may only serve as criticism and not be successful in increasing funding.

If a service has to be discontinued, it should be chosen based on the cost-effectiveness of the program. If an analysis is expensive to perform yet is not requested often and is available elsewhere for no cost, the laboratory may choose to discontinue the service. To determine the effect that this would have on the laboratory's stakeholders, a survey should be conducted. This serves two purposes. It informs stakeholders that a service may be discontinued as well as motivates them to speak against the reduction if it affects them significantly. The responses from the survey can be used as justification on why funding should be reinstated.

POLITICAL THREATS

When a laboratory has come under fire for analytical or managerial errors, they may be faced with political threats to reduce operating funds. This is common at the federal level where the media attention on agencies is more focused. When an agency is threatened with reduced funding based not on economics but due to political reasons, they may choose several approaches to manage the threat. When faced with a political attack, the laboratory may choose to fight the accusations by challenging them. They may present evidence that no errors were made or that the errors are isolated and do not reflect systemic problems. However, this approach may be risky and serve only to increase the agency's public perception as being inflexible and unable to accept criticism.

The laboratory or parent agency may choose to undertake an investigation to determine why the error occurred and how to keep it from occurring in the future. In addition to providing information to the agency, it also shows the public and the decision-makers that the agency is concerned about the quality of their work product and is not afraid to seek changes. The investigation can be performed by employees of the agency or from consultants external to the agency. Often if the laboratory is not accredited, accreditation will be sought as a means to minimize future errors. Another common finding of investigations is a need for increased funding to correct any perceived errors.

If a significant error occurs in an organization, a change in leadership is often sought as part of the solution. It is commonly believed that the management created an environment conducive to such errors and the only way to keep these errors from occurring in the future is to change the management. This change in management may also serve as evidence to the public as well as the decision-makers that the organization is concerned about the situation and should not suffer funding reductions because of it. As with many governmental organizations, a crime laboratory director may not be protected by civil service or a labor organization and is vulnerable to dismissal at will. This is especially true for fiduciary positions in crime laboratories operating under an elected official.

PROGRAM CUTS

When faced with severe budget cuts, it is even more important that a director knows which programs work and which do not. Program evaluation becomes an important tool in deciding which tasks may be cut. Barrett and Greene (2001) remind agencies that "If you've got all the money in the world, there's little need to set priorities; you can just throw more money at problems. But when money is short, knowing which programs work and which don't is of paramount importance."

When faced with budget cuts, laboratories that are part of a larger organization may find themselves at odds with other departments within the organization. The parent organization may choose to cut all departments equally so that each receives an equal percentage cut to their budget. If an organization chooses cuts based on other criteria, a laboratory could find itself experiencing larger or smaller budget reductions than other units.

Within a police department, personnel costs of commissioned officers are generally fixed. The department is less likely to lay off officers for fear of the effect that it may have on public safety or perception of public safety. Therefore, criminalists and other civilian staff within the crime laboratory may be more at risk for cutbacks. It is important for a laboratory to have the ability to present justification for personnel and operational funds. Program evaluations that show that the laboratory's services are essential to the agency's mission and that the laboratory is operated in an efficient manner will assist with this.

Often individuals who work within a crime laboratory have the impression that their work is so important that an agency would not dare cut their budget. As any director who has worked in a crime laboratory for any period of time remembers, while a laboratory's mission is important, when faced with a decision to cut officers or to cut laboratory supplies, it is the supplies that must go. A director must be able to motivate criminalists to find creative ways in which to save precious funds during tight times without affecting the quality of the work product.

PERSONNEL CUTBACKS

An organization may either choose to cut personnel expenses in an attempt to reduce operating expenses or they may be forced into it as a final option. All positions within an agency provide a service to the organization. When positions are eliminated, it directly or indirectly affects the effective operation of organization. This option requires an agency to consider equity issues among employees. An agency must be careful to choose an option that is not perceived as being unfair to any group of employees.

Many of the employees in crime laboratories are represented by labor organizations that have negotiated contracts that define the parameters of employment. Most contracts specify the rights of the employees as well as the rights of management. When cutbacks occur, they must comply with the agreed upon contract. Often laboratories that operate within law enforcement agencies are staffed by non-commissioned employees. The contracts covering the non-commissioned employees often have fewer restrictions regarding lay-offs than do the contracts covering commissioned employees. Because of these differences, as well as the appearance that the lay-off of officers will dramatically affect public safety, a law enforcement agency will likely choose to lay off non-commissioned workers first, including those in the crime laboratory.

Initially the government overseeing the agency or the agency itself may impose a hiring freeze so that existing vacancies will not be filled. The government or agency may also choose to offer early retirement to employees so that the higher salaries and benefits paid to long-term employees can be eliminated. A reduction of personnel expenses also occurs through attrition. When personnel retire or resign, the resulting vacancies are not filled.

Generally, the elimination of positions is based on seniority so that the last hired is the first to be laid off. An agency may determine that all cuts come from a specific job classification or bargaining unit. When determining which classifications will be affected, they may consider the public perception of each position. Forensic scientists may be perceived as more important to the agency's mission than other employees. If this is the agency's decision, the forensic scientists may not be directly affected but the clerical workers may be. If a crime laboratory's typist is laid off, it may mean that the forensic scientists will be required to perform clerical work. This creates additional challenges to analyzing cases in a timely manner. If an agency chooses to lay off employees disregarding job classification and based only on seniority, forensic scientists may be affected. If several DNA analysts were hired recently in order to address the backlog of DNA cases, lay-offs could claim several of the analysts and setback the progress of the DNA backlog elimination program.

GRANTS

In the United States most government laboratories, with the exception of federal agencies, have the opportunity to obtain funding through grants. Generally grants come from federal agencies such as the National Institute of Justice. However, some private foundations also provide grant funding for criminal justice agencies. Regardless of the source, grants are provided to forward a policy of the granting agency. They provide funds that allow an organization to implement a program deemed valuable by the granting agency. Grants provided by the federal government are generally proposed by the executive or legislative branch and support very specific purposes.

Federal grants may be awarded as block grants or discretionary grants. Block grants are given to states based primarily on their population. While they are intended for a specific general purpose, the details of the spending are not specified. The state granting agency determines the priorities for the state and determines which programs and/or local agencies receive funding. The Edward Byrne Memorial Law Enforcement Assistance Program is a block grant. The Bureau of Justice Assistance distributes funding to a state criminal justice agency specifying general guidelines for its use. The state agency then determines the priorities for the state. They keep a portion of the funding for use at a state level and distribute the remaining funds to local and regional granting agencies based upon the population of the region. The local agency then finally distributes the funding to local grantees based upon the priorities of the state as well as their own priorities.

Discretionary grants are distributed at the discretion of the federal agency entrusted with the grants administration. The priorities of a discretionary grant are determined at the federal level. State and local agencies compete for the funding through grant proposal applications. The federal agency administering the grant determines who is awarded funding based on how closely the proposal for funds meets the priorities of the grant program. No one agency or state is guaranteed funding. The DNA Improvement Act of 1995 provided for a discretionary grant program administered by the National Institute of Justice (NIJ). Within the legislation, Congress specified the priorities to be used in granting funds. State and local agencies were required to submit applications to NIJ specifying how they would use the funds if awarded a grant. NIJ then awarded grants based on how completely the proposals fulfilled the spirit of the legislation.

Equity issues exist in both block and discretionary grant programs. The block grants that go to each state ensure that all states receive funding. Further, this specific use for the funding can be decided based on the individual needs of the state. However, there are concerns that the lion's share of block grant funding stops at the state level and is not available to local jurisdictions. For crime laboratories this can mean that a state crime laboratory has an unfair advantage over local laboratories in obtaining funding made available through block grants.

Discretionary grants produce the opposite situation. The funding decisions are decided not by the state but by the federal agency administering them. Little flexibility is provided to the state and local governments for use of the funding. If a state's needs lie in something other than the priorities set at the federal level, they will likely not receive any funding. However, because the decisions are made by one federal agency, the agency can determine where the funding can be utilized in the most beneficial manner for the entire country. Because of this, all agencies, whether state or local, have an equal opportunity to be awarded funding.

The grant process can be intimidating to those who are inexperienced with the procedure. A proposal should be well planned and concisely written. It must convince the donor that a problem exists and the applicant can solve the problem with the proposed program. It should be directed to an agency with funds available to solve the particular problem. A proposal outlining a program intended to solve a clandestine laboratory problem will not receive funding through a DNA backlog grant program.

A University of Pennsylvania study found that donor agencies consider the project's purpose, feasibility, community need, applicant accountability and applicant competence to be "highly important" when evaluating proposal requests. Project logic, probable impact, language, money needed and community support were "important" criteria, while the least important criteria to donor agencies were working relationships, advocates, minority status, social acceptability, prior funding, and influence of acquaintances. In order to influence granting agencies, crime laboratories should focus on addressing the highly important and the important criteria in grant proposals.

A crime laboratory usually develops a project based upon the availability of a specific grant. If the NIJ offers a DNA backlog elimination grant, the laboratory will submit a grant proposal following the outline and time-line specified by NIJ. However, a laboratory may also take the opposite approach by first developing a project and then seeking donors interested in the project. If the project conforms to a specific funding area of a federal funding agency, the laboratory may choose to apply within that program. However, if the project does not meet their guidelines, the laboratory may look elsewhere for funding sources.

GRANT OPPORTUNITIES

Federal grants are the most commonly utilized grants for crime laboratories. Most federal grants have restrictions for the use of funds. In addition to using it for a stated purpose, many require matching funds. Some grants require a cash match where an agency must provide a percentage of the program cost with actual funds. Other grants accept in-kind matches where the agency's share of the program is supplied by non-cash contributions such as employees' salaries. Still other restrictions on the use of federal funds may include prohibitions against constructing or renovating facilities and supplanting an agency's operating expenses with those from the grant.

Another controversial source of federal funding exists through developing relationships with the legislators from the district in which the laboratory resides. All government laboratories have the opportunity to appeal to their own representatives to obtain special funding through a government appropriation. If the legislator is assigned to an influential committee such as Appropriations, the laboratory may be able to obtain an "earmark" in legislation. Earmarks generally mandate that a specific sum of money be provided to a specific organization for a specific purpose. Among laboratory directors, earmarks are extremely controversial. Historically, earmarks to specifically identified organizations have drastically reduced the availability of general funding for crime laboratory grant programs. A select few politically connected organizations are viewed as profiting while the majority of the crime laboratories suffer. At best, this action solicits jealousy and, at worst, hostility toward the laboratory obtaining the earmark.

Private grant sources may be available through local foundations and corporations. If the laboratory locates a funding source through a private corporation, the support may be in a form other than money. The corporation may be able to donate instrumentation or computers that will assist the crime laboratory. Corporate support can be particularly useful for short-term needs for which their support is seen as an investment and can be used as a marketing tool for them. For example, following the September 11, 2001 attacks, many corporations readily donated services and equipment to assist with recovery and identification of the victims. Crime laboratories should not be reluctant to approach private corporations when such needs arise.

Instrument manufacturers may also be willing to supply instrumentation for training courses. Other manufacturers may even supply personnel to provide training. This is especially beneficial to crime laboratories if the training covers a new technique. The manufacturer will benefit by introducing their instrument to the crime laboratories, and laboratory personnel will benefit with training regarding a new technique.

A laboratory seeking funding should be well informed about the granting agencies that it approaches. The laboratory should ensure that the interests of the donor agency are the same as theirs. A research project focused on forensics is not likely to receive funding from a foundation for the arts. When an agency with consistent interests has been identified, the laboratory should develop relationships with the personnel in the agency. Most granting agencies are willing to discuss their funding areas as well as provide suggestions, especially if there is no application deadline approaching. The laboratory should explain the project as well as ask for suggestions, criticism, and advice about the project.

GRANT PROPOSALS

Generally, a grant proposal should address a new area of concern or propose a different solution to an existing problem. When developing an idea for a proposal, a laboratory should determine if the idea has been previously considered by the funding agency for the specific locale. The laboratory should thoroughly develop the short- and long-term goals of the program.

Community support is important to a funding agency. Letters of endorsement for a specific project can help demonstrate community support. Letters should be requested from various stakeholders such as law enforcement agencies, prosecutors, defense attorneys, and community action groups which may be supportive of a new program. The letters should include how the new program will help them to achieve their goals. Some granting agencies require that a grantee employ an advisory panel to administer the grant. This panel would serve as a forum for discussion regarding the merits of the proposal as well as generation of data to support proposal and development of a strategy to generate broad support for the project.

While some problems are global in nature, it is important to address the local need as well. When applying for federal funding, it is important to cite the national need, but also the statistics from your local jurisdiction as well. Local statistics are also relevant to include in applications to local granting agencies who are especially concerned with how funding will help their own area. The proposal should predict quantitatively what would be solved with the project. This may include the number of backlogged cases that will be reduced or how many days will be reduced in the performance of controlled substance testing.

Grant proposals should include an honest portrayal of the project and what it will accomplish. The use of declarative verbs such as "can" and "will" rather than conditional verbs such as "if," "could," and "might" grab the attention of the donor. Measurement indicators should be outlined to demonstrate to the reader what will be accomplished. Proposals should be written in clear concise language and should not exceed the recommended page length. The proposal should demonstrate the problem but not make it seem insurmountable. The focus of the proposal should be on the opportunities that exist with the challenges. After the proposal has been written, it is always a good idea to have a knowledgeable individual review it for grammatical errors as well has for clarity of arguments and strength of reasoning.

A proposal should always be introduced using a cover letter on the laboratory's letterhead. The letter should be addressed to the individual responsible for the funding program rather than "To whom it may concern." It should provide an overview of the problem faced by the community as well as a brief description of the laboratory and program to be funded. Contact information of a responsible person should also be included. The total length of the letter should not exceed two pages.

Instead of extended grant proposals, some foundations prefer a summary of the proposal be submitted. From the summary the granting agency can determine if the proposal conforms to their grant requirements. If the project is deemed to meet the requirements, a more complete proposal will be requested. Generally the summary letter includes elements similar to a cover letter. It provides an overview of the laboratory as well as the problem, the project and how the project will solve the problem. It may also include the amount of funding needed for the program.

WRITING THE PROPOSAL

Generally, a grant proposal consists of eight basic components:

1. Proposal summary.
2. Introduction of organization.
3. Problem statement (or needs assessment).
4. Project objectives.
5. Project methods or design.
6. Project evaluation.
7. Future funding.
8. Project budget.

While this section provides general suggestions, a proposal should strictly follow all guidelines laid out from the granting agency, whether it is a governmental agency or private foundation. A sample grant proposal is included in Appendix E.

Proposal summary

The proposal summary appears at the beginning of the proposal and outlines the key points of the proposal. As it may be used as the deciding factor for future consideration, it is a critical element of the proposal. The summary should be brief and concise, not exceeding two to three paragraphs. It should also be interesting so as to draw the donors' attention. The proposal should be completely developed prior to writing the summary in order for all the key points to be included. The summary should provide a framework of the project upon which the rest of the proposal will build. It should include why the project is important to the local community and what alternatives exist in the absence of the requested support.

The summary should identify the grant applicant and include a sentence on the credibility of the applicant. While this may not seem important for traditional crime laboratories, it is necessary to reconfirm the importance of the laboratory to the community and criminal justice system. The summary should include a sentence on the problem, a sentence on the objectives of the program, and a sentence on the methods used to evaluate the program. It should include the total cost of the program including the funds available through the organization.

Organizational introduction

The introduction of the organization presents the crime laboratory as a credible applicant able to successfully manage the proposed program. Crime laboratories must compete with each other in order to secure scarce federal funds. This section should demonstrate that your laboratory is the best choice to execute the proposal. Prior program successes help the donor make these decisions. This section should not exceed one or two pages.

The organizational introduction should clearly establish who is applying for the grant. It should address the demographics of the jurisdiction that the laboratory serves as well as the services that it provides. It should address the clients who are served. Are only specific law enforcement agencies served or are services opened to defendants as well? Letters of support from these agencies should be included as appendices but should be referenced in this section.

Evidence to prior accomplishments should be presented along with statistical support of the accomplishments. The qualification of the laboratory and key staff in the program should be presented to demonstrate the laboratory's ability to accomplish the proposed program. Any other evidence of administrative competence should be included in this section and it should logically lead into the problem statement. As with all parts of the grant proposal, it should be truthful, concise and interesting.

Problem statement

In three to four pages, the problem statement assesses the need to be addressed. A formal or informal assessment should be included to develop the purpose for the proposal by discussing the nature of the problem. The problem cited should be limited in scope to what the proposal can solve. It should not be so broad as to be unreasonable.

This section should include information on how the community is affected by the problem, as well as how the problem hinders the crime laboratory from reaching its goals. It should include objective data regarding the problem. For a grant proposal aimed at reducing the backlog of controlled substance cases, this section may include the number of backlogged cases and the number of days it now takes to work the cases. It should also address the effect that the backlog has on the prosecution of cases, such as how many cases were continued because no laboratory report was received.

Assessments of the problem may include historical documentation, geographic or other statistical information. Additionally, studies performed regarding the problem can be cited. If this type of information is not available, case studies and anecdotal evidence can be presented. If the laboratory is currently attempting to address the problem, the processes currently being used, as well as its successes or failures, should be included. If the laboratory has a current funding stream for a project but is anticipating losing the stream, the laboratory should address what will happen as a result of losing the funding.

The problem statement should also address who will benefit from the program, and how. Development of the problem through a needs assessment of the affected community illustrates the laboratory's concern of the problem and adds to its credibility. If a needs assessment was conducted among law enforcement agencies, this should be cited as a means of developing the program. Statements from the agencies regarding the problem can be included in the problem statement section as well. Inclusions of such testimonials provide additional community support for solving the problem.

The problem statement should be free of scientific jargon. A crime laboratory should not assume that the proposal evaluator knows what a GC/MS is. It is equally important that the problem statement contains no unsupported claims. Don't say, for example, that *all* drug cases are late in getting to court. This type of over-statement is readily detected by the granting agency.

Project objectives

The problem statement should lead into the project objective section that delineates the specific program that is being proposed. The project objectives section should not exceed one or two pages and describes what will be achieved through the program, not the method to be used to achieve the objectives. The objectives should reflect the problem outlined in the problem statement. The objectives should be measurable and include time-lines in which they will be achieved. Objectives should also be reasonable. If the project is funded, these objectives may be used by the granting agency to evaluate the success of the program and influence future funding.

There are several types of objectives that can be used for the proposal, including behavioral, performance, process, and product objectives. A behavioral objective reflects one in which a human action is anticipated. An example would be that officers will submit cold DNA cases after grant funds are spent on educational material about the benefits of CODIS. A performance objective reflects a specific time-frame within which a behavior will occur. For example, "All cold cases requiring DNA analysis will be completed within one year of the grant award." A process objective is the manner in which something occurs as an end in itself. An example of a process objective would be that the laboratory would be able to search all cold cases containing DNA evidence against CODIS. Finally, a product objective is the creation of a tangible product. For example, "A manual for training law enforcement officers regarding evidence collection will be published with the grant funding."

Program design

The program design outlines the specific actions that will be taken to achieve the program objectives. This section should logically flow from the problem statement and program objectives to describe the specific methods employed to achieve the objectives and solve the problem. It may exceed four pages and should clearly describe the program activities as well as the time-lines in which they will be undertaken.

Personnel necessary to perform the activities should be listed. If a training program is to be employed, it may be helpful to include the curriculum vitae of the instructor if one has been selected. If direct funding for personnel is not allowed in the grant proposal, it may be acceptable to include their salary and benefits while working on the project as the agency's matching contribution.

If facility renovations are to be performed within the program, this should be noted and the time-line for completion considered. While most federal grants will not cover renovation costs to facilities, it may be acceptable for the agency to use the cost as matching funds.

The activities that are to occur, as well as the personnel needed to perform them, should be included. Program objectives should be measurable through performance of the activities. If important to the program, detailed descriptions of the activities should include why activities are undertaken in a particular order. It may be useful to include a flow chart or diagram to outline the succession of activities. If other activities could achieve similar outcomes, it is beneficial to describe why the selected course of action is preferable. Discussion of innovative actions may provide a distinction between one agency's proposal and others of a similar nature.

The program design should be reasonable and straightforward. The activities proposed should reasonably be expected to achieve the objectives within the time-lines presented. Detailed narratives may distract from the readability of the proposal. Appendices should be added to include timetables, work plans, schedules, activities, methodologies, or curriculum vitae of personnel.

Program evaluation

The evaluation section of the grant application addresses how the project's success will be assessed. The evaluation should address the effectiveness of each step of the project as well as the overall effectiveness of the project. The completed evaluation allows the agency to determine if the funds were well spent. A positive evaluation may influence a donor to provide continuing funds or new funds for a new proposal. The evaluation section of the application should be one to two pages in length and outline the evaluation design. The type of data to be collected and an explanation of how it assesses on the overall effectiveness of the project should be included. Additional attention should be paid to how the data will be collected, how it will be evaluated, and when evaluation reports will be issued.

The evaluation section should present a plan for evaluating the accomplishment of objectives. It should also address how evaluation methods will be modified as necessary as the project progresses. This section should also address when in the program that the evaluation will begin. Evaluations that are begun at the project's outset are beneficial because appropriate data collection can be assured. The data will be consistently collected throughout the term of the project. The evaluation design discussion should include if the evaluation is to be conducted by an internal staff member or an external consultant and how much time the evaluation will take, especially if the design is complex. It should describe how the assessor will be chosen.

Granting agencies may have set requirements for evaluations and should be included in the proposal. If specific data is required from the funding agency, this data must be included in the project's evaluation.

Future funding

The future funding section exhibits long-term planning. If funding will be required after the grant period, this section specifies where that funding will be obtained. If equipment is to be purchased with the grant funds, this section should address future maintenance and supply costs. This section is generally one half-page.

Most granting agencies are not willing to continue funding a program for an extended period of time. This section tells the granting agency that the applicant has given thought to how the program will continue past the grant period. It may be necessary to include letters of commitment from stakeholders who will continue to utilize and provide funding for the program. This may be the laboratory's agency stating they are willing to pay for maintenance, or from other stakeholders committing themselves to purchasing specific services.

Proposal budget

The budget outlines the expenses that will be incurred during the life of the grant. Federal grant applications usually have specific forms for fiscal information that must be completed. These may include listing of employees taking part in the program as well as their salary and fringe benefits; consultants or other personal service contracts as well as their hourly fee and the total cost for services; travel specifics to include mileage, airfare, meals, lodging, and miscellaneous travel expenses; equipment to be purchased; supplies required; office expenses; and any indirect costs. Cost projections should include inflationary increases but should be realistic. Costs of audits, development, implementation and maintenance of information systems necessary to collect required data should be included. Supplies and reagents should also be included.

All costs presented in the budget should be consistent with the objectives of the project. If the grant proposal includes hiring additional personnel, costs for additional space and office equipment should be included to accommodate personnel. Salaries and benefits for the personnel should be consistent with those currently employed. Federal grants may accept an agency's payment of personnel costs as matching funds if the personnel will be used exclusively for accomplishing grant objectives.

The proposal budget should provide detailed information on the project's cost. There should not be any unexplained costs for miscellaneous expenses. It should include all items requested from the granting agency as well as all items to be paid for by the applicant or other sources. The budget should include costs specific to the project. A laboratory's general operating budget should be separate from the project costs. The budget should be presented in tabular form, but justified with a narrative explanation.

Any other sources of income should be included. If it is expected that income will be obtained from the program, this should be included in the budget as well. If the laboratory will charge for services made possible through the grant, the revenue derived should be disclosed.

Appendices

Some appendices may be required in a grant application, either as a requirement from the granting agency or to support information provided by the applicant. Information to include in appendices are letters of support by law enforcement agencies or other clients, list of agencies that utilize a laboratory's services, and biographies of key personnel or trainers to be obtained with grant funds.

CONSORTIUM GRANTS

Consortium grants are awarded to several agencies working toward a common goal. For example, the grant may be awarded to several laboratories within the same state for the purpose of improving the DNA analysis within the state. These grants require a lot of coordination among agencies and agreement as to the goals of the program, how funding would be distributed, and what kind of analysis will be acceptable. Generally, in consortium grants not all laboratories receive equal shares of the grant award. However, if the goals and priorities were agreed upon prior to submitting the application, the consortium will more readily accept this inequity.

In states that have a statewide system as well as local laboratories, the state laboratory system is in a unique leadership position. The laboratory usually takes on the role of being facilitator and administrator for consortium grants. It is usually a thankless position because there are generally difficult decisions to be made that result in unsatisfied participants.

In return, state laboratories also have the unique opportunity to acquire funding more easily through state and federal legislators. Most state laboratories are under an elected official. These politicians generally wish to be re-elected and are eager to demonstrate a program that benefited their constituents. If a crime laboratory's actions assist the official in gaining reelection, the official may in turn provide the financial support needed to implement a program or upgrade their operation.

PARTNERSHIPS

Partnerships between public agencies and private corporations have become increasingly common. They are most common in the areas of transportation but may also provide unconventional avenues for the resolution of some of crime laboratories' budgetary concerns. For example, a crime laboratory may find that an instrument vendor is willing to sponsor a training class or provide instruments to use in the class.

When the public agency and the private corporation join together to accomplish a goal, they must be able to agree on the goal while respecting their different points of view. Kittower (2001) states, "What makes these partnerships successful, participants report, is research, comprehensive planning, willingness to share risks and understanding that the public and private sectors have – and always are going to have – different points of view." Successful public–private partnerships may not share a common goal for each organization, but may share a common commitment to the public good. Private corporations generally have profit as a motivation yet also make a commitment to improve the community in which they operate.

Laboratories should not expect to be approached by the private companies but should instead initiate the contact. Laboratories should approach a corporation seeking their advice regarding the proposed program. Behn (1995) states an old aphorism that "If you want advice, ask for money. If you want money, ask for advice." The corporation should be presented with information on how their partnering with the laboratory can be an investment for them.

When a private corporation partners with a public agency at the beginning of the program, they acquire a personal stake in it. Because they want it to succeed they will also participate as partners in acquiring public and legislative support for the program. Many corporations have extensive marketing and governmental affairs units that can provide training and assistance to a crime laboratory partner.

While a partnership can provide benefits to both the private corporation as well as the crime laboratory, there are precautions that should be taken to ensure that a mutual understanding exists regarding the goals of the program as well as the restrictions that must be in place. For example, a crime laboratory whose charter only allows for laboratory analyses to be performed for law enforcement agencies, cannot agree to perform handwriting analyses for the corporation to use in civil litigation.

Suggestions for other public–private partnerships that would enhance forensic analyses would be for public laboratories to partner with privately owned laboratories to accomplish research. In addition to partnering with an instrument manufacturer for training courses, the laboratory may allow the manufacturer to use their laboratory for marketing in exchange for instrument support. Also, a public–public partnership can be formed between a public crime laboratory and a local university. The crime laboratory could provide a facility for interns to gain real-world experience and the university could provide research facilities for forensic analyses.

Above all, a crime laboratory and its leadership should be comfortable with any partnership agreements. If the partnership appears to be an unethical relationship, it should not be entered into.

SUMMARY

A crime laboratory is expensive to operate. While personnel, supplies, equipment, and facilities are common everyday expenditures for case analysis, quality assurance processes and accreditation expenses are also necessary operating expenses for today's crime laboratory.

Public crime laboratories are appropriated public funds derived from tax revenues with which to function. Because of this they must be guardians of the public's trust by operating in an effective and efficient manner. They should periodically evaluate their program operation to ensure that they are making the best use of the available funding. Private laboratories also need to evaluate their programs to ensure that they are maximizing available operational funds and profit.

REFERENCES

Barrett, Katherine and Greene, Richard (2001) Bad News Budgeting. *Governing Magazine.* November.

Bartle, John and LaCourse Korosec, Ronnie (2001) Procurement and Contracting in State Government. Government Performance Project Working Paper Series.

Behn, Robert (1995) The Benefits of the Private Sector. *Governing Magazine.* June.

Developing and Writing Grant Proposals. URL: http://www.cfda.gov/public/cat-writing.htm [10-29-01].

Elements of a Grant Proposal. URL:
http://www.silcom.com/~paladin/promaster.html [10-29-01].

Grant Writing Tips. URL:
http://uscolo.edu/faccntr/tips.html [10-29-01].

Gurwitt, Rob (1998) Foundations with Strings Attached. *Governing Magazine.* April.

Key, V. O. (1992) The Lack of a Budgetary Theory. In: Albert C. Hyde (ed.) *Government Budgeting: Theory, Process, and Politics* (second edition). Wadsworth, Belmont, CA. 22–26.

Kittower, Diane (1998) Counting on Competition. *Governing Magazine.* May.

Kittower, Diane (2001) Playmakers Team Up, *Governing Magazine.* May.

Levine, Charles (1992) Organizational Decline and Cutback Management. In: Albert C. Hyde (ed.) *Government Budgeting: Theory, Process, and Politics* (second edition). Wadsworth, Belmont, CA. 369–380.

National Organization of State Purchasing Officials (1997) *Survey of State and Local Government Purchasing Practices, 1997.* Lexington, KY.

Reed, B. J. and Swain, John (1997) *Public Finance Administrators* (second edition). Sage Publications, Thousand Oaks, CA.

Rhoads, Steven E. (1995) *The Economist's View of the World.* Cambridge University Press, New York.

Tips for Grantwriting. URL:
http://grantproposal.com/tips_inner.html [10-29-01].

Walters, Jonathan (1999) People, Partnerships, and the Power of Performance. *Governing Magazine.* January.

Wildavsky, Aaron (1992) *The New Politics of the Budgetary Process* (second edition). HarperCollins, New York.

Wilavsky, Aaron (1992) Political Implications of Budgetary Reform. In: Albert C. Hyde (ed.) *Government Budgeting: Theory, Process, and Politics* (second edition). Wadsworth, Belmont, CA. 39–45.

CHAPTER 8

EFFECTIVE COMMUNICATIONS

Public opinion is everything. With public sentiment, nothing can fail. Without it, nothing can succeed. Consequently, he who molds public opinion goes deeper than he who enacts statutes or pronounces decisions.
(Abraham Lincoln)

It usually takes me more than three weeks to prepare a good impromptu speech.
(Mark Twain)

INTRODUCTION

The ability to effectively communicate is arguably the key factor to successful management. Communications with others both inside and outside of the crime laboratory is of vital importance in fulfilling the mission of the laboratory. Crime laboratory directors must communicate with employees so that all agree with and understand the goals of the organization. They must communicate these goals to their administration to gain financial support. Crime laboratories must also share their goals with others in the criminal justice system as well as seek the public's support for them.

Successful communications implies that a message is sent and received. The communicator has to be clear and the listener has to be receptive. President Ronald Reagan was known as the "Great Communicator." Michael Deavers (1996) discusses lessons that can be learned from him in "The 'Gipper's' Timeless Lessons on Communicating Effectively."

- *Understand who you are.* Not only is it important for an individual to know what they personally stand for but also what the goals and vision of their organization are. When these are clear, they are more easily communicated with others.

- *Know your strengths and weaknesses.* As with all personal behaviors, communication skills can only be improved when one is aware of their weaknesses. Additionally, an agency's leadership must be aware of the organization's strengths and weaknesses to adequately represent the agency in a public forum.

- *Speak only when you have something to say.* This is particularly relevant when deciding whether to address the media. At some point in time, the media will be critical of an organization. However, it may not be necessary for the agency to respond to every criticism. When responding in detail to all charges, the main message can be lost in the details.

- *Keep your goals limited.* It is not possible for someone to be all things to all people. Goals should be limited and repeated to others until they are well understood.

- *Keep laughing.* Humor may not be appropriate for all situations, but it can make some difficult situations easier. People appreciate someone who does not take themself too seriously. Small mis-steps made in a presentation can be smoothed over by acknowledging them through humor.

PUBLIC COMMUNICATIONS

Public communication includes all interactions with external stakeholders. It includes presentations to schools and community groups, media outlets, and elected officials. Effective public communications can make the difference in whether the goals of a crime laboratory are reached. Public communications build interest and support in the projects undertaken by the crime laboratory by illustrating how they help the community. The support built by these communications can assist in securing funding to make the project possible.

Public communications is necessary for teaching those outside the organization about the good things that an organization does for the community. It includes community relations, government relations, issues management, media relations, volunteer programs, and regulatory affairs. For private laboratories, communication with the public may be assigned to a Public Affairs Office. In public organizations, a Public Information Office may be assigned this responsibility. In all organizations, a planned approach to releasing information is needed.

A Public Affairs Office in a public organization generally has the task of increasing public awareness of the accomplishments of the agency. The office can present the positive achievements of the agency to the public and contradict negative press. An advertising campaign for the NEW IRS is an example of this. Typical tasks of Public Affairs Offices include publicizing the availability of the agency's services to the public or releasing the results of government research performed by the agency. They may also include educating the public about new laws or regulations. Public Affairs sections may also attempt to change undesirable behaviors, as is illustrated with anti-drug or safety belt campaigns.

While government agencies may not be allowed to lobby the legislature for increased funding or support of specific legislation, they are allowed to educate legislators regarding issues relevant to their missions. Often this task is assigned to the Public Affairs section. Conversely, Public Affairs units may also provide information to the agency regarding trends in public or legislative opinions that may lead the agency to make program changes. This early warning may also give the agency the opportunity to address concerns and propose a new program to the legislature just as the legislators become aware of it as an issue. The Public Affairs unit will also be responsible for publicizing this program to citizens and legislators whose support could ensure its successful funding.

Employees of government Public Affairs offices are placed in a unique position. As "public servants" they are required to serve the best interests of the public. However, as agency advocates they are also required to promote the agency's interests. While most of the time the public and agency interests agree, the public affairs professionals face ethical dilemmas when they conflict. The public affairs professionals employed by private organizations may face similar conflicts, but because their income comes from profits of the company, not citizen taxes, may feel less conflicted.

The Public Affairs Council has developed Ethical Guidelines to help public affair professionals determine the appropriate course of action when faced with conflicts. Hanson (1996) used these guidelines to suggest questions that can be used to reflect on ethical principles in public affairs. These are listed in Figure 8.1. Many of these same guidelines can be applied to the public communication policies adopted by crime laboratories. The information distributed by crime laboratories should be accurate and free of misconceptions. Criticisms should be responded to openly and in a timely manner. The public should be recognized as key stakeholders in crime laboratory operations and their views should be considered and balanced with those of the laboratory when addressing concerns.

In order to fully address the needs of the community it serves, a crime laboratory may wish to institute a formal public affairs program. If part of a larger organization, the organization may already have a public information unit. The crime laboratory director may have the ability to utilize that unit in developing

Figure 8.1

Ethical audit questions for public affairs.

On communication

1. Are all my communications accurate?
2. Are all my communications complete enough to avoid foreseeable misconceptions?
3. Do all my communications accurately reflect the organization's actual positions on key matters?
4. Have I selectively omitted certain information which should have been communicated?
5. Have I communicated to all groups who have an interest in or a right to know about my organization's plans/position?
6. Is my communication on the same subject to different stakeholders consistent?
7. Is my communication always timely?
8. Do I always disclose the identity of my client or employer?
9. Is my communication respectful of the positions of other participants in the public policy process? Do I disparage the interests or motives of others?
10. Have I sought to pre-empt, disrupt or drown out the communications of other legitimate interests?
11. Have I facilitated the communication of important perspectives which are not represented in the public policy process?
12. Do I respond to inquiries and criticisms openly and without rancor?
13. Do I refuse to use communication as a vehicle for retribution and revenge?

On two-way communication

14. Do I meet with and listen to outside groups who are legitimate stakeholders of my organization?
15. Do I present the views of outside groups to my own organization in a balanced way?
16. Do I counsel my own organization to heed outsiders' views when they are the ethical course of action?

On client relationships and employment

17. Do I work only for organizations whose mission and values are consistent with my own?
18. Do I inform all clients of my ethical commitments and that I would not lie, cheat, steal or misrepresent for them?
19. Do I resist pressures from clients to shade the truth or conceal information that should be disclosed?
20. Have I resigned an account when it was right to do so?

On legal and regulatory responsibilities

21. Do I fulfill all reporting requirement on my work required by law?
22. Do I know, respect, and abide by all federal, state, and local laws that apply to lobbying and related public affairs activities?
23. Do I know, respect, and abide by all laws governing campaign finance and other political activities?

a plan to promote forensic services as well as the services of the overall organization. Avery (1996) presents a simple approach for establishing a plan for addressing public affairs for a governmental agency. The approach calls for evaluating the organization's current situation and determining action needed to establish an effective program as listed in Figure 8.2.

Developing action plan
- Evaluate the agency's current situation.
- How is the agency perceived?
- How well does the agency know the people in their local community?
- How well does the agency communicate with the people in their local community?
- How well does the agency involve the people in their local communities in project analysis and project implementation?

Determining needed actions
- What are the short-term and long-term objectives that the agency needs to establish?
- What does the agency need to do to identify all the people with whom they should be communicating?
- What are the activities which the agency will conduct to improve their relationships with their local communities?
- How will the agency measure their success in improving our community relationships?
- What are the training needs for the agency to implement the action plan to improve relationships with their communities?

Figure 8.2

Developing an action plan and determining needed actions for working with communities.

In evaluating the agency's current situation, they must consider the perception that the community has about the agency. This perception is influenced by the media. If negative stories have appeared concerning the crime laboratory, the perception may be that the laboratory is poorly run or uses questionable techniques. If this is the case, the plan should include ways in which the perception can be turned around. They must also consider their relationship with the community that they serve. There should be ongoing participation between the laboratory and community groups as well as the community leaders and elected officials that they influence. The relationship includes a dialog between the laboratory and community groups where their concerns are addressed. The public should also be given an opportunity to comment on the programs implemented by the laboratory. This can be done through public forums or periodic organized tours of the crime laboratory for community groups.

Once the current state of the agency's public relations is understood, an improvement plan can be put in place. Avery (1996) also presents several issues to be addressed in setting the plan. They include the establishment of short- and long-term objectives for the public affairs program, identification of all the people with whom communication is necessary, recognition of activities that will improve relationships with the community, measurement of success, and identification of staff training required to improve relationships.

A Public Affairs unit can contribute to the strategic planning of an organization by bringing emerging trends and issues to the attention of the organization's leadership. The leadership can then address the issues by incorporating new programs in the strategic plan. If, for example, the Public Affairs unit within a law enforcement agency becomes aware that certain community groups are expressing a concern over an increase in burglaries, the agency can address those concerns by including plans to promote the use of DNA analysis to property crimes.

WRITTEN COMMUNICATIONS

Communicating a formal message is commonly done in written and oral forms. For criminalists, written communications generally entail reporting scientific results. When an individual is promoted to supervisor, they must learn a different way of writing correspondences. The scientific language required for forensic reporting is not appropriate for communications commonly required of crime laboratory management. Often the scientific language is not understood. If used in an attempt to garner support, it may actually cause interest to be lost due to a lack of understanding regarding the need.

Internal written correspondences performed by crime laboratory managers include memorandums sent through the organization to inform the administration of laboratory operations. They include periodic reports concerning routine casework or specific reports on particular issues. Other correspondences include requests for purchasing authorizations. They may also include responses to inquiries from administrators about controversial laboratory issues.

Outside correspondences may include thank-you letters for the services of others or letters to elected officials requesting their support for legislations. Other correspondences from laboratory directors may include letters requesting information concerning grants or a request for a grant. Directors may also write press releases outlining new programs instituted by the laboratory or editorials for a local newspaper.

Regardless of the purpose for the correspondence, it should clearly address the issue in a logical and objective manner. Often individuals write as they talk and, when read by others, the written message appears undeveloped and even unprofessional. Thought and review of all correspondences should be done prior to sending to ensure a thoughtful and professional approach. This is especially important when using electronic mail because it can be quickly sent and, once sent, is difficult to recall.

INTERNAL CORRESPONDENCE

Most organizations have accepted formatting guidelines for correspondences. While structural guidelines for internal memoranda vary, there are accepted conventions to be followed when composing all formal correspondence. These standards apply when composing letters or memorandum for either conventional (paper) or electronic mail.

First, the content of the letter should follow a logical order. The first paragraph establishes the purpose of the letter. The middle paragraphs provide information, answer questions, and state any action that is required. The last paragraph summarizes the contents of the letter.

In addition to proper spelling and grammar, a letter should convey a clear message in a concise manner. Individuals that tend to write in a verbose or disorganized manner should have their letters reviewed before sending. When writing a correspondence that explains the need for a piece of scientific instrumentation, the terminology in the letter should be understandable by the readers. Scientific explanations of the instrument's function should be abandoned for a more general description of its function and its benefit to the organization.

Letters expressing concern over the actions of an individual, unit, or private agency should follow the same format. The letter should first express concern over the unacceptable situation, provide justification for that concern, and finally express the action desired as well as time-lines for the actions. The language of the letter should be tactful yet directly reflect the desires of the writer. It should be kept in mind when internal memorandums are sent criticizing the actions of other units within the same agency that ultimately both units must work together. When defaming language is used in memorandums, the long-term working relationships of the units can be affected.

Letters requiring responses should be attended to as soon as possible. When responding to a correspondence, the original material must be well understood. The response letter should answer all questions asked in the original letter. Responses should be arranged in order of priority, where the most important questions are answered first.

EXTERNAL LETTER FORMATS

Increasingly, electronic mail is becoming the primary method for business correspondence. E-mail is faster than sending paper mail and therefore allows for faster responses. However, at this time in history there remains a need for paper correspondence. Currently, a business letter is still viewed as a more formal correspondence. When an important subject must be addressed, paper remains the primary choice among businesses and governmental agencies alike. For this reason, crime laboratory managers must be aware of the formats common to business communications.

There are many acceptable formatting styles used for business correspondences. Often a clerical professional is available to assist in the correct format of the letter. Also, word-processing software may automatically format a letter. A properly formatted letter reflects on the professionalism of the writer. If the letter is improperly aligned and contains multiple grammatical or spelling errors, the reader may lose confidence in the writer.

The modified-block style of letter is the most commonly used. With the exception of the date and the closing, all the contents of the letter are blocked to the left margin. The date and closing begin in the middle of the line. Whatever style of letter is used, the body of the letter should be aligned on the page so that it is pleasing to the eye. Shorter letters can have larger spaces at the top of the page to make them more attractive. When letters extend beyond one page, each additional page should have a header reflecting the letter's content. A commonly accepted practice is to include the name of the addressee, the date, and the page number on three separate lines in the header of each subsequent page.

The fashion in which a letter is folded also reflects on the professionalism of the person sending the letter. Using $8^1/_2$" × 11" paper and a legal size envelope, a simple tri-fold will work. The tri-fold can have both ends folded into the middle so that the text is enclosed, or the sender can fold the letter in an accordion fashion so that the heading of the letter is facing the reader when the envelope is opened.

If an $8^1/_2$" × 11" sheet of paper must fit into a letter-size envelope, it should first be folded in half to form a $5^1/_2$" × $8^1/_2$" sheet. This sheet can then be tri-folded to fit evenly in the envelope. If the bundle of papers to be sent is over three sheets, they should be sent unfolded in a large envelope.

PRESENTATIONS

The fear of public speaking is often ranked as one of the most common fears that humans experience. In order to present expert testimony, a forensic scientist learns not to fear public speaking. Scientists are generally stereotyped as introverts and may find that giving testimony is the most difficult part of the job. Most of the time, this fear diminishes with experience. The more often one performs any task, the easier and the more enjoyable it becomes.

As they are promoted to positions of greater responsibility, forensic scientists may find that their opportunities to speak before a group increase. Not only may they still be asked to provide expert testimony, but they will have to provide training to police officers and prosecutors, make presentations to schools, speak with journalists, give scientific papers at forensic scientist meetings, or promote a new procedure to their administrators. As laboratory directors they may also be called upon to persuade a decision-maker to fund a new program or even advocate legislation in front of a congressional body.

Presentations should be enjoyable for both the speaker and the audience. Everyone has experienced bad speakers who talk too loud or too soft, mumble and do not speak into the microphone, read directly from a prepared text, have no inflexion in their voice, have no energy, are too verbose with nothing to say, and have visuals that are hard to read or outdated. But everyone has experienced good speakers as well. They are relaxed but passionate about their subject, they have a lot of energy, they are entertaining with humor, they pause to make an important point, and have interesting visuals.

During presentations, as with all types of communication, there is a message that the presenter wishes to convey. Audiences for the presentation are present to gain information from the presentation. Both feel that they have wasted their time if the message is not delivered. By practicing and preparing, a speaker can maximize the quality of the presentation and make it an enjoyable experience for both themselves and the audience.

PREPARING FOR A PRESENTATION

The purpose of the presentation will determine its manner. Different events require different speaking styles. For example, when speaking to elementary schoolchildren about forensic science, a speaker should use short sentences with easily understood language. They should have lots of pictures and hands-on activities. To keep children's attention, they should walk around and possibly even kneel next to them to make a point. However, when speaking to a group of legislators at a congressional hearing, a much more formal approach with a prepared statement would be necessary.

When giving a presentation, a crime laboratory director should be aware of the power that they have. With the microphone comes a certain degree of credibility. One should double-check their facts and speak truthfully. If speaking about a controversial subject, the speaker should present credible and current sources to support their point of view. While not shocking the audience, the speaker should stand for his or her beliefs.

Practice

All public-speaking experts stress that practice is the most important step that a speaker can take in preparing for a presentation. The more a speaker practices, the more familiar they become with the material. The presentation will become easier and more enjoyable to give and listen to.

A presentation begins with a message to be conveyed. The presenter should determine what that message is when they begin preparing the speech. The audience will absorb no more than five key points, so the speaker should limit the presentation to that number. Preparation should begin as soon as possible, as the speaker can expect to revise the material over time as new ideas occur.

The speaker should be enthusiastic about the material presented. If the material to be presented is factual, the addition of appropriate humor can make even the most boring material interesting. However, inappropriate humor about controversial issues should be avoided. Additionally, while quotations can make a presentation more interesting, too many can bog down a presentation. Finally, when speaking to a group, the use of "you" instead of "he/she" draws the audience into the presentation and keeps their interest.

If the presentation is very important, the speaker may want to practice in front of a mirror or with a video camera until they are at ease with the presentation. If possible, the speaker may rehearse in front of a friend or acquaintance who will give honest feedback of the presentation and visual aids. What they find most memorable or usable should make the basis of the overview and summary slides used in the presentation.

Rehearsal should include noting the time it takes for the presentation. When using slides, a speaker should expect to spend at least ten seconds with a slide, but no more than 100 seconds. Often, presenters include too much material in their program, spend too much time on one subject, or go off the subject being presented. When this occurs, they go over their allotted time, causing the audience to become restless. This also throws off the time allotted for other speakers and may prevent them from giving their entire presentation because of time constraints.

If presentation software is used, the presenter should be thoroughly familiar with it. It is frustrating for an audience to watch a presentation where the speaker does not know how to use the presentation software. Audiences have actually groaned when a presenter struggles with the computer. During preparation, the speaker should develop a contingency plan in case technology fails. If all their notes are on the computer and the computer doesn't work, there is likely to be a disaster. An alternative such as using overheads or physical slides should be developed and practiced.

Finally, the more experience a presenter has at presentations, the more comfortable they will be getting in front of an audience and giving a speech.

Beginning presenters should accept as many speaking engagements as possible. There are always schools or community groups interested in forensic science that will be interested in speakers. Also, groups such as Toastmasters offer opportunities to hone presentation skills. Individuals who are nervous or lack other skills needed to give a good presentation could benefit from attending these types of meetings.

Before the presentation

On the day of the presentation, a presenter can increase their comfort level by becoming more familiar with their surroundings. They may wish to arrive early to discover the layout of the room. By standing on the stage they can become comfortable with what they will be seeing during the presentation. Presenters should also sit in several seats throughout the room to give them an idea of how comfortable the audience will be and how their view of the presenter will be. If they discover they will be presenting in a large room, where visual aids not projected on a screen will not be visual to those in the rear, presenters should consider walking among the audience while discussing these objects.

Voice amplification with a microphone is a necessity in a large room, but it can also add emphasis when speaking to any size group. If speaking to an unfamiliar audience, there may be hearing-impaired individuals who will benefit from its use. It also grabs the attention of attendees where the voice alone does not. If the presentation is held in a small room and the speaker possesses a strong voice, they may be able to bypass the use of amplification, but in most circumstances a microphone should be utilized.

If possible, run through the presentation using the equipment to be used. If multiple speakers are giving an electronic presentation, it is advisable for a common computer to be used for all presentations. It is awkward and time-consuming for each presenter to switch to their own computer. To facilitate an efficient flow of speakers, all presentations should be installed beforehand and the speakers should know how to switch quickly to their own presentation. It is also advisable to install desktop icons for each presenter to access quickly.

The audience also plays a part in making the speaker more comfortable. If there is an opportunity before the presentation, a speaker can make themself more comfortable by meeting the audience beforehand. The audience is there because they want to be entertained and learn something new from the presentation. By speaking with the audience beforehand, the speaker becomes acquainted with their expectations and may be able to incorporate additional information to help meet their needs. Also, when the audience feels that they know the speaker, they will feel a personal desire for the speaker to do well and may overlook small mis-steps.

Finally, a speaker should relax before the presentation. This is particularly important if they get very nervous, as an audience quickly detects nervousness through changes in the voice. Stress reduction techniques such as deep-breathing exercises can help relax a speaker. Never should a speaker believe that alcohol enhances their ability to entertain a group. Where one drink may relax a speaker, it can also decrease their ability to react on their feet and may even cause their speech to slur. An audience will quickly detect it and will lose respect for the presenter.

Giving presentations

To make a presentation interesting a speaker needs to do more than just stand in front of an audience and read information to them. A speaker should speak in a conversational style. When an audience feels that they can relate to a speaker, they are more interested in the presentation.

A speaker should face their audience and make eye contact. By observing the audience's behavior, the speaker can get an indication on how they are doing. While the public believes that forensics is always exciting, it can be boring if presented in a technical manner, especially to a non-technical audience. It is important, whether giving expert testimony or a presentation, that material is kept at the level of the audience. If the audience walks out (not allowable for jurors) or nods off, this is a strong indication that the presentation is not going well. It may be necessary to provide more examples of interesting cases with the technical information.

A presentation is more interesting when the speaker does not stand behind a lectern for the entire speech. A wireless microphone may be available and can be useful when speaking to large groups. This allows the speaker to walk around on stage and maintain the audience's attention as they follow the speaker with their eyes. If providing training to a smaller group of people, walking around the room provides stimulation for the audience. Additionally, the use of a remote mouse provides the speaker with the opportunity to take advantage of the computer while walking through the audience.

Another way to involve the audience in the speech is to refer to members of the audience in your presentation. When giving a speech to an organization, it is important to thank their leadership for the opportunity to speak. If appropriate, a humorous remark can be directed toward the president of the organization. The good-humored remark can play on a rivalry between the speaker's and president's hometown sport's team or other appropriate rivalry. This light humor can also help relax the presenter and the audience and prepare them for the presentation. The speaker should always avoid controversial or inappropriate language as well as subject matter when offering humorous remarks.

Though a speaker may be nervous, they shouldn't draw attention to it by apologizing for their nervousness. Also, if there are technical problems with the presentation, the speaker may be better off to joke about it rather than apologizing. An apology tends to draw attention to an area that the audience may have been unaware of, prompting them to look for other signs of nervousness. Instead of concentrating on nervousness, a speaker should concentrate on the message that they are presenting. Usually, it will be an area that the speaker cares a lot about. Concentrating on the message will divert the speaker's attention from their nerves and allow them to calm down.

While reading from a prepared text is usually boring for the audience, there are times when it is necessary, such as when making a presentation to a legislative body. The text of the presentation will be recorded and therefore should be read exactly as the written text. To make a presentation of this sort more interesting for the audience, it should be practiced until the speaker is familiar with the pauses and inflexions needed to make the speech sound natural. Written words are often not used in everyday conversation; practice sessions should include determining if the words sound natural and changing them as necessary.

When reading from a prepared text or using notes, the proper type-font can enhance the readability of the text. As capital letters can be difficult to read, both upper- and lower-case letters should be used. Words or phrases to be emphasized in the presentation should be annotated throughout the notes. The text can also be double spaced and short paragraphs should be used to assist with readability. A page of notes should end with a complete sentence or paragraph to avoid confusion when reading. While reading the text, the speaker should ensure that pages are not stapled. The pages should be slid smoothly to the side when the speaker has finished them as picking the paper up and placing it beneath other pages can be distracting to the audience.

When giving the presentation, the speaker should set the groundwork for questions. They should state at the beginning if they prefer questions as they arise, or at the end of the presentation. If an audience member asks a question on subject material that will be covered later, it is acceptable for a speaker to say so. If a member of the audience asks a question that is not related to the subject matter or would take too long to answer, the speaker can say so but invite the member to meet with them after the presentation to discuss the matter. If a question is asked for which a speaker does not have the answer, they should admit it. However, they should invite the questioner to leave contact information so that the information can be sent to them. Often, following a presentation, an audience member will approach a speaker concerning a subject that was brought up during the presentation. It is for this reason that speakers should make themselves available after presentations for these discussions.

A presenter not only wants the audience to receive useful information but also to act on the information when they leave the presentation. In order to make this probability more likely, there are several things that a speaker should do. First, the speaker should be aware that everyone is busy and people can walk out if they don't perceive that they are getting useful information. The speaker should therefore thank them for their time. The speaker should also provide materials for them to take with them and include their contact information so that the audience can reach them at a later date.

Feedback from an audience is important in order for a speaker to improve. It is not always appropriate to ask for feedback from the entire audience. The size of the audience as well as the formality of the presentation dictates whether evaluations are appropriate. If giving a keynote address, it is not generally desirable to hand out evaluations to the audience. However, as a workshop presenter, it works very well. Feedback or evaluation forms should ask the audience if they obtained the information that they expected. It should ask if there was information that they expected to be presented but was not. Feedback should also include constructive suggestions on how a speaker could improve their overall presentation and presentation skills.

Visual aids

Visual aids can enhance the understanding of the topic, add variety and give the presentation greater impact. Not only do they enhance a presentation, but slides are useful as memory aids in a presentation. They allow the speaker freedom to move around the room and make the presentation more enjoyable for the audience. Visual aids need not be confined to slides. Professional speakers use everything from balls to balloons to make their points. For crime laboratory employees who make presentations, the use of spent bullets or other items that can be handled by attendees can make a presentation more enjoyable.

The first visual aid that a speaker brings to a presentation is themself. The clothes that the speaker wears as well as their grooming, gestures, voice, facial expression, and demeanor are very important to giving a good presentation. A speaker's dress should reflect the formality of the presentation. While it is not appropriate to wear jeans to a congressional hearing, neither is it appropriate to wear a suit to a picnic.

If possible, the speaker should provide items that the group can take home to remind them of the message. Most commonly this includes handouts of the slides used or other summary of the presentation. Handouts can be referred to by the speaker and can be used by the audience to record notes. Handouts should be distributed before or after the speech so as not to disturb the flow of the presentation. Some speakers give them out beforehand so that the audience can use them to make notes. Others prefer to give them out afterwards so the audience will not be distracted from reading them. Other handout items could include "prizes" for the person who answers a particular question. The prize could be an item such as a patch or cup from the crime laboratory or agency. The audience is encouraged to pay attention when they know that they could win something.

Other visual aids that can be used are graphs, charts, and photographs. Some can be included as part of a computer slide presentation or can be presented by themselves on foam board. If a presenter wants to write something as they speak, they may choose to use flipcharts for permanent recording, or an overhead transparency. Additional visual aids include the use of films, videos, audiotapes, or other electronically recorded material. Clips from television or movies can be used to make a point, as can certain musical pieces.

When preparing visual aids, it is important to use them correctly. Slides that contain too many words in small fonts are difficult to read. The audience members in the back of the room cannot read the slides. At times, the font is so small even the speaker has difficulty reading the material on the slide. As a general rule of thumb, when making slides that will be used for an audience, a title should be 24 point font, subtitle should be 18 point font, and other text should be 14 point font. For handouts, titles should be 18 point font, subtitles 14 point font, and other text 12 point font. When making transparencies for use in a presentation, the title should be in 36 point font, subtitles in 24 point font, and other text in 18 point font. These font sizes are illustrated in Figure 8.3. If writing on a flipchart, the title should be 3 inches high, subtitles should be 2 inches and all other text should be 1.5 inches. This will assure that the audience can easily read the text.

If slides are used they should be balanced and pleasing to the eye. The text should use both upper- and lower-case to make the slide easier to read. Color should be used, but certain combinations are very difficult to read. Bright red letters on a bright blue background appear to move and are difficult for the audience to focus on. Light-colored backgrounds with black letters generally work well for reading.

To effectively utilize visual aids, they should be practiced with the presentation. The speaker should integrate them into the presentation, knowing their placement in the speech. Visual aids should not be displayed until the speaker is ready to use them, and they should be promptly removed when they are finished with. When presenting slides or overhead transparencies, the presenter should stand to the side of the aid, facing the audience, instead of directly in front of it where their body can block the view. When referring to the aid, the speaker should point to it to guide the audience's attention to it as well.

When using slides, it is proper to present a summary slide(s) at the beginning of the presentation consisting of the information to be presented. After the presentation, another summary slide should be offered to reiterate the material

Figure 8.3

Font sizes for visual aids.

Slides

Titles: 24 font
Subtitles: 18 font
Text: 14 font

Handouts

Titles: 18 font
Subtitles: 14 font
Text: 12 font

Overhead transparencies

Titles: 36 font
Subtitles: 24 font
Text: 18 font

presented. As people will remember no more than five items, the summary slide(s) should consist of no more than five key points. This reinforces the material that the speaker wishes the audience to retain and act upon.

While acceptable, notes should not be used to a great extent as it can be distracting for the audience as the speaker searches their notes for the information that they wish to convey. Instead, the speaker should practice the presentation to the extent that it can be presented without reading from notes. If note cards are used, they should not include long sentences or paragraphs. Only the key points and factual material that the speaker wants to report accurately such as quotations and statistics should be included on the cards. If used, note cards should also be numbered to avoid disaster in case they are dropped.

Visual aids should supplement the speech – not become the speech themselves. The weight of the presentation lies on the information and the manner in which the speaker relays the information. The presenter should be well informed and well practiced. In doing so, they will be relaxed and able to present their material in an interesting and informative manner.

MEDIA RELATIONS

A crime laboratory director can spread a message to several hundred people through public speaking engagements, or to several hundred thousand by speaking with the media. The media plays a pivotal role in developing public opinion. The crime laboratory should consider the media as a partner in influencing the public to support their goals. A reporter is looking for an interesting story to help the station gain an audience. A crime laboratory director wants the audience to be interested in their organization and how their activities affect the audience. Through mutual cooperation, both the reporter and the director can achieve their goals.

While speaking with the press has advantages, it can also be intimidating. Some believe that journalists are untrustworthy and will only present negative stories. Because of this, they will avoid speaking with the press altogether. Negative stories are generally only presented when a controversial event occurs. To minimize adversarial meetings during bad times, liaisons should be formed with journalists in good times. Crime laboratories should present themselves as reliable sources of background information regarding forensic analysis and a willing provider of interesting story material.

If the organizational culture allows, directors should take a proactive approach to contacting the media regarding new programs. Every organization has different guidelines regarding media relations. An agency may have a public information office and all press releases must be approved by that office. Others are much less structured but still have guidelines for releasing information. If a crime laboratory has access to a public information office, they can be useful in providing suggestions about how to effectively speak to the press. They can also assist in preparing press releases regarding new procedures and their impact on public safety.

It is important when issuing press releases, that all reporters receive the same information and the same professional courtesy. At times, if an agency feels that a specific news outlet always presents a slanted story, there is a temptation to deny information to that outlet. By holding information from an outlet that is perceived to be unethical, they are given an opportunity to criticize the agency further by making accusations that the information is being withheld because of its damaging nature.

PREPARING FOR INTERVIEWS

As with public speeches, interviews with the news media also require preparation. If the interview is not initiated through a press release, a reporter's call may occur unexpectedly at any time. In either case, the laboratory director should use the interview as an opportunity to present a message to the public. If the laboratory's largest challenge is obtaining funding for a specific new procedure, this message should be repeated multiple times during the interview.

When preparing for an interview, the objectives to be advanced by the interview should be identified. Often the laboratory director has only a few minutes to prepare for an interview. Given this inevitability, the director should always have objectives identified to be advanced in media interviews. These may likely be the same objectives listed in the laboratory's strategic plan. Responses to probable inquiries should be prepared that include these objectives. A message should be from the public's perspective and delivered in a way that will make the public feel that the crime laboratory's objective could be beneficial to them as well. For example, if a laboratory's goal is to obtain additional drug analysis instrumentation, they should make the public aware of the backlog and how the instrument will help achieve more timely justice. To avoid confusion, an interview should promote no more than three key objectives.

There are specific state and federal rules and legislation on what constitutes public information. Divulging information regarding an ongoing investigation may compromise the investigation and is generally not considered to be public information. However, depending on the situation, an agency may decide to release some material in order to obtain more information that may lead to solving a case. A laboratory may choose to never release case-sensitive information but instead refer inquiries to the officer in charge of the investigation. A laboratory director should nonetheless be aware of what constitutes public information in their jurisdiction and should be careful to protect information important to the case. Questions regarding public information can generally be directed toward a public information officer or the agency's legal counsel.

Often a request from the media results from a highly publicized crime or event either in the local area or from another jurisdiction. Even if a laboratory director cannot honor their request for information because of agency guidelines, they should reply promptly in light of the reporters' deadlines. Television reporters generally request interviews for the same day so that the story can air during the evening news. The quick response, even if in the negative, will be appreciated by reporters who can then seek answers elsewhere and meet their deadlines.

When responding to a reporter, it is important to know which outlet the reporter is representing and what specific issue they are interested in. Often a reporter will want to discuss an ongoing case. Generally laboratories or law enforcement agencies will not discuss these matters. However, the laboratory may be willing to discuss the general techniques involved in performing the type of analysis that is important to the case. For example, if a paint comparison was the critical piece of evidence in a hit and run, the laboratory may not give specifics of the case but may give an interview concerning how paint is analyzed.

Often the reporter calls at a time that is not convenient for the laboratory. Generally this happens when a newsworthy crime comes to the attention of the reporter. Their request for an interview comes just as the laboratory is analyzing the evidence on the specific crime. If the laboratory has resources to accommodate the reporter, they may choose to do so. Otherwise they may respectfully decline the interview based on their workload. If the laboratory wishes to foster a positive liaison, they may be able to give the reporter a contact in another laboratory that can provide background information.

As with all presentations, it is important to practice interviewing skills. This is particularly important if the interview is regarding a significant or controversial subject. A public information office can be very useful in providing suggestions on how to respond to adversarial questions. It may also be desirable to prepare a detailed question-and-answer sheet for the journalist to refer to as they are preparing their story. This will help them avoid presenting incorrect information to the public.

GIVING THE INTERVIEW

Even if nothing controversial is at issue, interviews can be intimidating. As with presentations, even with practice, things do not always go as planned. As soon as the microphone and camera go on, the words do not flow as smoothly as they did in practice. Above all, an interviewee should be themselves and present accurate information focusing on the message to be delivered. Journalists seek sound-bites and quotable quotes to add to their stories. With this in mind, responses to questions should be concise and less than 15 seconds in length. When longer responses are given, the answer may be edited and your message distorted.

Interviews should not be given just to answer a reporter's questions. Selected messages should be worked into the responses to as many questions as possible. Often a message concerning a lack of funding can be woven into responses to questions regarding almost anything. If a reporter asks about DNA analysis in the laboratory, a crime laboratory director can respond that "we could do more if we had additional funds."

As with all professions, forensics has its own jargon. When giving an interview, jargon uncommon to the public should be avoided. Even words such as CODIS are unknown to the public. This is also important because reporters rarely have scientific expertise. They cover stories because they are available. If they don't understand the technical terms used, the opportunity for reporting errors increases. Simple but descriptive words should be used to carry a message. As forensic scientists often experience with juries, the majority of the public will also lose interest when the operation of a gas chromatograph/mass spectrometer is discussed.

When responding to questions, the answers should always be honest. If a question seems to call for a misleading response, the interviewee should rephrase the questions and answer in a way that will reduce the risk of misinterpretation. Also, hypothetical questions should be avoided by emphasizing the facts of the situation. If a crime laboratory director were asked to comment on apparent improprieties occurring in another laboratory, they would be wise to avoid commenting on the other laboratory but instead discuss how their own laboratory uses quality processes to minimize errors.

Additionally, those giving interviews should assume that all comments are on-the-record. If a reporter asks a question about an ongoing case, an interviewee should avoid giving any information even if the journalist says that it is off the record. If a journalist perceives an answer to be interesting, they will use the statement. Instead of giving specific "off-the-record" information, general information suitable for public viewing should be offered.

All good interviewers, whether homicide investigators or journalists, know that most people are uncomfortable with silence and will fill it with talk that can lead to additional questions. When asked a question, the appropriate answer should be given and the interviewee should then wait for the next question. Information should not be volunteered when there are gaps in the conversation.

Because reporters have the opportunity to edit responses, interviewees have the opportunity to pause before answering questions. This pause allows an interviewee time to consider the question and phrase an appropriate response to include the message to be conveyed. Knowing that the pause is allowable is also useful when responding to difficult questions. Even though it seems that a reporter is seeking a specific response, an interviewee should not allow a reporter to put words in their mouth that can lead to misinterpretation. Their response should be direct, while weaving in their message.

A reporter has a right to phrase a question in any manner that they choose, just as an interviewee has the right to respond to the reporter's questions as they choose. If the interviewee gets angry at a question or the way that it was asked, it will come across in the interview. Instead, if the question calls for a negative response, the interviewee can rephrase the question in a positive light before answering. This is particularly important when dealing with damaging information. Additionally, a key message can be inserted in the response. For example, a laboratory director may be asked why a particular analysis was "botched." Depending on the circumstances of the case and the steps taken by the laboratory, the director may respond with, "Our laboratory is careful with all analyses that are performed. The analysis in this case is no different and was performed using all quality processes in place at the time. Additional processes have been added to continue to improve the quality of our analyses." The fact that the laboratory considers quality analyses to be important is repeated several times in the response. It also answers a negative question in a positive manner.

During an interview, it is possible that the reporter will ask a question for which the laboratory manager does not know the answer. They should admit that they don't know the answer but should volunteer to get back with the reporter later. They may also choose to send them to another source or call on another member of the laboratory to provide the necessary information.

ISSUES SPECIFIC FOR EACH MEDIUM

Television

Each communication medium has specific needs that are important to their audience. Television requires interesting visuals, while radio requires interesting sounds. More compelling interviews will result when these needs are considered. When a television interview is conducted at the laboratory, the interviewee should look for eye-catching visuals that can be filmed to supplement or to act as a background for interviews. Crime laboratory tours are always useful for the reporter to pick a location that they believe will appear appealing on camera.

When giving a television interview, the interviewee should look and talk to the interviewer, not directly at the camera. They should maintain eye contact at all times and avoid actions that may cause them to appear uncomfortable such as licking lips, squinting, rolling the eyes or excessive blinking. A normal voice volume should be used when speaking, varying it as in normal conversation. Speech that can be distracting to an audience such as the use of "ums" and "ers" should be avoided. Also actions such as using hand motions when speaking can be distracting and should be avoided. If this comes naturally to an individual, they should consciously hold their hands in their lap or clasp them together.

The physical stance that the interviewee takes can give positive or negative impressions to the audience. When being interviewed sitting at a desk, the interviewee should lean slightly forward, placing forearms on the table and clasping the hands. This position shows that the interviewee is involved in the discussion and cares about the subject matter. When someone leans back, they appear too relaxed and nonchalant about the interview and it distracts from their credibility. If they are interviewed in an armchair, an interviewee's legs should be crossed at the knees and they should lean forward with their hands clasped in their lap. When standing, their feet should be about 12 inches apart, with one leg slightly in front, and their arms should either be at the side or held motionless.

The face is the primary mode for an interviewee to make a point. The facial expressions should come across naturally and will help to enliven the interview. While the hands should be held motionless, nodding the head or raising an eyebrow can emphasize a point. However, facial expressions can also betray underlying emotions when an interviewee is faced with difficult questions. Actions that may reveal awkwardness such as lip-licking and excessive blinking should consciously be suppressed. When an interviewee can anticipate difficult questions and prepare a response before the interview, they will be more comfortable and their facial expressions will reflect those of a credible response.

Some individuals may even get nervous when speaking on camera when not faced with difficult questions. As with any public-speaking opportunity, stress reduction exercises such as deep breathing and stretching may help promote relaxation prior to the interview.

When given an opportunity to pick the clothing for the interview, business attire is always appropriate. Men should wear light shirts with conservative ties, and women should wear light-colored clothing. Reflective jewelry or jewelry that clanks or jingles appear ostentatious. Also, clothing with intricate patterns of contrasting shades or colors can appear to shimmer on the screen and should be avoided. Crime laboratory personnel always have the opportunity to appear on camera in a laboratory coat. Care should be taken that the coat be neat and clean of stains. Also, when forensic scientists appear on camera performing analytical techniques, all appropriate protective equipment such as gloves and eye protection should be worn.

Print

When speaking to a print reporter, there is less stress and attention to appearance because the interview does not take place in front of a camera. Additionally, fact sheets and background information can be provided to a print reporter that a television reporter may not be able to use. The reporter may wish to record the interview if it concerns a controversial subject. If this is the case, the interviewee should assume that the tape is always running. As with all interviews, nothing should be said that is not for public information. If the interview is not being recorded, the interviewee should speak slowly so that the reporter has time to take accurate and detailed notes. As with television interviews, the silences between questions should not be filled with chatter that can give the reporter controversial information to be used in the story.

Radio

Radio interviews will always include an audio recording. The interviewee should speak in a normal voice, providing inflexions to emphasize a point. A constant distance should be maintained when speaking in front of a microphone, especially in a studio interview. The head and body should not be allowed to sway back and forth or from side to side so that the distance to the microphone is varied and the voice level fluctuates. As with all interviews, nothing should be said that is not for broadcast to the public. The interviewee should always assume that the tape is running.

OTHER MEDIA INTERACTIONS

In addition to face-to-face or telephone interviews with media representatives, a message can be delivered in other ways as well. Press releases highlighting a message can create interest in an issue and perpetuate interviews. Often press releases will draw attention to research that has been conducted regarding a specific subject. An objective survey of crime laboratory directors regarding crime laboratory needs can be publicly released to media outlets to bring attention to deficiencies in funding. In order for a study to be credible, the research should be objectively conducted and presented. If a media outlet airs a flawed survey and is criticized for it, they will be unlikely to accept information from that source in the future.

The print media provides opportunities to convey a message without being interviewed. "Op Ed" pages, the page traditionally located opposite the editorial page, prints letters to the editor and other articles intended to draw attention to issues. A crime laboratory director may wish to submit a piece for publication on this page when requesting public support for an issue. They should be careful to write the piece from the public's point of view; specifically, how the issue affects the operation of the local crime laboratory and the services provided to the public.

CORRECTIONS

Many have the impression that journalists are not to be trusted and will present a slanted story if it will make the piece more controversial and therefore more interesting to their audience. This is not true for most journalists who attempt to present a story from a neutral point of view. They do not want to get something wrong, nor do they want to gain a reputation as an unethical reporter. They view their sources to be important and wish to treat them fairly, especially if they expect to use the source for future stories. However, reporters will make mistakes because of misunderstandings or incomplete information. When this occurs, they have an obligation to issue a correction.

When corrections are presented, they are usually done with much less fanfare than the original story. In print media, there can be frustration when the original story with incorrect information appeared on the front page but the correction appears in small print in an obscure part of the newspaper. Most likely, an interviewee will not have the opportunity to review a story prior to publication; therefore they should ensure that the reporter has a clear understanding of the information and message that is being presented.

Whenever interacting with the press, crime laboratory managers should ensure that they weave in no more than three key messages. These messages should serve to advance the laboratory's strategic goals. Additionally, a crime laboratory should always leave the audience with a positive impression of the organization. Even when addressing large backlogs or an embarrassing situation, positive aspects should be emphasized.

WHEN THINGS GO WRONG – ISSUE MANAGEMENT

While crime laboratories never expect to experience a publicly embarrassing situation, it will happen. It may be a small incident where the completeness of a single examination was questioned or one in which the nation's attention is directed at the laboratory and their overall operations are placed under scrutiny. A crime laboratory director must put preventive actions in place but should be prepared to respond when an unexpected issue arises. It is important for organizations to publicly manage issues in an honest and direct manner in order to maintain the public's confidence.

Chase and Crane (1996) have defined an issue to exist when there is a "gap between corporate action and stakeholder expectations." For a crime laboratory, stakeholders expect that all analysts behave ethically at all times. If an analyst is discovered stealing controlled substances for personal use, the action deviates from the stakeholders' expectation and an issue arises. A gap exists between what is expected and what has occurred. In some circumstances, the gap may be slight, such as when the public perceives that crime laboratories have the ability to analyze all evidence as quickly as they do on television, when in reality this is not the case. In other situations, the gap may be much larger, as when the public perceives that the laboratory bases conclusions on sound scientific data and it is discovered that analysts are failing to completely perform the analysis required to reach such a conclusion. Issue management closes the gap that exists between the public's perception and the organization's performance.

When something goes wrong, an issue arises. It is clear that the performance goals of the organization have not been achieved. The organization should evaluate what was the goal and what actually happened to establish the performance gap. Additionally, the organization should determine the reputation that they wish to have and evaluate the public perception of the organization. This establishes the gap in the public's perception. Strategies must be devised to narrow the gap in public perception as well as the gap in performance. When something goes wrong, the crime laboratory's public reputation is damaged, as is the laboratory's internal performance goals for excellence. Both gaps must be closed for the laboratory to regain its reputation.

The performance gap can be narrowed through implementing new policies and procedures to correct deficiencies and prevent future occurrences. The project management steps of identifying the issue and determining and implementing the appropriate solutions should be followed. The perception gap can be narrowed by sharing these corrective actions with the public through press releases, interviews, and other informational activities.

When communicating with the public regarding an issue, Koch and McGee (1996) recommend against throwing statistics at perceptions and emotions. When the public feels strongly about an issue, they will disregard the statistics presented to dissuade them from their opinion. Koch and McGee cite a study performed by the Center for Risk Communications that lists four key factors that influence public trust and credibility. Perceived caring and empathy that can be assessed in the first 30 seconds of a public statement is of primary importance to the public. After empathy, competence and expertise, honesty and openness, and dedication and commitment are equally important in influencing public trust. When an issue is discovered that harms a laboratory's reputation, instead of quoting the number of cases worked and the percentage that were correct, the public will be more accepting by first expressing concern over the errors that were made and how they feel about the citizens who may have been harmed. After that, disclosure of corrective actions and commitment to those actions will assist in returning the public's confidence to its original level.

It is important to speak to the media regarding the issue of concern in order to maintain the public's confidence. The media will continue to request interviews on stories that they perceive to be in the public's interest. Replying "No comment" or remaining silent regarding the situation will only intensify the speculation of wrongdoing. Instead, a responsible position should be taken by expressing honest concern, stating the facts as known, and reporting back as the problem is investigated and solutions are obtained.

During interviews concerning controversial situations, many difficult and adversarial questions may arise. Prior to the interview, an agenda should be devised that focuses on key messages that will enhance public confidence.

Honest concern should be expressed as well as how the problem is being investigated and what is being done to correct future occurrences. All questions should be answered with a factual statement followed by a key message relevant to the question. Mistakes should be admitted to but followed up with how future occurrences will be prevented. As with all interviews, honesty and directness apply to adversarial interviews as well. The interviewee should remain polite and respectful when addressing the reporter's questions.

Answers should be short in order to minimize the likelihood that they are taken out of context. When questions are asked that demand release of confidential information, the interviewee should state as much. If the reporter asks the same question over or in a slightly different way, the interviewee should remain calm and give the same response. If questions are ambiguous, the interviewee should interpret as they like and answer the question as they desire. The reporter will follow up if they intended a different interpretation.

Within a crime laboratory director's career, it will be likely that a situation will arise where the laboratory's operations are questioned and its reputation is damaged. To regain the public's confidence in the laboratory's abilities, the director must be prepared to approach the issue in a proactive manner while addressing the concerns of the public.

GOVERNMENT RELATIONS

Until recently, a crime laboratory director was not required to be politically astute. It was enough that they were knowledgeable of the technical aspects of forensic analysis and management of personnel. However, in the last few years, the nature of the job of crime laboratory director has changed to include being politically active. The result of this activity has been increased governmental support for forensic science activities.

A crime laboratory director may be seeking support for their own agency or for the entire community. Either way, they must be aware of the political processes followed at a federal level as well as at their state and local level. There are particular times in the legislative cycle when a legislator is more receptive to considering requests for support. There are also particular legislators that are more important to a crime laboratory director.

The United States federal government is divided into three branches: executive, legislative, and judicial. All states in the United States are organized in the same fashion. The three branches are equally important in running the government. Each has control over the other branches through specific actions listed in the United States constitution. Occupying these positions are elected and appointed officials with various beliefs on how the government should function and on what role it should play in the lives of its citizenry. Generally, the officials hold views reflecting the dogma of the two major United States political parties, Democratic and Republican. The opposing points of view on all issues are debated in formal and informal ways and the final outcome is usually a negotiated compromise between the two extremes.

The executive branch of the federal government consists of the Office of the President, the cabinet departments and the independent government agencies. The President proposes the budget based upon his policy priorities. The cabinet departments and independent agencies administer the laws enacted. One of the agencies most familiar to crime laboratories is the Department of Justice and Department of Treasury. Within the Department of Justice are the Federal Bureau of Investigation, the Drug Enforcement Agency, and the National Institute of Justice. The Bureau of Alcohol, Tobacco, and Firearms is located within the Department of the Treasury, as is the Secret Service.

The Legislative branch of the federal government consists of the two houses of Congress, the House of Representatives and the Senate. Both houses are composed of representatives elected from each state. The House of Representatives is composed of representatives elected based on the state's population. A census is completed every ten years to determine changes in population and is the singular determinant in assigning the number of representatives from each state. The district from which Representatives are elected are drawn by politicians within a state. Drawing congressional district boundaries is a very complicated process and a very political activity. Some districts have been known to take extremely unusual shapes to include voters who historically vote for a specific party. The party in power that has drawn the district hopes to elect more representatives of their party in order to carry on the policies of that political party. The Senate is composed of two Senators from each state. The Senators represent the entire state, not just a district, as do Representatives.

The Judicial Branch consists of the United States Supreme Court, the court of appeals and district courts. A crime laboratory analyst may testify in a United State District Court during a criminal trial for a federal offense. The Supreme Court is composed of nine justices appointed for life. The appointment of federal judges is also a political exercise. The President nominates judges who he feels will support legal decisions that support his party's policies. Judges' nominations are often challenged by legislators of the opposing party who fear this very thing.

The balance between the branches has been set by the constitution or by judicial decision. Neither branch has ultimate authority over the others, nor does any have power to control the actions of the others. The President nominates federal judges and appointees to run bureaucracies but Congress must approve the President's nominations. Congress also has the authority to impeach both judges and Presidents and to remove them from office. Finally, the Supreme Court has the authority to declare laws passed by the Congress and signed by the President as unconstitutional.

It takes both houses of Congress, House of Representatives and Senate, to pass laws. Laws may be for any purpose but of the most important is legislation that appropriates funds to operate the government. While Congress passes laws, the President must sign the law for it to be enacted. While the President has the right to veto a law, the Congress can subsequently pass it over the President's veto.

The executive, legislative, and judicial branches must work together to effectively run the country. The interactions between the three are very complex and very political. Each branch operates independently but is acutely aware of the control that the other branches have upon their operations.

The actions of all three branches will affect crime laboratory operations at certain times. The bureaucracies in the executive branch control federal laboratories such as the Federal Bureau of Investigation, the Drug Enforcement Administration, and the Bureau of Alcohol, Tobacco, and Firearms. Also among these bureaucracies is the National Institute of Justice which is generally responsible for distributing grant funds for local and state crime laboratories. The agencies in the executive branch control the rules under which the state and local crime laboratories and other law enforcement agencies must abide. Among these are health and safety requirements.

The executive branch and its agencies can recommend that a new federal program such as those to fund crime laboratory improvement be enacted. Depending upon their dedication and passion for the program and their influence in Congress, they can persuade Congress to pass legislation to enact their proposal. The Community Oriented Policing Service, or COPS, is an example of this. Originating under President Clinton, the program sought to place "100,000 cops on the street." While many in Congress doubted the legislation's ability to make that number an actuality, and others had concerns about the future of the officers that were hired after the grant funds ran out, Clinton's influence carried the legislation through many years. Each year the Congress threatened to discontinue funding, but in the end, funding was maintained throughout the Clinton presidency.

The Supreme Court has the authority to decide if a law enforcement practice is constitutional. These decisions can influence whether a crime laboratory can continue to perform specific tests. For example, if the court should rule that collection of DNA-convicted offender samples is a violation of the individual's civil rights, it could dramatically affect the laboratory's ability to identify suspects through DNA analysis.

Crime laboratories often interact with the federal bureaucracies such as the National Institute of Justice but also may interact with the Congress. Among the many elected officials and committees in Congress, some are more important to crime laboratories. In the Senate, most of the authorization legislation affecting crime laboratories originates from the Judiciary Committee, specifically the Criminal Justice and Oversight Subcommittee. Appropriations for this legislation is granted by the Appropriations Committee – specifically the Commerce, Justice, State, The Judiciary, and Related Agencies Subcommittee (CJS). In the House of Representatives, authorizations derive from the Judiciary Committee, Subcommittee on Crime. Appropriations result from the Appropriation Committee, Commerce, Justice, State, and Judiciary subcommittee. While legislation concerning crime laboratories may originate from any congressional member, it must go through these committees to be enacted.

HOW A BILL BECOMES A LAW

The textbook description of how a bill becomes a law follows a simple path. The bill is introduced by a member of Congress in either the House of Representatives or in the Senate. The bill is then referred to the appropriate committee where it may be referred to an appropriate subcommittee. It is likely that no further action will be taken on the bill. If this occurs, the bill is said to "die in committee."

If a bill does not die in committee, the subcommittee studies the bill. Hearings may be held to consider the merits of the bill. Interested parties, including officials in federal agencies, may be called upon to testify for or against the bill. The subcommittee may revise the bill prior to approval. Once the majority of the subcommittee agrees to the final language of the bill, it is returned to the full committee. The full committee may also amend the bill and the majority of the committee must approve of the bill before sending it to the House or Senate floor for a vote.

If the bill is in the House of Representatives, the bill is sent to the Rules Committee which assigns rules for debating the bill when it is presented to the House floor. The House leadership schedules when the bill will be presented to the House. At that time the entire House debates the bill and amendments may be offered. A vote is then taken on passage of the bill. If the bill passes, it is sent to the Senate.

If the bill is in the Senate, it does not go through a Rules Committee but is scheduled for debate before the whole Senate by the leadership. As with the House, the Senate membership may offer amendments prior to the vote. If the bill passes, it is sent to the House.

Generally a bill passes the House and Senate in two different versions. It is then sent to a Conference Committee composed of members from both the House and Senate. The Conference Committee resolves discrepancies between the versions and the bill is then returned to both Houses for voting on the compromise bill. If both Houses pass the bill, it is sent to the President for action.

The President may sign the bill, at which time it becomes law. If he has objections, he may veto the bill or send it back to Congress noting his objections. If two-thirds of the members in both the House and Senate vote to approve the bill, the Congress may override the veto and the bill will become law.

In addition to the progression of a bill through Congress, it is also important to understand how the Congress is organized. Members in the House of Representatives are elected for two-year terms. The two years are considered to be a "Congress." For instance, the 2001–2002 period made up the 107th Congress. If a bill is introduced but not considered in that period of time, it is not automatically carried over but must be re-introduced and the entire process begins anew.

Another important distinction is the difference between authorization bills and appropriation bills. An authorization bill authorizes money to be spent for a specific purpose but does not provide the funds to be spent. The authorization must be included in an appropriation bill for the money to be available for spending. Authorizations may be passed at any time during the Congressional sessions but Appropriations are only passed once a year, during late summer and early autumn.

ADVOCACY

The textbook description of the law-making process in the United States does not address many of the intricacies and realities. There is considerable discussion and negotiation that occur at all stages of the process. Along the way interest groups assist in keeping the bill alive. It is a common misconception that interest groups purchase legislators' votes with campaign contributions and are to blame for all the problems in government. The reality is that all citizens belong to some interest group and rarely contribute to campaigns. A citizen's interests may lie in the government's policies on education, prescription drugs, or tax reform. How actively they advocate the issue will depend on how strongly they feel about it.

Crime laboratories and law enforcement agencies have a direct interest in certain criminal justice legislation. This is true for legislation that will have a positive or negative effect on the agency's resources. Some legislation will require more of the agency's resources to comply with the legislation. Other legislation provides more resources for the agency in the form of grants. Charles Mack (1996) defines lobbying as "the advocacy of a point of view on a matter of public policy." Law enforcement and forensic organizations and agencies actively engage in lobbying when they try to influence Congress by supporting or opposing legislation.

Interest groups may be represented by professional lobbyists. If interest groups carry a poor reputation, lobbyists are considered even worse. Lobbyists provide interest groups with access to the elected officials. Generally, they reside in Washington, DC and are familiar with the staff and the processes necessary to forward a bill. They can be instrumental in influencing Congress to hold hearings or to include an issue in legislation.

Individuals and groups generally lobby for specific purposes. They may lobby for legislation to obtain an advantage that they cannot obtain by themselves in the private sector. Individuals concerned that pharmaceutical companies exert too much power and are charging too much for prescription drugs, lobby for legislation that will regulate the companies and keep costs contained.

Groups may also lobby for economic advantage. Private forensic laboratories may lobby for legislation that provides funding for subcontracting of forensic analyses. Instrument manufacturers may also lobby for legislation that would provide funding for crime laboratories to purchase their instrumentation. This is especially true for manufacturers within specialty markets such as ballistic image systems or DNA typing instruments that are selected by federal agencies for use at a national level.

Often public agencies lobby for new programs that they believe would be beneficial for the public and their agency. Many law enforcement agencies, as well as organizations to which they belong, such as the International Chiefs of Police, lobby for grant programs that will provide funds for new computer technology. They view the computers to be essential in the effective tracking of criminal activity and effective law enforcement. Without the new programs, they would be unable to obtain these computers and therefore lobby for passage of the legislation.

Finally, groups lobby for actions that only government can take. Some issues are truly global in scope and cannot be effectively confronted at a local level. These include environmental and national defense issues. The use of databases in law enforcement has transformed many forensic analyses from local to global issues. In order for information to be shared, it must be compatible and require federally mandated guidelines that apply to all jurisdictions.

Lobbying can be direct or indirect. Direct lobbying consists of directly communicating with a public official in an attempt to affect pending legislation. The contact could be in person or in writing with an elected lawmaker or their staff. This is the commonly thought-of form of lobbying where professional lobbyists act on behalf of an interest group to influence a Congressional vote.

Indirect lobbying takes place at a "grassroots" level. A large number of individuals across the country are encouraged to express support or opposition to their own elected officials. This is particularly useful if the elected member of Congress sits on an influential committee. If a crime laboratory serves the constituents of a member of the Appropriations Committee, the laboratory's request for support for a bill providing funds to crime laboratories may be particularly influential in obtaining the member's support for the bill.

Often those with similar interests join together to more effectively advocate an issue. The "States Coalition" was formed as a group of law enforcement agencies from across the United States that were concerned about the lack of funding for forensic laboratories. The "Consortium of Forensic Science Organizations" shared a similar concern. They were composed of organizations that shared common interests in forensic analyses. Together these groups, as well as others, successfully promoted legislation to grant funds to crime laboratories.

The interaction between Congress and interest groups is not one-sided. Interest groups seek a legislator's support for their issues but are also valuable sources of information to legislators regarding issues. Legislators view the groups as the experts regarding a particular issue and will seek their opinion prior to supporting legislation that affects them. They may call upon the group for research or other studies that support their issue. Federal agencies are also considered to be interest groups and are pivotal in providing information to legislators. Independent interest groups may be called upon to comment regarding the operations of the federal agency.

DRAWING ATTENTION TO ISSUES

In addition to expressing support of public policy to decision-makers, lobbying can be done by calling on the support of others through the mass media. The public's opinion on issues can be impacted through television, newspaper and radio, and in turn, the public's opinion will impact governmental policy decisions. In addition to only those with a direct interest in forensic analyses, those with an indirect interest could be motivated to express support when they read an article about the enormous backlog of cases awaiting analysis. Public attention to issues may be obtained through other means as well. Having a celebrity act as a spokesperson for the issue can draw the public attention. Forensic issues have been championed by author Patricia Cornwell and actor William Peterson.

Formal organizations often educate their members about the political process and pending legislation in which they may be interested. This education provides congressional representatives with more informed and active constituents. Education takes place through personal contact, newsletters, conferences, and through the Internet.

The Internet is valuable to groups in many ways. Organizational web pages provide immediate information regarding pending legislative action. Links to a reliable source of legislative information such as the Library of Congress website can be included that direct an individual to the proposed legislation. Organizational websites can elicit political action from their members and even include templates for letters supporting or opposing legislation. The website can also encourage members to promote the issue to their own community through use of media contacts. Organizational mail exchanges as well as websites can provide forums for members to share thoughts, ideas, and information regarding specific issues. This exchange of information can provide members with solutions to problems they are facing in their own organizations. It may also provide training ideas or aids to be used for the organizational member to educate others about a public policy issue.

The Internet also provides a rapid source for obtaining information. Research can be conducted quickly through mail exchanges between those with similar interests. On-line surveys can be conducted and anecdotal evidence can be sought that can immediately be provided to legislators.

Often legislation that has an indirect effect on crime laboratory operations is passed without consulting the law enforcement or forensic community. The Internet provides a "highway" to inform others that such legislation is being considered and action is required on their part to support, change, or oppose the proposal.

MEETING WITH LEGISLATORS

A crime laboratory director should get to know their local members of Congress or their staff. Further, these relationships should be treated as another continual duty of a crime laboratory director. Continual attention is required because there is constant turnover in legislators and their staff. In many jurisdictions term limit legislation accelerates the process. Each new legislator must be informed regarding issues relevant to crime laboratories as well as their local laboratory's ability to serve as a source for new issues.

Many agencies have prohibitions against their employees directly contacting elected officials. A director should ensure that they are allowed to make such contact. If not, requests should be directed to the head of the agency requesting their signature on a letter of support or other appropriate demonstrations of support such as directly contacting the member of Congress through telephone or in person.

Congressional staff

As elected officials are very busy, their staff members take on important roles. Generally a crime laboratory director will not get to speak with an elected official but must present the issue through a staff member. Within a Congressional office, various positions are held. The Chief of Staff or Administrative Assistant is usually in charge of office operations. They report directly to the member of Congress and are responsible for the final evaluation of the political outcomes of legislation as well as constituent requests.

The Legislative Director (also called Senior Legislative Assistant or Legislative Coordinator) monitors the legislative schedule and makes recommendations regarding the legislation to the Chief of Staff. An office may have several Legislative Assistants, each with expertise with a particular issue.

A member of Congress may also employ a Press Secretary to oversee media and constituent communications, an Appointment Secretary to schedule meetings or appearances, and Caseworkers to work with constituent requests.

Contacting members of Congress

Contacting a member of Congress may be done by telephone, letter, e-mail, or in person. Legislators and their staffs are extremely busy and all communication should be brief and direct. The reason for the contact should be stated early in the communication. When seeking a legislator's support for a particular piece of legislation, it should be requested up front.

Telephone calls

Telephone calls to members' offices are usually answered by a staff member. Unless one is familiar with a particular individual, they should ask for the staff member who handles the issue on which they are calling. A crime laboratory director will generally request the staff member who is responsible for criminal justice issues. Once introduced, they can become an ongoing point of contact.

Common etiquette calls for immediate identification of the caller and their agency (if allowed). If the caller is a constituent, that should be noted that as well. After the introduction, a brief message expressing support or opposition for a piece of legislation should be left. For example, "Please tell Senator/Representative X that I support/oppose Senate bill S# or House resolution HR#." A brief justification may be offered especially regarding how it will affect the citizens in the member's district. After establishing a relationship with a staff member of elected official, the communication will become more informal and additional information supporting or opposing the legislation can be offered.

Telephone calls can also be made to invite the member or staff member to a crime laboratory. When members are on recess, they return to their home district. This can be an opportunity to invite the member to the crime laboratory that serves their district and to show them how their support has helped the laboratory and their constituents. The visit can also reveal deficiencies in service and serve as an opportunity to gain their support. Either purpose for their visit will generally garner their support. Most elected officials will find the crime laboratory a fascinating place and will be grateful for the invitation.

A telephone call may also be made to set up a meeting during a visit to Washington. Unless it is a particularly busy time, legislators and their staff will agree to set up a meeting, especially if it is with a constituent. As the legislator is usually very busy, unless they are personally interested in the subject matter, the meeting will likely be with a Legislative Assistant, not with the elected member.

Writing to a member of Congress

Written communications to a member of Congress either through electronic or conventional methods should also be brief and direct. When writing in support or opposition to a specific piece of legislation, the legislation should be specified and the contents of the letter restricted to that issue. The letter should include justification for support or opposition of the legislation and should be limited to one page.

Meeting with members of Congress

When requesting a meeting with a legislator, it should be first submitted in writing. However, a telephone call is usually required to confirm and finalize the meeting. When a specific date and time has been set for the meeting, the attendees should be selected. It may be only the crime laboratory director, or they may wish to bring along others who support the issue. The attendees should be limited to three or four people. Often the meeting room is small and too many people will be uncomfortable. If too many people are in attendance, the legislator may feel unnerved or intimidated.

Prior to the meeting, all attendees should agree on talking points to be presented. The group should also plan the details of the meeting, including such details as who will start the conversation. It is also advantageous to have an informational handout that can be left with the staff member or member of Congress. The packet should include a copy of the bill that the group is advocating as well as how it will affect their constituency.

When arriving for the meeting, attendees should be prompt but also be prepared to wait or even have the meeting rescheduled at the last moment. As with other forms of contact, the meeting should be direct and brief. If appropriate, the spokesperson of the group should begin by expressing their appreciation regarding the legislator's past support on issues relating to crime laboratories. Research regarding their voting record may have to be performed prior to the meeting. If a meeting attendee is a constituent, brief casual conversation regarding the legislator's district or history may be appropriate. If the legislator was a Prosecutor prior to being elected to Congress, it may be likely that the laboratory director or other laboratory staff is personally familiar with him and his work.

The staff member or legislator may choose to extend the meeting by asking questions but attendees should be prepared to spend only ten or twenty minutes with them. Honest answers should be given to their questions. If attendees don't know the answer, is should be stated that they will find out the answer and get back with the information as soon as possible.

A sincere thank-you should be offered at the end of the meeting as well as an invitation to visit their local crime laboratory. They should be reminded that the attendees are a valuable source for all forensic issues. Immediately following the meeting, a letter should be sent to the staff member or legislator thanking them for their time and outlining the key points of the discussion. Attendees should follow up with the legislator at key points in time as the legislation moves through Congress.

BUREAUCRACIES

Within the executive branch are bureaucratic agencies that perform the day-to-day work of the government. While these agencies report to the President, they are created and funded by Congress. Congress therefore has considerable oversight power over the bureaucracies' policies. Bureaucratic agencies are also important to Congress. They are often called upon to provide information to Congress as they are considering legislation. Congress may also rely on the agencies to assist constituents resolve problems and make rulings that benefit the interest groups that politicians like.

Bureaucracies may implement policy and act as regulators. For example, Congress appropriates funds for dissemination as grants but does not specify detail regarding the granting policy. The bureaucratic agency responsible for dissemination is also responsible for the rules by which state and local agencies must apply for the grants. The agency may also set priorities as to how the grants will be disseminated. For example, for grants available through the DNA Improvement Act of 1995, the federal granting agency gave priority to consortium grant applications from several agencies over grant applications from single agencies.

Bureaucracies may also be assigned regulatory authority. Crime laboratories must dispose of hazardous waste per regulations promulgated by the Environmental Protection Agency as well as comply with quality assurance regulations for DNA testing promulgated by the FBI. State bureaucracies also often set rules governing the testing of breath and body fluids for use in intoxicated driving cases.

Other bureaucracies maintain crime laboratories. These include the Department of Justice which operates the FBI and DEA and the Department of the Treasury which operates the BATF, the Postal Laboratory; and the Secret Service laboratory.

The United States operates under Federalism. Federalism organizes the nation so that two or more levels of government have formal authority over the same area and people. States and local governments share power with the federal government and crime laboratories must comply with legislation from all three governments. One of the common points of disagreement among politicians concerns the appropriate ratio of power between the states and the federal government. One of the ways in which crime laboratories are affected by this discussion is in the way that grant funds are made available. Block grants are issued to states generally based on their populations. The premise behind block grants is that states know their needs and should decide how to best spend the funds. Discretionary grants are usually administered by a federal agency. The federal agency sets priorities as to the use of grant funds for the nation by interpreting the spirit of the legislation. Funding is distributed based on how closely the grant proposal meets the priorities. For discretionary grants, the states are generally not given the opportunity to determine how the funding would best be utilized in their state.

There is disagreement about which type of funding best meets the needs of the crime laboratories. This is especially true for smaller laboratories that may not receive grant funds as often as larger state laboratories. One point of view is that discretionary grants are not influenced by political authorities in the state. State laboratories are generally under the ultimate authority of an elected official who has direct or indirect influence over the state granting agency. It is a disputable belief that the majority of block grant funds go to state crime laboratories because of this influence. Discretionary grants therefore give equal consideration to both state and local laboratories.

The other point of view contends that under a block grant dissemination of funds, all states receive funding. This is not necessarily true with discretionary grants. The state and local crime laboratories can then work together to set priorities for the state, and funding can be disseminated as determined by the state priorities.

Another forensic area affected by state versus federal oversight concerns administration of databases. The establishment of federal databases is important because criminals do not respect boundaries: they readily move between cities and states. Therefore it is necessary for the federal government to maintain databases where information can be exchanged. However, they are reliant upon the states and localities to enter data. The Combined DNA Indexing System is overseen by the federal government; each state has a CODIS administrator usually located in a state laboratory; local laboratories perform analysis and input data into the database. All levels of government must work together to make the database successful.

THE NATIONAL FORENSIC SCIENCE IMPROVEMENT ACT

The National Forensic Science Improvement Act can be used as a demonstration of government processes in the United States. In 1997, a group of law enforcement executives realized that their crime laboratories were in desperate need of assistance. A "States Coalition" was formed to forward the idea for federal legislative support. It was decided that the Coalition must use political leverage and raise public awareness to obtain the needed assistance from the federal government. Among the leaders was "Buddy" Nix, the Director of the Georgia Bureau of Investigation. Director Nix was passionate about the issue and his enthusiasm spread to those around him. Director Nix dedicated the resources of GBI into the development and passage of the National Forensic Science Improvement Act. One of the original drafts of the National Forensic Science Improvement Act (NFSIA) called for $768 million to be appropriated to state and local crime laboratories "to improve the quality, timeliness, and credibility of forensic science services for criminal justice purposes."

Working alongside of the States Coalition, the board of the American Society of Crime Laboratory Directors became politically active. Grassroots lobbying efforts were urged of their members. Several visits were made to discuss the NFSIA with federal legislators. In the early visits, the group encountered resistance not to the idea but the amount of money requested. However, in response to the visits, Sentator Mike DeWine (Ohio) amended the Crime Identification Technology Act of 1999 (CITA) to include authorization for forensics. The purpose of the CITA legislation was changed to "To provide for the improvement of interstate criminal justice identification, communication, and forensics." That year $250 million was appropriated to CITA. Of that, however, very little went to forensics. It was clear that more lobbying was needed by all interest groups to expand the appropriations to the forensic sciences.

In 1999, the States Coalition used political influence to have the National Forensic Science Improvement Act introduced in both the House of Representatives and the Senate. Paul Coverdell (Georgia) introduced Senate Bill 1196 and Sanford Bishop (Georgia) introduced House Resolution 2340. Several years were spent building support in Congress as well as with other organizations. Among the organizations that supported the legislation were the International Association of Chiefs of Police, the National Sheriffs Association, the

National Association of Attorneys General, and all the national and regional forensic organizations.

In 2000, seven organizations joined together to form the Coalition of Forensic Science Organizations. These organizations were the American Society of Crime Laboratory Directors, the American Academy of Forensic Sciences, the American Society of Crime Laboratory Directors – Laboratory Accreditation Board, the National Association of Medical Examiners, the International Association of Identification, the National Forensic Science Technology Center, and the National Center of Forensic Sciences. The CFSO represented the vast majority of forensic science practitioners. With consolidated funds, they contracted with a professional lobbying corporation to assist with the promotion of forensic science legislation.

In July of 2000, an event occurred that was to have a major impact on the future of the National Forensic Science Improvement Act. One of the initial supporters of the Act, Paul Coverdell, Senator from Georgia, died suddenly of a cerebral hemorrhage. This tragedy was turned into an opportunity by the States Coalition which proposed that Senator Jeff Sessions (Alabama) introduce a new bill in Coverdell's memory. In September 2000, the Paul Coverdell Forensic Science Improvement Act was introduced with a press conference. In an attempt to gain media attention, the press conference featured mystery writer, Patricia Cornwell. However, the bill introduction was late in the two-year session of Congress and many legislators would be returning to their home jurisdictions to campaign for their re-election. After the appropriation bills were passed, they would be adjourning for the year and no new legislation would be passed. It was agreed that passage of the Coverdell FSIA would be difficult, if at all possible.

In November 2000, fate stepped in again with the disputed Presidential election. Since it was uncertain which political party would take the White House and therefore which policies would be adopted, no action was taken regarding appropriations and the Congress did not adjourn. Taking advantage of this extended session, the Act was passed by the Senate on October 27, 2000 and the House of Representatives on December 7, 2000. It was enacted as law when it was signed by President Clinton on December 21, 2000, literally days before he was to leave office.

With an authorization bill as law, the work to obtain appropriations began. The legislation authorized nearly $500 million, with $35 million to be made available the first year. During 2001, lobbyists working for the Consortium of Forensic Science Organizations persuaded the Senate to conduct hearings on crime laboratory needs. These hearings included leaders of the forensic science community and featured another celebrity, William Peterson, an actor on a popular television series about forensic investigations.

When the Appropriations law of 2001 was signed, only $5 million was appropriated for the Coverdell FSIA. This amount was disappointing to the many that had worked hard for passage over the four years since inception. No doubt in the years to come, additional work will be directed at increasing the amount of funding for the Coverdell FSIA as well as other crime laboratory improvement programs.

SUMMARY

One of the most important roles of the crime laboratory director is to be an advocate for the laboratory. This requires that a laboratory director give presentations that will result in funding for a new procedure or instrument; essentially to become a salesperson. In the United States, salespeople are often placed on the same rung of the societal ladder as lobbyists. However, like lobbyists, salespeople serve a valuable role in society.

As no one is self-sufficient, acquiring goods and services from others is essential to living. No one has the ability to purchase everything they desire or need. In order for a consumer to make a decision regarding what to buy with their limited resources, they must be convinced that they want or need what they are buying. The entire field of marketing is dedicated to determining the best way to influence consumers. A consumer's decision can be based on many factors, including product name recognition, quality, and price. The individuals who manufacture and sell a product should be passionate about it. Their enthusiasm and knowledge about it can sway a consumer into choosing one product over another.

When crime laboratories purchase scientific equipment, they face a buying decision. Often their knowledge regarding a manufacturer's past service as well as the instrument's performance is a primary factor in reaching a decision. The manufacturer's sales representative can also affect a decision. A representative's honesty, knowledge and enthusiasm about the instrument can be the deciding factor between two equal items.

Crime laboratory directors should think in these same terms when acting as advocates for their crime laboratories. As do consumers, agency and legislative decision-makers have limited resources to spend. They want to spend their resources on what they desire most. Crime laboratories can help decision-makers decide to spend resources on forensics by being enthusiastic sales representatives for the laboratory. By effectively communicating a message of a crime laboratory's importance to legislators through public and media outlets, the director can play an influential role.

REFERENCES

Adams, William C. (1996) The Importance of Media Relations in Public Affairs Planning. In: L. Dennis (ed.) *Practical Public Affairs in an Era of Change.* University Press of America, New York. 75–87.

American League of Lobbyists. *Code of Ethics.* URL: http://www.alldc.org/ethicscode.htm [3-7-02].

Avery, Gary *et al.* (1996) Public Affairs in the Public Sector. In: L. Dennis (ed.) *Practical Public Affairs in an Era of Change.* University Press of America, New York. 169–177.

Chase, W. Howard and Crane, Teresa Yancy (1996) Issue Management: Dissolving the Archaic Division between Line and Staff. In: L. Dennis (ed.) *Practical Public Affairs in an Era of Change.* University Press of America, New York. 129–141.

Communicating with Elected Officials. URL: http://www.capwiz.com/alliancecm/issues/basics/?style=comm [10-13-01].

Communicating More Effectively. URL: http://www.dummies.com/Money/Career/Communication_and_pu.../0-7645-5253-8_0011.html [1-17-02].

Deavers, Michael (1996) The "Gipper's" Timeless Lessons on Communicating Effectively. In: L. Dennis (ed.) *Practical Public Affairs in an Era of Change.* University Press of America, New York. 347–353.

Drebinger, John W. Jr (1997) *Mastering Safety Communication.* Wulamoc Publishing, Galt, CA.

Feierman, Art, *Presenting Solutions – Effective Presentations,* URL: http://www.presentingsolutions.com/effectivepresentations.html [10-14-01].

Greenhalgh,Diane, *Tips for Meeting with Legislators,* URL: http://www.alliancecm.org/policy/meetingtips.htm [10-13-01].

Gove, Bill and Siebold, Steve, *Seven Ways to Boost your Onstage Charisma*, URL: http://www.govesiebold.com/speaking/speakingtips/stage_fright.htm [10-14-01].

Gove, Bill and Siebold, Steve, *Ten Tips to Overcome Stagefright*, URL: http://www.govesiebold.com/speaking/speakingtips/stage_fright.htm [10-14-01].

Hanson, Kirk (1996) Ethics and Public Affairs: An Uneasy Relationship. In: L. Dennis (ed.) *Practical Public Affairs in an Era of Change.* University Press of America, New York. 423–434.

Hill Basics: Congressional Staff Roles. URL: http://www.legislators.com/physicians/staff.html [10-13-01].

Koch, William and McGee, Patrick (1996) Public Affairs and Risk Communications. In: L. Dennis (ed.) *Practical Public Affairs in an Era of Change.* University Press of America, New York. 157–168.

Kraus, Margery (1996) Government Relations in the 90s and Beyond. In: L. Dennis (ed.) *Practical Public Affairs in an Era of Change.* University Press of America, New York. 89–100.

Laskowski, Lenny (1996) *Overcoming Speaking Anxiety in Meetings and Presentations,* URL: http://www.ljlseminars.com/anxiety.htm [10-14-01].

Laskowski, Lenny (1998) *Four Common Ways to Remember Material,* URL: http://www.ljlseminars.com/remember.htm [10-14-01].

Library of Congress. URL: http://thomas.loc.gov

Lineberry, Robert *et al.* (1995) *Government in America: People, Politics, and Policy,* Brief Version (second edition). HarperCollins, New York.

Mack, Charles (1996) Lobbying and Political Action. In: L. Dennis (ed.) *Practical Public Affairs in an Era of Change.* University Press of America, New York. 101–113.

Madison, James (1995) The Federalist No. 10. In: Cigler, Allan J. and Loomis, Burdett A. (eds) *American Politics.* Houghton Mifflin Co., Boston, MA.

Meier, Kenneth J. (1992) *Politics and the Bureaucracy* (third edition). Wadsworth Publishing, Belmont, CA.

Nelson, Richard (1996) Activist Groups and New Technologies: Influencing the Public Affairs Agenda. In: L. Dennis (ed.) *Practical Public Affairs in an Era of Change.* University Press of America, New York. 413–422.

Neuman, Robert and Arnold, Kenneth (1996) Interfacing with Peers, Trade Associations and Professional Societies. In: L. Dennis (ed.) *Practical Public Affairs in an Era of Change.* University Press of America, New York. 291–303.

O'Neil, Kathleen (1996) Research Designed for Public Release: A Powerful Tool for Public Affairs and Public Relations. In: L. Dennis (ed.) *Practical Public Affairs in an Era of Change.* University Press of America, New York. 63–73.

Politics 101, URL: http://www.tcul.org/legislative_toolbox.htm [10-13-01].

Pullen, Dale. (1999) *US Congress Handbook.* Barbara Pullen, McLean, VA.

Rice, Jean (1998) *Tips on Talking to the Media.* URL: http://www.dealconsulting.com/salesmktg/tips.html [10-13-01].

Rozakis, Laurie (1999) *The Complete Idiot's Guide to Public Speaking* (second edition).
Alpha Books, New York.

Shiller, Ed (2000) *Media Tips.* URL:
http://www.home.the-wire.com/shiller/tip-earlier.html [10-13-01].

Society of Professional Journalists. *Code of Ethics.* URL:
http://www.spj.org/ethics_code.asp [3-7-02].

State Government Affairs Council. *Guidelines for Professional Conduct.* URL:
http://www.sgac.org/page02.htm [3-7-02].

Ten Tips for Successful Public Speaking. URL:
http://www.toastmasters.org/tips.htm [10-14-01].

Tips for When the Media Calls. URL:
http://www.capcollege.bc.ca/admin/Formedia/tips/ [10-14-01].

Virtual Presentation Assistant project. *Using Visual Aids.* URL:
http://www.ukans.edu/cwis/units/coms2/vpa/vpa7.htm [10-14-01].

Websters New World Secretarial Handbook (1989) (fourth edition).Prentice Hall, New York.

Wilson Group Communication (2000) *Five Tips for a Successful News Media Interview.* URL:
http://www.wilson-group.com/articles/fiveTips.html [10-13-01].

Working with the News Media. URL:
http://www.umr.edu/~newsinfo/campus/working.html [10-13-01].

CHAPTER 9

SAFETY IN THE FORENSIC LABORATORY

Michael W. St Clair

INTRODUCTION

This chapter discusses various elements of environmental health and safety issues in the forensic laboratory. It is not meant to be an in-depth discussion of every issue related to environmental health and safety in the forensic laboratory. Instead, it is designed to provide awareness of the issues that may arise in the laboratory and as an overview of the ways to make the forensic laboratory a safer place for employees and visitors. The elements covered in this chapter include the safety culture in the laboratory, common physical hazards, common chemical hazards, chemical management, spill control, biological hazards, facility safety equipment, and personal protective equipment.

SAFETY CULTURE

Because the water is still, you must not think there is no crocodile there.

(Old Malaysian proverb)

The above proverb is indicative of the approach one should take towards safety in the forensic laboratory. Do not be fooled by the fact that everything seems to be going smoothly and no accidents have happened in your forensic laboratory. Lack of safety vigilance can contribute to an accident in the laboratory at any time. Safety should be part of the culture within your forensic laboratory. The goal should be to prevent incidents that threaten health or the environment. It is imperative that the culture in the forensic laboratory be one where safety is that which is done each day. It is important that each person in the forensic laboratory understands and practices safety on a daily basis. One person in a forensic laboratory who does not practice safety puts every other employee and visitor to the laboratory at risk for injury.

This culture is not an easy level to achieve. It is a process that typically takes many years to accomplish. A culture change does not have a beginning and an end. A culture change is a lasting change that is embraced by the entire organization. It is a change that perpetuates itself no matter the number of times the laboratory staff changes. Through continuous hard work, the change can happen in any laboratory situation.

Management support is key in conveying to the employees that safety is a number one priority within the organization. Safety in the forensic laboratory is dependent upon the teamwork of the individuals and management within the laboratory not only for an individual's safety, but also the safety of everyone's neighbor. As with any process of change, it is important to establish a vision of what is desired and to communicate this vision throughout the organization. A strategy should be developed with input from all employees within the organization to assess the strength and weaknesses of the current culture and to develop a strategy to implement the desired changes identified in the vision. Management bears a large responsibility for safety in the forensic laboratory including the clear communication of safety responsibilities for all laboratory and holding personnel accountable for meeting these responsibilities. As with any continual process of improvement, an analysis of the progress and changes to the implementation should be made on a periodic basis, keeping the end result in mind. Throughout this process the employees must be empowered to manage their own safety processes with every employee as an equal partner. When the culture change is accomplished, management will have more time to concentrate their energies on other management requirements. When this change becomes part of the culture, personnel within the laboratory will be thinking of working safely as part of their everyday regimen.

As noted earlier, the laboratory director should clearly communicate and hold personnel responsible for their actions as they relate to safety and environmental issues. In addition, the laboratory director should supervise the preparation of procedures for dealing with accidents, provide input into appropriate control practices to be used for safe work, and provide oversight for the preparation of a safety plan for the laboratory.

The health and safety officer for the laboratory should be an integral part of any safety program. This person should assist the laboratory director in surveying the laboratory to help determine hazardous operations that exist. In addition, the health and safety officer should make sure all employees have a copy of the safety plan and rules, and review the standard operating procedures for laboratory activities that require the use of hazardous materials. This person should ensure all employees are trained on the safety procedures and safe work practices and help the laboratory director to monitor safety performance of the staff. The health and safety officer should conduct formal laboratory inspections for safety and environmental compliance and aid the laboratory director in arranging for workplace monitoring when required. Finally, the health and safety officer should document compliance activities and help to develop rules and procedures for safe work practices.

Employees should be required to understand and act in accordance with the safety requirements established for the laboratory and wear the personal protective equipment necessary to perform the tasks in the laboratory in a safe manner. Finally, employees should be required to report any incidents and all facts pertaining to any incident to the laboratory director and the health and safety officer.

The ultimate responsibility for ensuring a safe work environment rests with the employees. The employees must maintain an active role in keeping the work place safe. When all the different roles and responsibilities come together, the safety goals of the laboratory are usually successful in protecting the personnel in the laboratory.

PHYSICAL HAZARDS

There are many physical hazards in the forensic laboratory environment. The first priority in any safety program is to identify the hazards present in the forensic laboratory. Once the hazards have been identified, the risk posed by each hazard should be evaluated in order to identify the necessary steps to be taken to minimize or reduce the risk. One must remember that a hazard analysis should not just focus on the most severe hazards in the forensic laboratory. The hazard analysis must take into account all degrees of risk, including minor risks, since they comprise the majority of accidents in the forensic laboratory. To be discussed in this section are some of the most commonly found physical hazards in any forensic laboratory.

SLIPS, TRIPS AND FALLS

Slips, trips and falls are consistently one of the highest rated causes of injuries and death each year in the workplace. Typical causes of slips, trips and falls in the forensic laboratory include: water; cleaning chemicals and spills on the floor; improper footwear; objects in the pathway; objects projecting into the pathway; poor lighting; and uneven surfaces.

In order to prevent these causes it is recommended that some simple rules be followed. These rules include the need to keep walkways clear and to promptly clean up all spills. Personnel in the laboratory should be notified of any foreign substance on the floor. A good practice is to use signage to warn of wet floors or other potential causes of slips and falls. In addition, the installation of non-skid surfaces is helpful in preventing slips and falls. Finally, sufficient lighting in the laboratory along with the repair of any uneven flooring will also provide help in preventing slips, trips and falls.

ELECTRICAL HAZARDS

Electricity is accepted as a source of power without much thought to the hazards encountered. It is important that electrical equipment be free from recognized hazards that are likely to cause death or serious physical harm to employees.

The safety of electrical equipment that may be used in the laboratory should be determined using many considerations. These considerations include the suitability of the equipment for the use intended, including any listings or other approvals that indicate the suitability of the electrical equipment for its intended use. In addition, other considerations include the mechanical strength and durability of the parts designed to enclose and protect the equipment, the electrical insulation provided with the equipment, any heating effects under conditions of use and any arcing effects that may be experienced during use. Finally, the classification by type, size, voltage and current capacity are other considerations that should be used to determine the suitability and safety of electrical equipment that may be used in the laboratory.

Only grounded outlets should be used. Adapters for ungrounded plugs should not be used since most people do not connect the neutral line on the adapter to a real ground. In addition, some type of ground fault circuit interrupter should be used when near a water source. A ground fault circuit interrupter detects leakage of electricity and stops the flow before electrocution can occur. Standard outlets should not be located inside fume hoods or in an area where a flammable atmosphere might occur. If outlets are necessary in an area where a flammable atmosphere is possible, an explosion-proof outlet should be installed and used with only explosion-resistant or explosion-proof equipment.

It is always advisable to unplug equipment before making modifications or repairs to the equipment. Frayed or damaged cords or wiring should be replaced as soon as it is recognized and only a qualified person should complete any repairs to electrical equipment.

Contact with energized circuits should be avoided when working in the forensic laboratory. If a person comes in contact with energized circuits, the energized circuit must be disconnected or turned off before removing the injured person from the hazardous area.

A refrigerator or freezer used for storing flammable chemicals should be rated for the storage of such flammable materials. Likewise, stirring and mixing equipment used in all types of forensic laboratory work should be used in such a way as to prevent sparks from occurring, especially when used near flammable chemicals. Spark-free motors should be used in these devices when working near an area where fire may occur due to sparks from the motor.

Eliminating the use of extension cords in the forensic laboratory is one way to reduce not only the electrical hazard, but also eliminate slips, trips and falls due to extension cords that impede a clear walkway. In addition, extension cords are for temporary use only and should never be used as a permanent fixture in a forensic laboratory. When using any type of cord, make sure it is protected from damage. The cord should be inspected on a regular basis to make sure there are no cuts, breaks or cracks in the cord. If any damage is found, the cord should be replaced immediately. Electrical safety in the forensic laboratory consists of many easy to follow, commonsense rules that when followed will help to make the laboratory a safer place.

COMPRESSED GASES AND COMPRESSED GAS CYLINDERS

A compressed gas is a material or mixture, which is a gas at 20°C or less at an absolute pressure of 101.325 kPa and has a boiling point of 20°C or less at a pressure of 101.325 kPa. Compressed gases can be categorized as non-liquefied, liquefied, compressed gases in solution and compressed gas mixtures. These materials are under tremendous pressures and represent a major risk in the laboratory when handled in an improper manner. Training should be provided for persons working in areas of the forensic laboratory where compressed gases are stored, used or otherwise handled. The training should include information on the physical and chemical properties of the materials as well as the appropriate response for personnel should an emergency related to the compressed gases arise.

Working with compressed gases involves handling materials that are under tremendous pressures. A safety feature that every user should be familiar with on some compressed gas cylinders are pressure relief devices. Pressure relief devices may be built in to some compressed gas cylinders to facilitate venting of the cylinder should excess pressure build up in the container. Typical pressure-relief devices include spring-loaded safety valves, frangible discs and fusible plugs.

Care should be taken not to expose personnel to the high pressures associated with compressed gas cylinders by venting or opening compressed gas cylinders without the proper equipment attached. This equipment includes regulators, tubing, connectors and the reaction vessel. Regulators are designed to reduce the high pressure and flow found in the compressed gas cylinder to an acceptable pressure and flow for the forensic laboratory experiment or process. Regulators are connected to the outlet on the compressed gas cylinder and typically will indicate two pressures, the tank pressure and the delivery pressure. The screw on the front of the regulator typically controls the delivery pressure. The flow control valve on the outlet of the regulator helps to control the flow to the forensic laboratory analysis or process. Every regulator is designed for a specific gas and is not to be used on a compressed gas cylinder for which it was not designed. Check the regulator for any evidence of damage or foreign objects in the threads before use. Special care should be taken to make sure no oil or grease is used on any regulator attached to oxidizing gases such as oxygen. A fire or explosion may result from the contact of oil or grease with high-pressure oxidizers. The delivery pressure control should be set to allow no pressure or flow into the regulator before turning the compressed gas cylinder on. After turning the compressed gas cylinder on, the pressure may be raised slowly to the desired pressure for the analysis or process. Many different materials are available to help check for leaks in a system using compressed gases. These materials used should be compatible with the gas that is being used in the system.

Regulators for corrosive gases such as hydrogen chloride or chlorine are different from most other regulators and are made from corrosion-resistant materials. These regulators do not typically contain pressure gauges due to the corrosive nature of the gases. A corrosive gas regulator should be removed between uses to prevent excessive corrosion to the regulator and should be discarded if the regulator becomes corroded in a manner that might compromise the safety of the regulator.

Compressed gas cylinders should be separated by the type and hazard class of the gas. They should be stored in a dry, well-ventilated and lighted area. Hazard classes should be separated to prevent unwanted outcomes such as fire or explosion should a compressed gas cylinder leak during storage. For example, oxidizing gases should be separated from flammable gases since the combination of the two may have unintended consequences. Compressed gas cylinders should be kept out of direct sunlight, excessive heat and away from open flames. All compressed gas cylinders should be clearly labeled. Do not try to identify a compressed gas cylinder by color since the color of compressed gas cylinders change with time and supplier. If a compressed gas cylinder is received that is not clearly labeled, return it immediately to the manufacturer.

Each compressed gas cylinder typically comes with a valve protection cap in place. Valve protection caps should be kept in place when the compressed gas cylinders are in storage. The valve protection cap should only be removed when the compressed gas cylinder is in use and should be replaced when it is no longer in use. The cap protects the valve from being sheared off in an accident and turning the compressed gas cylinder into a missile.

It is advisable to keep storage of compressed gas cylinders in the forensic laboratory to a minimum. Only compressed gas cylinders in use and connected to the equipment or process should be in the forensic laboratory at any time. The rest of the compressed gas cylinder stock should be stored in an appropriate remote location.

Empty compressed gas cylinders should be marked and removed from the forensic laboratory at the time they are deemed empty. Do not forget that even "empty" compressed gas cylinders contain pressure and may be hazardous. It is important to replace the compressed gas cylinder valve cap before the cylinder is removed from the area. A compressed gas cylinder cart or other appropriate device for moving cylinders should be used. It is not advisable to roll or drag cylinders by hand when transporting them from one place to another.

All compressed gas cylinders, whether in use or in storage, should be secured from tipping over by restraints intended for this use. The compressed gas cylinder should be kept clear of electrical equipment and live circuits. Any system using compressed gases should be checked for leaks, and any necessary adjustments or repairs should be made at once in order to stop a leak in the system. Only the manufacturer or other trained personnel should repair a compressed gas cylinder, valve or regulator.

At a minimum, eye protection should be worn when working around compressed gas cylinders. Additional personal protective equipment and engineering controls may be necessary depending on the chemical characteristics of the gas being used. Due to the nature of compressed gas cylinders and their potential for great harm when mishandled, every precaution possible should be taken to prevent a mishap and injury when using, handling or storing them.

HYDROGEN

Hydrogen is a common gas used in forensic laboratory instrumentation. Hydrogen is a gas that burns in air with an almost invisible flame. The flame is typically a pale blue. This gas has a very wide flammability range in air of 4 percent to 75 percent. Hydrogen is non-corrosive and can be stored at room temperature.

The same general safety rules apply to hydrogen as with other gases, but some additional care should be taken with this gas in particular. When opening a hydrogen cylinder, it is not advisable to crack the cylinder valve before installing the regulator. This is due to the fact that hydrogen may self-ignite under these circumstances. Instead, the regulator should be put in place first with the regulator valve closed and the pressure-adjusting screw turned out. The cylinder should then be opened slowly with the outlet pointed away from the person opening the valve as well as others in the laboratory. The cylinder valve should be opened fully and then the regulator pressure and valves can be adjusted slowly.

Hydrogen should be stored according to the local fire and health and safety regulations. Should a cylinder of hydrogen start to leak even when the valve is closed, the cylinder should carefully be moved to an outside area away from any ignition sources and the cylinder supplier should be contacted for further instructions. In addition, the cylinder should be clearly marked with a sign indicating there is an uncontrollable leak. When moving the cylinder to an outside area one must take great care in avoiding any ignition sources since any flame would be almost invisible.

If storing hydrogen cylinders in a remote location, the cylinders should be inspected on a periodic basis to make sure none of the cylinders are leaking or are damaged. If damaged or leaking cylinder(s) are discovered, the cylinder(s) should be returned to the supplier as soon as possible. Finally, as with all cylinders, never attempt to repair or work on a cylinder. This responsibility should be left to the professionals who are trained to handle cylinders and their special hazards.

CRYOGENIC LIQUIDS

Cryogenic liquids are substances with boiling points less than $-90°C$ at an absolute pressure of 101.325 kPa. Cryogenic liquids can include liquid nitrogen, liquid oxygen, liquid helium and liquid argon. These liquids are typically stored in low pressure, multi-walled containers with vacuum-insulated walls in order to keep them in liquid form.

Since cryogenic liquids are at extremely low temperatures, care should be taken to handle them safely because they may freeze human skin on contact. In addition, the extremely cold temperatures may cause materials such as plastic and rubber to become brittle. Gloves, eyewear and other personal protective equipment may be necessary to prevent contact with the skin during handling. These liquids will also expand quickly as they turn to gas at room temperature. This situation can be hazardous if these liquids are in a sealed container with no means of pressure relief. In addition, cryogenic liquids can displace oxygen from a room if a significant amount of liquid is spilled in a small area. Therefore, these liquids should be handled in appropriate containers in well-ventilated areas.

Additional care should be taken when handling cryogenic liquids that are also oxidizing (i.e. liquid oxygen). When in contact with grease, oil or other hydrocarbons, fire or explosion may result under optimum conditions. Cryogenic liquids may be handled safely in the laboratory provided appropriate safety precautions are in place and are followed.

CHEMICAL HAZARDS

STORAGE/INCOMPATIBILITIES

There are many types of chemicals found throughout laboratories. The classes of chemicals discussed in this section are limited to classes that may be typically found in forensic laboratories. Additional information on incompatibilities can be found in the references at the end of this chapter. Table 9.1 lists many of the classes of chemicals that may be found in forensic laboratories along with their incompatibilities.

Class of chemicals	Incompatible classes
Acid Anhydrides	Alcohols, Aldehydes, Amines, Caustics, Ethers, Inorganic Acids, Oxidizers
Alcohols	Acid Anhydrides, Aldehydes, Halogens, Inorganic Acids, Oxidizers
Aldehydes	Acid Anhydrides, Alcohols, Amines, Caustics, Halogens, Inorganic Acids, Ketones, Organic Acids, Oxidizers
Amines	Acid Anhydrides, Aldehydes, Esters, Inorganic Acids, Ketones, Organic Acids, Oxidizers
Aromatic Hydrocarbons	Halogens, Inorganic Acids, Oxidizers
Caustics	Acid Anhydrides, Aldehydes, Esters, Halogens, Inorganic Acids, Ketones, Organic Acids, Oxidizers
Esters	Amines, Caustics, Halogens, Inorganic Acids, Oxidizers
Ethers	Acid Anhydrides, Inorganic Acids, Oxidizers
Halogens	Alcohols, Aldehydes, Aromatic Hydrocarbons, Esters, Inorganic Acids, Ketones, Olefins, Oxidizers
Inorganic Acids	Acid Anhydrides, Alcohols, Aldehydes, Amines, Aromatic Hydrocarbons, Caustics, Esters, Ethers, Ketones, Olefins, Organic Acids, Oxidizers
Ketones	Aldehydes, Amines, Caustics, Halogens, Inorganic Acids, Oxidizers
Olefins	Halogens, Inorganic Acids, Oxidizers
Organic Acids	Aldehydes, Amines, Caustics, Inorganic Acids, Oxidizers
Oxidizers	Acid Anhydrides, Alcohols, Aldehydes, Amines, Aromatic Hydrocarbons, Caustics, Esters, Ethers, Halogens, Inorganic Acids, Ketones, Olefins, Organic Acids

Table 9.1

Classes and incompatibilities of commonly used chemicals.

The storage of chemicals should be by the hazard class of the chemical. The hazard class of a chemical may be determined by different means including knowing the properties of the chemical being used, reading the label, looking in reference books or reading the safety information provided by the manufacturer. Although many situations occur where chemicals are stored in alphabetical order, there is the possibility of many unwanted severe reactions taking place when chemicals are stored this way. Table 9.2 shows the possible outcome of storing chemicals by alphabetical order rather than by class of chemical.

Table 9.2

Possible reactions between chemicals stored in alphabetical order.

Storage	Incompatible reactions
Acetic Acid, Acetaldehyde	Small amounts of acetic acid will cause the acetaldehyde to polymerize releasing heat
Acetic Anhydride, Acetaldehyde	Can lead to an explosion
Aluminum, Ammonium nitrate	Potential for explosion
Aluminum, Bromine	Aluminum foil reacts with bromine vapor at room temperature and incandesces
Ammonia vapor, Bromine vapor	Forms an unstable compound, nitrogen tribromide, and explosion may result
Ammonium nitrate, Acetic Acid	Mixture may result in ignition
Barium, Carbon tetrachloride	Violent reaction
Calcium hypochlorite, charcoal	Mixture can result in explosion
Carbon, Any bromate or chlorate or iodate	Potential explosive detonated by heat, percussion or friction
Cupric sulfide, Cadmium chlorate	Explosion on contact
Hydrogen peroxide, Ferrous sulfide	Vigorous, highly exothermic reaction
Lead perchlorate, Methanol	Explosive mixture if agitated
Mercury (II) nitrate, Methanol	Forms explosive mercury fulminate
Nitric acid, Magnesium	Reacts with explosive force
Silver metal, Tartaric acid	Explosive mixture
Silver oxide, Sulfur	Potentially explosive mixture
Sodium nitrate, Sodium thiosulfate	Mixture of dry material can result in explosion

It is important that chemicals in the laboratory are stored correctly in order to prevent adverse reactions. Proper storage will aid in providing a safe work environment for all persons involved in the use of chemicals in the laboratory.

CARCINOGENS

Carcinogens are materials that are capable of causing cancer. Examples include such materials as acrylamide, arsenic compounds, benzene, chromium compounds, formaldehyde and vinyl chloride. Personal protective equipment should be worn at all times when handling these materials and should be properly disposed of as soon as the work is completed. Areas in the laboratory where carcinogens are used should be designated in some way so all personnel are aware of the potential hazards that exist in the area. In order to avoid these issues, it is advisable to substitute a non-carcinogenic material when possible in any laboratory work.

REPRODUCTIVE TOXINS

Reproductive toxins have adverse effects on reproduction. These effects may include death to a fertilized egg, embryo or fetus, malformations and other deficiencies. Since there is little protection to the fetus during pregnancy from these toxins, it is recommended that pregnant women avoid working with these materials. In addition, men may experience side-effects including sterility from exposure to certain reproductive toxins. Reproductive toxins may include materials such as arsenic compounds, cadmium compounds, formamide, lead compounds, mercury compounds, toluene, vinyl chloride and xylene. Care should be taken by anyone handling these materials to avoid all exposures to this type of toxin. Personal protective equipment and engineering controls including but not limited to the use of gloves, eyewear and local exhaust ventilation should be used to limit exposure to these materials.

FLAMMABLE LIQUIDS

Flammable liquids are those that catch fire easily and are typically defined by their flashpoints. Generally, flammable liquids are those that have a flash point less than or equal to 38°C. The flash point is the lowest temperature at which a liquid has sufficient vapor to form an ignitable mixture with air near the surface of the liquid.

In addition, every flammable liquid also has flammability limits. These are the upper and lower percentage limits at which the material will burn in air. If there is excessive flammable vapor in the air mixture, the mixture is too rich and will not support combustion. Conversely, if the mixture has too little flammable vapor, it is too lean and will not support combustion either. Typical flammable liquids used in the laboratory include acetone, diethyl ether, ethyl alcohol, isopropyl alcohol, methyl alcohol, methyl ethyl ketone, toluene, and xylene.

When working with flammable liquids, keep in mind that in order to support combustion, four items must be present. The items are fuel, oxygen, a source of ignition and a chemical chain reaction. This is typically referred to as the fire tetrahedron. If any one of these is eliminated, combustion cannot be supported. When working with flammable liquids, the easiest item to control is the source of ignition. Ignition sources should be kept out of the immediate area during flammable liquids use. Ignition sources in the forensic laboratory may include Bunsen burners, electrically powered equipment such as hot plates and, in some cases, static electricity.

In addition to the control of ignition sources, it is important to control flammable vapors. Flammable vapors should be kept under control through the use of engineering controls such as fume hoods and keeping the bottle of flammable liquid closed when not in use. These controls will aid in the control of the vapor and thus control the fuel portion of the fire tetrahedron, reducing the risk of fire. Also keep in mind that most flammable vapors are heavier than air and can travel long distances along the ground, floor, or tabletop with air currents to create a flammable atmosphere near an ignition source.

Flammable liquids should be stored in cabinets that are specially constructed for this use. Typical flammable storage cabinets are designed to protect the contents against involvement in a fire for up to one hour if the integrity of the cabinet is maintained. Flammable liquids should be stored with compatible materials only. Compatible materials usually consist of other flammable or combustible liquids. It is important to check the material that is being stored in a cabinet or area against the rest of the materials in the storage cabinet or area in order to make sure all materials are compatible with each other. Storage of flammable liquids with oxidizers, acids, bases and reducers should be avoided. These materials are incompatible and may cause a fire if mixed. Flammable liquids should be stored in a cool, dry place and should not be placed in refrigerators that are not designed for flammable liquids storage.

CORROSIVE CHEMICALS

Corrosive chemicals in the laboratory are substances that cause destruction to tissue at the site of contact. Corrosive chemicals are among the most widely found chemicals in the typical laboratory. They are used in many disciplines including drug chemistry, firearms analysis and trace analysis. Corrosive chemicals have several hazards associated with them beyond the destruction of tissue. These hazards include reactivity, toxicity and instability. Commonly used corrosives in forensic laboratories include acetic acid, hydrochloric acid, nitric acid, sulfuric acid, ammonium hydroxide, sodium hydroxide and potassium hydroxide.

Many corrosive chemicals are very reactive and can cause adverse consequences if not handled properly. Corrosive chemicals are incompatible with many other chemicals found in the typical laboratory including flammable liquids and should be kept segregated during storage and use. In addition, when strong corrosives come in contact with metal or metal shavings the reaction usually liberates hydrogen. This reaction can be a fire hazard if large amounts of hydrogen are generated but is usually not of concern when small amounts of corrosives are used in the restoration of serial numbers from metal objects.

Corrosive chemicals may react with each other. For example, acids and bases may react with each other to generate great amounts of heat, creating the potential for a fire. Some acids such as acetic acid and perchloric acid may react with each other causing violent reactions. Acids such as perchloric and nitric acids are strong oxidizers and have an added degree of incompatibility. Oxidizing acids should be stored away from materials that are incompatible with acids and oxidizers. Additional general information on chemical incompatibility was covered earlier in this section.

The proper handling of corrosive materials is very important. They should be transported in a bottle carrier, stored below eye level, and stored in a corrosion-resistant cabinet separate from incompatible chemicals. When using corrosive materials, acid should be added to water and plastic bottles should be used as a container when possible. Other important handling rules include the need to keep ignition sources away from many corrosive chemicals, the use of secondary containment when possible, a requirement to use appropriate personal protective equipment and a need for an eyewash/safety shower nearby. When handled appropriately, corrosive chemicals pose a reduced risk to employees and laboratory visitors.

REACTIVE CHEMICALS

Reactive chemicals are a class of chemicals that produce unwanted reactions when exposed to light, moisture, shock, friction, air or time. The typical categories of reactive chemicals found in forensic laboratories include peroxide formers, oxidizers and water reactive chemicals. Peroxide formers are chemicals that naturally decompose to form peroxides on exposure to air, water or other impurities. The typical chemicals found in forensic laboratories that form peroxides include diethyl ether and tetrahydrofuran. Peroxide formation occurs typically without a visible reaction. These compounds become shock-sensitive at very low concentrations, with some compounds being shock-sensitive at part per million levels. Peroxide formation will occur more quickly and become more concentrated upon evaporation or distillation of the chemical.

All containers of chemicals that may form peroxides should be dated upon opening the container. Regular inspection and testing of these chemicals may be required in order to determine the peroxide content. Commercial test strips as well as several chemical testing procedures that use chemicals such as potassium iodide may be employed to check the peroxide content of the container.

Since peroxides may be friction sensitive, it is not advisable to open a container suspected to contain peroxides. The container should only be opened or handled by personnel trained to open and handle these containers. Storage of peroxide-forming chemicals should be in accordance with manufacturer's recommendations and typically include storage away from heat, sunlight and sources of ignition. Recommendations also include storing these chemicals in a tightly closed container. Table 9.3 contains examples of storage periods for different peroxide-forming chemicals.

Table 9.3

Safe storage periods of common chemicals.

Common chemicals used in laboratories	Length of storage
Diethyl ether	12 months
Dioxane	12 months
Isopropyl ether	3 months
Potassium metal	3 months
t-Butyl alcohol	12 months
Tetrahydrofuran	12 months

Oxidizers are typically prevalent in chemical laboratories. These chemicals are typically stable when handled and stored properly, but may react violently when they come in contact with incompatible materials. Oxidizers also provide their own source of oxygen to any potential fire situation. Oxidizers may spontaneously ignite when they come in contact with combustible materials. These reactions generally produce large amounts of heat that may be enough to ignite items such as paper, wood and other combustible materials.

As discussed in the section on chemical incompatibility, oxidizers are incompatible with acid anhydrides, alcohols, aldehydes, amines, aromatic hydrocarbons, caustics, esters, ethers, halogens, inorganic acids, ketones, olefins and organic acids. Thus, oxidizers should be stored away from these types of chemicals. Secondary containment is a recommended practice when storing oxidizers. Storage of oxidizers should be according to the manufacturer's recommendations and health and safety regulations that apply to the laboratory. Typically, oxidizers as well as other reactive chemicals should be stored in a cool, dry location and should be protected from incompatible situations.

Water reactive chemicals may form explosive mixtures when in contact with water, may violently react with water, may form toxic gases on contact with water or may form flammable vapors on contact with water. Examples of water reactive chemicals include sodium, potassium, hydrides and carbides. These materials should be handled and stored with great care. This class of chemicals should be stored in watertight containers and segregated from incompatible situations including storage away from any water supplies. Fires involving water reactive chemicals will typically require a special class of fire extinguisher, Class D, in order to extinguish a fire involving this class of chemical. If storing or handling water reactive chemicals, preparation for an adverse event is critical in order to control these materials. All reactive chemicals can be handled safely in the laboratory provided proper precautions are taken before and during their use.

CHEMICAL MANAGEMENT

POLLUTION PREVENTION

Pollution prevention consists of practices that reduce or eliminate the creation of pollutants. This may be accomplished through the efficient use and conservation of resources. A successful pollution prevention program will help a forensic laboratory to achieve regulatory compliance, economic benefits and health and safety improvements.

A good pollution prevention program will aid in regulatory compliance by helping to eliminate permitting burdens. This program will also ease record-keeping requirements and decrease your legal liability as it relates to the handling and disposal of chemicals from the forensic laboratory.

A successful program provides economic benefits to a forensic laboratory by reducing the costs associated with the disposal of waste chemicals and materials. Additional savings may be found in the costs for reduced amounts of new chemicals purchased and increased efficiency in forensic laboratory processes. The increase in forensic laboratory efficiency will also aid in the possible reduction of storage space requirements, material handling requirements and maintenance requirements.

A good pollution prevention program will also aid in the improvement of health and safety in the forensic laboratory by reducing the amount of hazardous materials in the laboratory. This reduction will decrease the potential for exposures to employees and make the workplace more desirable for future employees.

Finally, a pollution prevention program may be required or preferred by the customers of the forensic laboratory. Many organizations are moving toward certifications through the International Organization for Standardization and other accrediting bodies throughout the world that may require pollution prevention programs. In addition, pollution prevention programs may be required by local government regulations. Laboratories should check local regulations in order to verify laboratory compliance.

The two most widely recognized methods of pollution prevention are source reduction and recycling. Since source reduction is the most desirable of the means to achieving pollution prevention, it is the method that will receive the greatest focus here.

SOURCE REDUCTION

Source reduction is an activity that reduces or eliminates the generation of wastes at their source. The typical means of source reduction include product substitution, product conservation, process change, and management practices. Product substitution is the practice of substituting a non-hazardous or less hazardous product in place of one that is considered to be hazardous and is currently in use in the forensic laboratory. Product substitution is an ideal way to reduce the use of hazardous materials in the laboratory and should be investigated and implemented whenever possible. Product conservation is the use of lesser amounts of a hazardous product in a process while achieving the same experimental results. An example may include the use of micro-scale processes during the analysis of materials. Process changes include any changes in the analysis process that may lead to less use or no use of hazardous materials. Examples include automation of equipment for analysis, changes in equipment to generate or use less of a hazardous substance.

Management practices are usually simple operating changes that can be implemented in order to control the use and generation of hazardous substances in the forensic laboratory. These may include inventory management, material exchanges, purchasing control, waste segregation, improved scheduling and housekeeping practices. An inventory of chemicals in the laboratory should be kept up to date at all times. This will allow anyone requiring additional chemicals to check the inventory to make sure that the material is not currently available in the laboratory. If the material is not available and if a small amount is needed, it might be feasible to get the material from a material exchange with another forensic laboratory in the area. When the purchase of new material is the only option, purchase only the smallest amount necessary for the analysis or the smallest amount that will be used in a short period of time. This will help to eliminate the need to dispose of material that will never be used or material that is out of date.

When waste materials are generated in the forensic laboratory, make sure that hazardous substances are segregated from non-hazardous substances. This will eliminate the requirement to treat any mixture of the two as a hazardous material.

Improved scheduling may also help to reduce the amount of hazardous wastes produced in the forensic laboratory by eliminating the need to make up several different batches of reagent to run several analyses when a group of analyses can be done at one time using a single batch of reagent.

Good housekeeping results in less spillage of materials, less contamination in the laboratory, and less hazardous material exposure to employees. Less spillage of materials leads to less waste generated and thus an economic benefit for the laboratory. This in turn leads to less contamination in the laboratory which results in less hazardous exposure to laboratory personnel. All of these factors lead to a cleaner and more efficient laboratory that personnel are more apt to want to work in, making for more satisfied employees.

DEVELOPING A POLLUTION PREVENTION PROGRAM

The first step in developing and implementing a pollution prevention program is to obtain management support. Management support is essential to the success of any program and should be expressed through a policy statement by the management. When management needs help to understand the importance of such a program, concentrate on the economic benefits, regulatory benefits and liability reduction found in all pollution prevention programs.

Management should not express its support for such a program by only supporting a policy statement. Management should show other visible support means such as encouraging workers to initiate pollution prevention activities in the laboratory, focusing on continual improvement in source reduction by measurable means, choosing vendors based on pollution prevention commitments when possible, and being a model forensic laboratory in pollution prevention. Additional ways to support these programs is by assisting other laboratories in the development of pollution prevention programs, by promoting pollution prevention to other forensic laboratories and by involving the public when practical in the pollution prevention program in the laboratory.

In addition to management, employees must buy in to the pollution prevention program. Employees may have many concerns when the program is first proposed. The employee concerns may range from "We have always done it this way," to worries about customer acceptance to the new process that has been proposed, to worries that not enough time is available to implement these changes. As with all change, employee concerns are to be respected and solutions found in order to get employees to buy in to the program. Without the employees' support, a pollution prevention program will not be successful.

After management commitment and employee buy-in is accomplished, the next step is to identify the waste sources in the laboratory and to set priorities to see if each source of waste can be reduced or eliminated. A pollution prevention team should be formed at this point in order to get the maximum value from the program and to keep the momentum of the program going. The team should consist of management, employee and fiscal representatives. The team should document the current processes in the laboratory that create hazardous wastes. Additionally, the cost of each operation should be identified including not only the monetary costs but also the cost of manpower and other organizational resources that may be necessary in dealing with hazardous wastes. Determining the costs associated with the handling and disposal of hazardous waste should include not only the direct cost for disposal, but should also include the cost for storing the waste on-site, the costs associated with materials such as drums, containers, labels and other materials needed to safely store the waste, cost of transportation to the disposal site, cost of training workers to properly handle wastes, cost of record-keeping, cost of medical surveillance for workers, if required, and any liability or exposure to the regulations. The use of current documentation that is available in the laboratory will help in this process. There is no need to reinvent the wheel. The available documentation may consist of such items as standard operating procedures, purchasing records, timekeeping records, regulatory inspection documents, and documented methods.

From the information gathered, the next step is to analyze the processes for potential improvements in the area of source reduction. The most costly waste stream should be examined first to see if there are savings that can be obtained by changing the process or improving the process to generate less waste. Some of the most frequently identified areas for saving are inventory management, housekeeping, spill prevention, purchasing control, product substitution, equipment modification and process modification.

Once the processes have been analyzed, setting priorities for successful pollution prevention is the next step. Begin by choosing the items that take minimal effort and have the highest potential for quick success and savings. This will help to build credibility for the pollution prevention program. One way to help determine what option for pollution prevention gets the highest priority is to develop a matrix with weighted rating criteria. This will help to take all of the factors that are important into account and compare the options on an equal basis. During this process some of the factors that may need to be taken into account include whether the change is technically feasible, does it reduce overall costs, is the process economically feasible, does it reduce hazards in the laboratory, how easy is it to implement, does the change require additional funding and does the change improve productivity.

When the priorities have been set, the next step is implementation of the first identified priority. This step may require the justification of the change in order to secure additional funding. The documentation obtained during the steps to this point should help the justification for additional funding. This may be a long process and should be taken on by someone who will continue to support the priority selected.

Now it is time to start the implementation of the first priority. As mentioned before, it is important to start with a couple of priorities that will be successful since it is much easier to implement more difficult priorities on previous successes. Document and publicize the successes whenever possible. Celebrate the success with the employees in order to keep momentum for change. This will also make it easier in the future to implement the more difficult tasks and changes. Finally, review what has been accomplished and solicit feedback from any groups, internal and external, involved in the process change and the pollution prevention program. Document the reviews, cost implications, pitfalls, and feedback. This will be an aid during the next planning phase for the next set of projects for pollution prevention. Once the process appears to be finished, it is time to start the process again. New priorities can be chosen as well as analysis of the changes that have just been completed to see if more change is needed. This process works like a continual circle and can be summarized as analyze, plan, implement, check.

SPILL CONTROL

Spills are incidents that will most probably happen in any laboratory. Despite any precautions taken, a spill will happen in the laboratory at some time. The preparation necessary in every laboratory to control spills is a very important aspect in any safety program. Government regulations may influence the actions that may be taken by laboratory personnel in a spill event. These regulations may also mandate the training that is required for spill cleanup. The spill control program put into place in the laboratory should be in concert with these regulations should they apply.

Generally in any spill control program, the hazards of all materials used in the laboratory should be known before work begins with these materials. It is too late to determine the hazards involved with a chemical once the spill has occurred. The chemical hazards should be determined for each material used and the material should be classified by the hazard class such as toxic, corrosive, oxidizer, flammable, pyrophoric, reactive, radioactive, biohazardous, etc. An important consideration in this process is to take into account the precautions needed when working with these hazardous materials in order to make sure minimal exposure occurs to the employee during a spill event. These precautions should include the use of personal protective equipment and other administrative controls as well as engineering controls to minimize the danger of a spill.

Every person in the laboratory should know where the emergency equipment is located in the laboratory and how to use it. The location of spill control equipment, exits, fire extinguishers and other safety equipment should be posted. Emergency telephone numbers should be posted near each telephone to remind personnel whom to notify in the event of a spill or other emergency. Spill response procedures should also be posted in order to provide additional reminders of what to do in a spill event.

The appropriate spill control equipment should be kept on site and all personnel should be trained on how to use the equipment as well as the limitations for the equipment, since different spill kits are good for different types of spills. The spill kit should include the necessary personal protective equipment for the spill that the kit is designed to control. Since there are many kinds of absorbents in spill kits, it is important to make sure that the absorbent in the kit is appropriate for the spill it is to be used to control. The spill kit should also include the tools needed for cleaning up or controlling the spill. For example, non-sparking tools are required for flammable spills and non-porous tools are required for the cleanup of radioactive materials. In addition, the containers used for disposal should be included in the spill kit. The containers should be compatible with the material that will be placed in the container, and government regulations may require that certain types or rated containers be used for the spill materials.

A spill control plan should be put into place before any spill event occurs. Beyond the training for the employees on the spill equipment available and how to use it as well as the personal protective equipment required, the spill control plan should address the type of spill that will be handled by personnel in the laboratory. Generally, 1) if the spill is not life threatening, 2) if the spill is of a size deemed manageable by the spill control plan, 3) if the appropriate training has been provided and 4) if there is appropriate and sufficient spill cleanup equipment available, most facilities will clean up the spill using laboratory personnel. If any of these conditions cannot be met, the laboratory should use specifically trained local professionals with the expertise to control and clean up the spill. If there is any doubt about handling the spill event, it is better to call a local professional than to take a chance that the cleanup and control can be done safely.

If the cleanup of the spill will take place internally, the general steps used by most professionals to clean up a spill are the assessment, containment, cleanup and the decontamination of the area. During the assessment phase, as much information as possible is gathered regarding the hazardous material involved, as well as what surrounding items may impact the spill adversely. Also included in the assessment is the volume of the spill in order to ensure that the appropriate amount of spill cleanup material is available before the cleanup begins. A hazard assessment of the hazardous material is undertaken to determine the specific hazards involved with the material and the risk this poses to the person cleaning up the spill. This hazard assessment will also help to determine the type of personal protective equipment required to clean up the spill. During this phase it is important that the appropriate notifications be made to personnel identified in the spill control plan. In addition, the spill area should be controlled so access is prevented and thus exposure to the material is minimized.

The containment step helps to limit the spread of the spill. Upon using the appropriate absorbent materials and engineering controls, the spread of the spill can be limited to the immediate area in most cases. When applying absorbent to the spill it is important to remember to apply the absorbent along the outer edges of the spill first and then proceed to work towards the center of the spill. This will prevent the spread of the spill during the application of absorbent materials. The appropriate absorbent should be applied for the spill material.

During the cleanup and decontamination portions of the process, the hazardous material is absorbed or removed from the contaminated surface, packaged and then the surface is decontaminated to remove any lingering contamination. The container the spill is to be placed in during the cleanup phase should be appropriately labeled, compatible with the material to be placed in it and should be sealed when the cleanup is complete. During decontamination, generally soap and water is applied to remove any residual contamination from the surfaces. Depending on the type of spill, testing may be required to confirm the surface is completely decontaminated. At the completion of the decontamination process, the person cleaning up the spill, including any personal protective equipment, should be decontaminated before exposing others to any contamination. All of the decontamination materials as well as the spill cleanup should be disposed of in a proper manner in accordance with the applicable government regulations in your area.

Preparation is the key to success in any spill situation. The more preplanning and training that has taken place before a spill event, the smoother the process will be in remediating the spill and returning the situation to normal.

BIOLOGICAL HAZARDS

When working with materials in the laboratory that are potentially infectious, containment becomes the most important method to reduce or eliminate potential exposure to the laboratory worker. All personnel who work with potentially infectious materials must be aware of the hazards involved and must be trained to handle these materials in a safe manner. Standard operating procedures that are developed for the handling and analysis of potentially infectious materials should not only identify the potential hazards, but should also identify the practices and procedures for the safe handling and analysis of these materials.

Safety equipment used in the containment of potentially infectious materials may range from biological safety cabinets to alternative engineering controls designed to reduce or eliminate the potential exposure to the laboratory worker. Personal protective equipment is also a part of the safety equipment employed in the laboratory to contain any potential exposure. Personal protective equipment is often used in conjunction with other types of safety equipment in order to further decrease the risk of exposure. Two of the viral agents that may pose risks to those handling blood and body fluids include Hepatitis B and HIV. Biosafety Level 2 practices and procedures should be implemented for the handling of blood and body fluids that may be present in forensic laboratories.

Biosafety Level 2 practices and procedures include the use of biological safety cabinets when manipulating materials that may produce an aerosol or splash hazard. In addition, personal protective equipment should be used that may include a splash shield, gloves, garment protection and face protection. Procedures that include universal precautions should be implemented to reduce any potential exposure. Finally, government regulations may require additional precautions or procedures to be used when working with potentially infectious materials. It is always important to check these regulations before any work is performed to make sure that the appropriate rules and regulations are being followed.

FACILITY SAFETY EQUIPMENT

VENTILATION

The use of appropriate and adequate ventilation in forensic laboratories is of extreme importance when working with potentially hazardous and infectious materials. There are typically three types of local exhaust ventilation used in laboratories. These are chemical fume hoods, biological safety cabinets and other types of local exhaust.

Chemical fume hoods

Probably the most common source of local exhaust ventilation in laboratories is the chemical fume hood. This type of local exhaust is designed to contain and remove contaminants generated within the hood to provide protection for the user. Typical laboratory fume hood systems are made up of many different types including bypass, auxiliary air and variable air volume. Typical laboratory fume hoods also may have vertical or horizontal sashes.

Several factors should be taken into account when placing a fume hood in the laboratory to ensure proper operation and maximum protection for the user. Since the user stands in front of the hood during use, eddy currents are formed around the body and may draw contaminants from within the hood through the breathing zone of the user. Combined with room air currents, these two factors greatly affect the performance of the laboratory fume hood. For this reason, the face velocity of air flowing into the fume hood should be between 60–100 cfm/sq ft with good air distribution. This level of performance can limit the breathing zone exposure to the user to less than 0.1 ppm. For uniform distribution of air within the fume hood, the baffles in the fume hood should be adjusted so the air flow velocity at the face of the fume hood varies by less than 10 percent from point to point across the face.

Fume hoods should be located away from heavy traffic areas and away from aisles and doorways. If it is necessary to install the fume hood near a doorway, the fume hood should not be located in a room without a second means of egress from the room. In addition, the traffic pattern in front of the fume hood should be kept to a minimum and the door should normally be open. Fume hoods should be equipped with a flow-monitoring device in order to alert the user that the fume hood is operating properly. This device will typically alarm if the flow velocity drops below a safe level, thus alerting the user to not use the hood until it can be serviced to restore it to the proper operation.

Appropriate work practices for the use of chemical fume hoods should be followed at all times in order to aid in the proper performance of the equipment. It is best to keep any operations in the fume hood at least six inches back from the face. The user should never place their head inside the fume hood when contaminants are being generated within the hood. Chemicals or other apparatus should not be stored in the hood. Instead these items should be stored in an appropriate location. During use, the hood sash should be kept as closed as possible and the baffles should be kept free of obstruction by equipment or other items. When using flammable materials in the fume hood, all receptacles or other potentially sparking devices should be kept outside the hood and only approved spark-proof plugs and receptacles should be used.

Biological safety cabinets

Biological safety cabinets are enclosures that are designed to minimize the exposure to a hazardous biological material. A biological safety cabinet should be used in the laboratory to provide containment of infectious materials during manipulation. There are three classes of biological safety cabinets: Class I, Class II and Class III. Class I and II cabinets provide the primary barrier needed to offer significant protection to laboratory personnel when used appropriately. Class II cabinets offer added protection for the materials in the cabinet from external contamination. Class III cabinets are airtight and provide the highest level of protection.

A Class I biological safety cabinet is designed as a negative pressure cabinet that is ventilated with a face velocity of at least 75 linear feet/minute. The exhaust travels through a high-efficiency particulate filter (HEPA) and either exhausted to the outside or back into the room. This type of cabinet is designed for infectious agents of low or moderate risk and is not suitable for materials that are vulnerable to external airborne contamination.

A Class II biological safety cabinet is designed for a face velocity flow of 75–100 linear feet/minute. In addition to the same protections as a Class I biological safety cabinet, a Class II biological safety cabinet provides protection for the materials in the cabinet from external airborne contamination. Class II cabinets are also designed for use with low to moderate risk infectious agents. These cabinets if configured and operated properly may also be used to handle some types of radionuclides and some toxic chemicals.

A Class III biological safety cabinet is fully enclosed and airtight. This cabinet is designed for the highest risk agents and offers the highest protection for personnel of all the classes of biological safety cabinets. All manipulations within the cabinet are typically performed with arm-length rubber gloves. These cabinets are operated under negative pressure with extensive HEPA filtration and treatment systems for all materials leaving the cabinet.

EYEWASHES

When chemicals are present in the laboratory and are being handled, the possibility exists for an accident. In the case of chemicals splashed in the eyes, eyewashes are a mandatory piece of safety equipment. Many chemicals cause rapid damage to the eyes and require irrigation in order to reduce or control the damage. Eyewashes are used to facilitate this requirement. Several types of eyewashes are available in the marketplace including the two major types, plumbed and self-contained. There are many different government regulations related to the installation and use of eyewashes. Consult these regulations as well as the manufacturer's recommendations before installing or using any eyewash.

Plumbed eyewashes typically deliver the greatest volume of water in the shortest period of time. This type is preferred in most laboratories. The eyewash should provide ample amounts of potable water in a controlled and uninterrupted flow. The water used should also be tempered in order to facilitate the length of time needed to completely flush the eyes in an incident; usually at least 15 minutes. Plumbed eyewashes have advantages because of the amount of water that can be supplied to the eyes in a short period of time, typically 7 to 13 liters per minute. Additional advantages include the facts that the water can be tempered and plumbed eyewashes are easily tested for proper operation.

Self-contained eyewashes usually deliver much less water than the plumbed version. In addition, this type does not usually temper the water and may be cold or hot depending on the surrounding air temperatures. Self-contained eyewashes also require preservatives to be placed in the water to prevent microbial contamination from multiplying and creating as much or more damage than the chemical exposure. This type of eyewash is a must when using chemicals in an area where a plumbed eyewash cannot be placed.

All eyewashes should be tested on a weekly basis and logged as part of a preventive maintenance program. This testing enables the user to verify that the flow is sufficient and the eyewash does not contain any blockages that might hinder proper flow to the eyes in an emergency. In addition, testing cleans the dirt and corrosion from the water lines and does not allow the water to become stagnant. All eyewashes should be clearly marked and should have highly visible signs placed in the area of the eyewash. All eyewashes should at a minimum be located in areas where corrosive chemicals are used and be located in an area free of obstacles and tripping hazards. In addition, the eyewash should not be placed next to electrical equipment or electrical outlets. Finally, all personnel in the laboratory should be trained on the location of the eyewashes, how to use the eyewash, how to inspect the eyewash, how to help others wash their eyes in case of an accident and how to get medical attention as soon as possible to the site of the accident.

SAFETY SHOWERS

Safety showers, shown in Figure 9.1, like eyewashes, are essential equipment in any laboratory handling chemicals. This safety device is designed to deliver large amounts of water to the whole body in a short period of time, washing away any contamination. The typical time required for decontamination is 15 minutes of washing. A safety shower is designed for use in the event of an exposure to a chemical over a large part of the body. When using the shower the exposed individual should remove any contaminated clothing and continue to wash under the shower until it is deemed that the person has been decontaminated. Safety showers should be placed close to the hazard, usually within a 10-second travel time or within 100 feet of the hazard. This is a general rule and may not be sufficient for protection based on every situation in the laboratory. Safety showers should be tested weekly to ensure proper operation and should be repaired immediately if any problems are discovered during testing. In addition, the testing should be documented and kept on file with other safety equipment-testing documentation. All personnel in the laboratory should be trained on the proper operation, use and testing of safety showers in the laboratory. There may be specific government regulations regarding safety showers. These regulations should be consulted before installing and using any safety shower in the forensic laboratory.

Figure 9.1
A safety shower.

FIRE EXTINGUISHERS

Fires may occur in a laboratory at any time when all of the necessary elements to support combustion are present. Many different fire hazards exist in the typical forensic laboratory, including flammable chemicals, combustible materials, electrical components and equipment, and reactive chemicals. Since most fires in the laboratory start as a small fire that can be contained, fire extinguishers are an important piece of safety equipment in every laboratory (Figure 9.2).

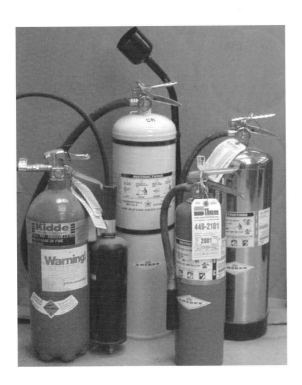

Figure 9.2

Fire extinguishers are essential for safety, as many different fire hazards exist in the typical forensic laboratory.

There are four major classes of fires; A, B, C, and D. The classification is divided according to the fuel involved in the fire event. Class A fires involve combustible materials such as paper, wood, cloth and plastics. Class B fires are fires that involve flammable liquids such as acetone, toluene and xylene. Class C fires involve the use of energized electrical equipment, and Class D fires involve combustible metals such as sodium or magnesium. Fire extinguishers are rated by the class and the size of fire that they can extinguish.

There are six common extinguishing agents used in most fire extinguishers. They are water, carbon dioxide, foam, dry chemical, halogenated agents, and metal-extinguishing agents. The correct type of extinguisher should be chosen based upon the type of fuel involved in the fire.

Water removes the source of ignition or heat leg from the fire tetrahedron by cooling the fire in order to extinguish it. Water is rated for Class A fire, which consists of common combustible materials. Although water is readily available and inexpensive, it has relatively little value in extinguishing a typical laboratory fire. Most flammable liquids will float on top of the water and thus continue to burn and spread the fire if water is used as an extinguishing agent. Water also conducts electricity, making it hazardous to use around the high density of electrical equipment found in every laboratory. Finally, water will intensify a fire involving flammable metals, causing the production of more hydrogen and thus more fuel for the fire.

Carbon dioxide is used for Class B and Class C fires involving flammable liquids and energized electrical equipment. Carbon dioxide works to remove the oxygen leg from the fire tetrahedron. One of the major advantages to the use of carbon dioxide is that it leaves no residue and thus will not damage many types of equipment in the laboratory.

Foam is another type of extinguishing agent used for Class B fires. Foam also works to remove the oxygen leg from the tetrahedron, but works in a different way than carbon dioxide. Carbon dioxide works to displace the oxygen while foam smothers the fire by creating a barrier between the fuel and the air. In addition, foam does provide some cooling effect on the fire. Foam leaves behind a large amount of residue that will require cleanup after the fire is extinguished.

There are two types of dry chemical available in fire extinguishers, standard and multi-purpose. Standard dry chemical is used for Class B and C fires while multi-purpose dry chemical is used for Class A, B and C fires. Both types of dry chemical bind the oxygen involved in the fire, thus extinguishing the fire. Standard dry chemical usually consists of potassium or sodium bicarbonate. Multi-purpose dry chemical agent is usually composed of ammonium phosphate. Both standard and multi-purpose agents leave a powdery residue in the laboratory after use and should be cleaned up immediately since their composition makes the extinguishing agents corrosive to many items in the laboratory. Neither agent should be used around sensitive electrical equipment since the equipment will usually have to be disposed of after use of one of the agents.

Halogenated agents, including halon and its substitutes, interfere with the chemical chain reaction to extinguish the fire. These agents work to extinguish Class A, B and C fires and leave no residue, making it the agent of choice for sensitive electrical equipment such as computers. In addition, relatively small amounts are needed to extinguish a fire. These agents are extremely expensive and limited due to environmental regulations related to stratospheric ozone depletion.

Metal-extinguishing agents are special agents designed to control Class D fires involving flammable or combustible metals. Typically the agents are specific to the fuel involved in the fire and work to form a crust or barrier over the burning metal to remove the oxygen component from the fire. Since metal fires are extremely hot, these agents take some time to completely extinguish the fire. Sand has been used in order to extinguish metal fires, but one should be careful when using sand since the fire may obtain oxygen from the silicon dioxide in the sand and can continue to burn long after the metal is completely covered. In addition, care should be taken when extinguishing a metal fire to make sure the metal is covered on all sides with the extinguishing agent and not just on top. It is advisable to cover the fire with the extinguishing agent first and then to spread a layer of agent on the floor next to the fire. Then the fire and extinguishing agent can be placed on top of the layer spread on the floor by shoveling the metal and then covering the entire area again, making sure to seal any cracks that have formed in the crust. This technique will help to prevent the metal fire from burning through the flooring or surface where it started.

Fire extinguishers should only be used by trained individuals who understand the proper techniques for extinguishing the fire. In general, trained laboratory personnel can extinguish fires when:

1. the fire is small;
2. the fire does not block the only exit from the area;
3. the correct extinguisher is being used; and
4. the individual using the extinguisher understands the proper use of the extinguisher.

The PASS acronym can be used to remember the steps to extinguish the fire. First, **P**ull the pin on the extinguisher. Second, **A**im the nozzle at the base of the fire. Third, **S**queeze the handle and fourth, **S**weep the extinguishing stream back and forth over the fire until the fire is extinguished.

Fire extinguishers should be inspected and serviced on a regular basis. Many regulations exist on the frequency required for inspection and service, so checking with the local rules and regulations would be advisable. Inspections typically involve checking the pressure gauge when one exists, checking the seal to make sure it has not been broken, making sure the extinguisher is visible and accessible, checking the general condition of the extinguisher to make sure the shell has not been damaged, checking that the appropriate class of extinguisher is available, and finally checking the hydrostatic test date on the extinguisher.

PERSONAL PROTECTIVE EQUIPMENT

When engineering controls are not adequate, personal protective equipment is the next step in protection. Personal protective equipment has become commonplace in most laboratories and is essential in order to provide a safe working environment. It should be the responsibility of the employer to provide the appropriate personal protective equipment and to train the employees on the equipment's correct usage, limitations and how to properly wear the personal protective equipment. It is the responsibility of each employee to use the provided personal protective equipment in an appropriate manner. Personal protective equipment comes in all shapes, sizes and varieties. A few of the more commonly used items are discussed in this section.

GLOVES

There is an endless variety of gloves available in the marketplace today (Figure 9.3). The appropriate glove for the job at hand is usually chosen based on the material the glove is made of, the chemical resistance and permeation properties of the glove, the size of the glove and any special qualities required for the job.

Figure 9.3

The proper gloves should be worn at all times in the laboratory.

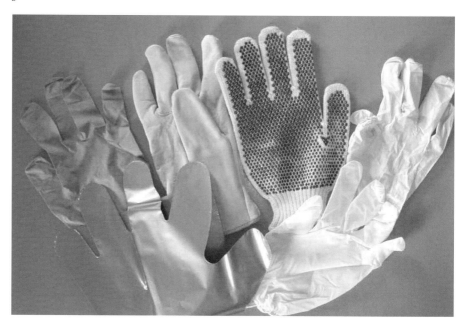

Gloves are made of a variety of materials including leather, cloth, Kevlar, nitrile and latex, to name a few. In the selection of the proper glove for the job, the selection of the appropriate material is the most critical. Gloves used for a task that consist of an inappropriate material will give the user a false sense of security and may unnecessarily expose the user to a hazardous situation. For example, leather is typically not a good choice of material for handling chemicals. Leather provides excellent protection from many hazards, but does not provide protection from chemical hazards since the chemicals absorb into the leather. A glove with chemical-resistant properties is usually the best choice in this situation.

Picking a chemical-resistant glove may be a very complex task. Manufacturers publish guidelines on permeation and chemical resistance for the gloves they produce. It is important that you consult the chart specific to the manufacturer since all gloves of the same material are not necessarily created equally. The chemical resistance and permeation properties of any glove are affected by the chemical that the glove is exposed to, the thickness of the material, the condition of the glove, the length of exposure for the glove and the amount of dexterity needed to perform the task at hand.

Different types of gloves typically used in laboratories include latex, nitrile, polyvinyl alcohol, polyvinyl chloride, laminates, butyl rubber and neoprene. Latex gloves are commonly used in medical laboratory situations to protect from blood and body fluids. They allow a great degree of dexterity because of the minimal thickness of the glove and the glove's ability to easily shape to different forms. Latex gloves typically provide limited resistance to some acids and bases. Latex is not appropriate for most chemicals because it does not provide permeation protection. In addition, one of the drawbacks to latex is that some people develop latex allergies that may range from rashes to serious health conditions.

Nitrile gloves provide a fairly wide degree of chemical resistance. They typically provide good resistance to oils, aqueous solutions and some solvents including xylene and limited resistance to toluene. Nitrile does not provide protection for solvents such as benzene, methylene chloride and most ketones. It is very important to check the glove manufacturer's guidelines for their specific properties. Nitrile gloves are usually very inexpensive since they are disposable. In addition, these gloves provide good dexterity since they mold to the shape of the hand. Nitrile gloves can be found in many thicknesses and types. It is important to make sure the nitrile glove chosen meets the criteria for the job to be done.

Polyvinyl alcohol gloves provide excellent protection against most organic compounds including ethers, chlorinated solvents, aromatics and most ketones. Acetone and alcohols are exceptions to this rule. Polyvinyl alcohol gloves are very permeable to many alcohols and will dissolve in water solutions. In addition, polyvinyl alcohol gloves are typically very expensive for a disposable glove.

Polyvinyl chloride gloves typically resist acids, bases, alcohols and aqueous solutions. Polyvinyl chloride is a poor choice to protect against most solvents since they permeate the gloves quickly. Polyvinyl chloride gloves are usually low cost but do not provide protection needed in most chemical laboratories that handle solvents.

Laminates are a class of gloves that usually offer excellent protection for the widest range of chemical substances for the longest periods of time. The drawbacks to laminate gloves are that they are usually expensive, do not provide a high level of dexterity and typically do not fit properly. Laminate gloves should be used in combination with another type of tight-fitting glove in order to increase the dexterity level and provide for a better fit.

Butyl rubber gloves provide excellent protection from aldehydes, ketones and most polar organic solvents. They do not provide protection from chlorinated solvents or other hydrocarbons. Butyl rubber gloves are very expensive and allow very limited dexterity for the user.

Neoprene gloves offer wide protections from solvents, bases, alcohols and many acids. They are commonly available as disposable gloves and are not usually extremely expensive. These gloves only provide limited dexterity and limited cut or abrasion resistance.

There is no ideal glove that will work in every situation. Since all gloves are permeable to chemicals at some point, it is very important to review the manufacturer's recommendations regarding the gloves intended for use in the laboratory. Choosing the right glove for the job may require that two gloves be used together. For example, a laminate glove may be needed for protection, but since it provides little dexterity, a tight-fitting glove such as a disposable nitrile glove may be required as a second glove worn over the laminate. It is important to match the glove to the chemical being used in order to not provide a false sense of security that may endanger the user's life. Finally, all gloves should be inspected before use and reusable gloves should be cleaned regularly. If damage is found in the glove that will compromise the safety of the glove, it should be discarded.

EYEWEAR

There are many varieties of eye protection available in the marketplace. Each type of eye protection is designed with a specific task in mind. It is important, as with gloves, to match the eye protection to the hazard to be encountered. The correct eye protection will protect the user from hazards such as flying objects, liquids, vapors, lasers and ultraviolet light sources (Figure 9.4). Eye protection

Figure 9.4

Various eyewear is available and should be matched with the hazard that can potentially be encountered.

should be worn at all times in the laboratory where there are hazards, should be correctly fitted and be of the correct type. Eye protection usually must comply with a government standard for its use. Check the local regulations in the area to make sure any eye protection used meets these standards.

Eye protection for flying debris usually consists of glasses with carbonate lenses and side shields attached to the glasses and are the most common form of eye protection seen in many workplaces. These glasses can be found in many types, sizes, colors and varieties. They can be basic plastic, glass or other resistant material. This type of eye protection is not suitable for protection against liquids since the liquid can enter the eye in the event of a liquid splash. It may be necessary to wear a face shield in order to increase the protection needed from flying debris. Face shields should not be worn alone; they should always be worn in conjunction with other eyewear appropriate for the hazard.

Eye protection from liquids usually consists of chemical splash goggles. This type of eye protection may also protect the user from splashing body fluids. The drawbacks to this type of eye protection are that they may be viewed as uncomfortable, visually unappealing and liable to fog on occasion hindering the visual field. Many types of goggles are treated to prevent fogging and in all actuality are not uncomfortable once the user gets accustomed to them. They may not be visually appealing, but they may save the user's sight in the event of an incident. If the user is working in an area where the potential for splashing is extreme, goggles should be worn with a face shield for added protection. If working with chemicals that represent a vapor hazard as well as a splashing hazard, unvented chemical goggles should be worn to protect against this combination of hazards.

Special eye protection is required to protect the user when working with lasers, ultraviolet light and infrared radiation. Exposure to these hazards without the proper eye protection may cause permanent damage to the eyes without being immediately detected by the user. The lenses in this type of eye protection are wavelength dependent. It is important that you match the eyewear in this situation to the specific wavelengths of light being used in the laboratory. In addition, if there is the possibility that light scattering may occur during operations using these types of radiation, wavelength-specific side shields may also be required to the protect the user.

Eye protection should be inspected on a regular basis for damage and should be replaced should the damage create a safety hazard for the user. Eye protection is a must in all forensic laboratories but this type of protection only works when it is being worn. Although the act of wearing eye protection may not be popular, each person in the laboratory has but one set of eyes and must protect them at all times in the laboratory.

LABORATORY SAFETY APPAREL

Laboratory apparel is some of the most widely used personal protective equipment in existence. This apparel includes such items as lab. coats, shoes, apron and gauntlets. The purpose of the protective clothing is to protect the body from chemical exposures in the laboratory mainly resulting from splashing of chemicals. Although personal clothing is not usually considered to be personal protective equipment, it does provide a barrier in case of the chemical splash situation. Proper personal clothing in laboratories should consist of clothing that covers the legs and body as well as closed toed shoes that provide a barrier for the feet. Many times dropped bottles and drips from bottles are overlooked as potential exposures for laboratory personnel. This type of exposure can be very common and is why open-toed shoes should not be allowed in the laboratory where chemicals are handled.

Lab coats provide an extra barrier for the skin and also provide protection for personal clothing during chemical handling. Lab coats are usually made of cotton and may be treated to provide a small amount of protection in case of fire because they do not melt, as many synthetic fabrics will do in a fire situation. One drawback is that the lab coat will absorb chemicals spilled on it and will react with strong acids and bases. The strong acid or base will burn through the cotton and continue to damage the clothing or skin beneath the lab coat.

When handling strong acids and bases in the laboratory, chemical-resistant aprons or gauntlets are suggested personal protective clothing. These items are worn over the lab coat and provide protection from chemicals that will react with the cotton found in lab coats. All personal protective clothing should be cleaned regularly and inspected for damage. Any damaged item that compromises the safety of the clothing should be replaced before it is worn again.

HEARING PROTECTION

Engineering controls should be the first choice for controlling noise in the laboratory. When engineering controls are not practical, hearing protection may be required. Hearing protection is usually not required in most laboratories, although forensic laboratories present a special circumstance in many instances. The analysis of firearms may require firing a weapon and thus will require appropriate hearing protection (Figure 9.5). Thus, high levels of noise for an extended period of time may cause hearing loss.

There are different types of hearing protection available including earplugs and ear muffs. Each type, style and manufacturer has rated the equipment with a noise-reduction rating. Many government entities have regulations related to hearing protection and hearing protection programs. The regulations related

Figure 9.5
While not required in many laboratories, hearing protection may be necessary in certain circumstances.

to laboratory operations should be consulted before hearing protection is selected and used.

Ear plugs are made of different types of materials including formable foam, premolded soft rubber or plastic and custom molded ear plugs. Foam plugs are disposable and usually very inexpensive to use. They have a wide range of noise-reduction ratings. They expand in the ear canal to form a tight fit in most cases. Premolded ear plugs are touted as a universal fit type of ear plug. They may provide excellent protection, as do formable plugs in most cases. One of the drawbacks to this type of hearing protection is that irregular ear canals may defeat the protection factor for premolded ear plugs. Many of the premolded plugs are designed to be reused but should be washed after each use and checked by the user to make sure there is no damage to the plug. In addition, premolded plugs may shrink or become hard, thus defeating the protection factor of the plugs.

Ear muffs come in a wide variety and are made to be reused. These items are more expensive on a per pair basis than disposable ear plugs but may be less expensive over the life of the muffs. Each pair should be inspected before use to make sure the seals have not been damaged. If the seal has been damaged or shows excessive wear, then another pair should be obtained and the damaged pair should be discarded. Personnel who wear glasses typically will not be able to wear muffs since the arms of the glasses break the seal between the muff and the skin.

After an analysis of the type and strength of the unwanted noise, consideration should be given to the type of hearing protection and engineering controls that should be put in place. If hearing protection is required, certain circumstances may create a necessity to combine ear plugs and muffs to provide additional noise reduction. If this is the case, it may be advisable to consult an expert in noise reduction strategies in order to implement further engineering controls if possible. In all cases requiring hearing protection, these devices should be selected based on several factors including the attenuation characteristics of the device, the consideration for other requirements for additional personal protective equipment, and the user's acceptance for the work setting.

SUMMARY

Safety and environmental awareness should be part of the culture within the forensic laboratory. It is important that each person in the forensic laboratory understands and practices safety and environmental protection on a daily basis. One person in a forensic laboratory who does not practice safety puts every other employee and visitor to the forensic laboratory at risk of injury. The personal safety and health of each employee in the laboratory and protection of the environment should be of primary importance. The prevention of injuries and illnesses as well as environmental protection should be given precedence over operating productivity whenever necessary. The laboratory should maintain an environmental safety and health program conforming to the best management practices of other forensic organizations with a program that embodies the proper attitudes toward protection of employees and the environment. Only through such a cooperative effort can an environmental safety and health program in the best interest of all be established and preserved.

REFERENCES

American Conference of Governmental Industrial Hygienists (1988) *Industrial Ventilation*. American Conference of Governmental Industrial Hygienists, Ohio.

Bretherick, Leslie (1995) *Bretherick's Handbook of Reactive Chemical Hazards*. Butterworth-Heinemann, Massachusetts.

Compressed Gas Association (1990) *Handbook of Compressed Gases*. Chapman and Hall, New York.

National Research Council (1995) *Prudent Practices in the Laboratory – Handling and Disposal of Chemicals*. National Academy Press, Washington, DC.

Plog, B. A., Niland, J. and Quinlan, P. J. (1996) *Fundamentals of Industrial Hygiene*. National Safety Council, Illinois.

Richmond, J. Y. and McKinney, R. W. (1999) *Biosafety in Microbiological and Biomedical Laboratories*. US Government Printing Office, Washington, DC.

Stricoff, R. S. and Walters, D. B. (1990) *Laboratory Health and Safety Handbook*. John Wiley and Sons, New York.

American Academy of Forensic Sciences
Code of Ethics and Conduct

SECTION 1 – THE CODE

As a means to promote the highest quality or professional and personal conduct of its members, the following constitutes the Code of Ethics and Conduct which is endorsed and adhered to by all members of the American Academy of Forensic Sciences:

a. Every member of the American Academy of Forensic Sciences shall refrain from exercising professional or personal conduct adverse to the best interests and purposes of the Academy.

b. Every member of the AAFS shall refrain from providing any material misrepresentation of education, training, experience or area of expertise. Misrepresentation of one or more criteria for membership in the AAFS shall constitute a violation of this section of the code.

c. Every member of the AAFS shall refrain from providing any material misrepresentation of data upon which an expert opinion or conclusion is based.

d. Every member of the AAFS shall refrain from issuing public statements which appear to represent the position of the Academy without specific authority first obtained from the Board of Directors.

SECTION 2 – MEMBER LIABILITY

Any member of the American Academy of Forensic Sciences who has violated any of the provisions of the Code of Ethics (Article II, Section 1) may be liable to censure, suspension or expulsion by action of the Board of Directors, as provided in Section 5h. below.

SECTION 3 – INVESTIGATIVE BODY

There shall be constituted a standing Ethics Committee (see Article V for composition) the primary function of which will be:

a. To order or conduct investigations and, as necessary, to serve as a hearing body concerning conduct of individual members which may constitute a violation of the provisions of Article II, Section 2.

b. To act as an advisory body, rendering opinions on the ramifications of contemplated actions by individual members in terms of the provisions of Article II.

SECTION 4 – INVESTIGATION INITIATING ACTION

The following are the principal forms by which the Ethics Committee may initiate investigative proceedings:

a. A member of the Academy may submit a formal written complaint or allegation of violation(s) concerning a member to the Secretary of the Academy (see section 5, Rules and Procedures, below) or to the Chairman of the Ethics Committee.

b. The Ethics Committee may institute an inquiry based on any evidence brought to its attention which in its opinion indicates the need for further query or action under the provisions of these Bylaws. Appropriate to this form of action, Section Officers, upon receipt of a complaint or allegation concerning the professional or personal conduct of a member of their section, may refer the complaint or allegation to the Ethics Committee in writing, accompanied by a recommendation, if any, concerning the need for further investigation. Such recommendations, however, shall not be binding on the Ethics Committee.

SECTION 5 – RULES AND PROCEDURES

The following procedures shall apply to any written complaint(s) or allegation(s) of unethical or wrongful conduct against a member of the Academy whether initiated by a member or resulting from an inquiry originated by the Ethics Committee:

a. Written complaints or allegations against a member if delivered to the Academy Secretary, shall promptly be transmitted to the Chairman of the Ethics Committee.

b. The Ethics Committee shall determine whether the complaint(s) or allegation(s) fall(s) within its jurisdiction and whether there is probable cause to believe that the complaint(s) or allegation(s) may be well founded.

c. If the Ethics Committee, in its preliminary determination, finds that it does not have jurisdiction or that there is a lack of probable cause to believe that the complaint(s) or allegation(s) may be well founded, it shall dismiss the complaint(s) or allegation(s). It shall issue a report of such determination to the Board of Directors, setting forth the basic facts but omitting the names of the parties, and stating the reasons for its decision to dismiss. Notice of the filing of the complaint or allegation shall also be given to the accused.

d. If the Ethics Committee finds that it has jurisdiction and that there is probable cause to believe that the complaint(s) or allegation(s) may be well founded, its shall give notice of the filing of a complaint(s) or allegation(s) to the accused, and, in accordance with Rules and Regulations formulated by the Ethics Committee and approved by the Board of Directors, assemble such written data from both the accused and the accuser(s) which will permit the Ethics Committee to determine whether the complaint(s) or allegation(s) requires further investigation.

e. The Ethics Committee may appoint an Academy Fellow or Fellows to investigate the complaint(s) or allegation(s) and, if necessary, to present the charge(s) on behalf of the Academy to the Committee.

f. If, as a result of an investigation, the Ethics Committee decides to dismiss the charge(s) without a formal hearing, it may do so. It shall notify the accused and the accuser(s) of its decision and shall issue a report to the Board of Directors setting forth the basic facts but omitting the names of the parties and stating the reason(s) for its decision.

g. If the Ethics Committee decides to formally hear the charge(s), it shall give both the accused and the accuser(s) a reasonable opportunity to be heard and to confront each other. It shall then make a decision and notify both parties of its decision. The Ethics Committee shall then make a report to the Board of Directors on its decision including reasons and any recommendation for further action.

h. Following receipt of a report of the Ethics Committee and upon a vote of three-fourths (3/4) of the members of the Board of Directors present and voting, the party accused of unethical or wrongful conduct may be censured, suspended or expelled. No member of the Board of Directors who is the subject of a pending accusation under the provisions of this Article shall sit in deliberation on any matter concerning ethics. Suspension of the accused will be qualified by the permissible method of reinstatement.

i. The accused has the right to appeal from the action of the Board of Directors to the membership of the Academy. In effecting an appeal, the appellant must file a brief written notice of the appeal, together with any written statement he may wish to submit in his behalf, with the Academy Secretary not less than one hundred twenty (120) days prior to the next Annual Meeting of the Academy. The Secretary shall immediately advise each member of the Board of Directors of the appeal and shall forward to each a copy of the supporting papers submitted by the appellant.

j. The Board of Directors shall then prepare a written statement of the reasons for its actions and file the same with the Academy Secretary not less than forty (40) days prior to the next Annual Meeting.

k. Within twenty (20) days thereafter, the Academy Secretary shall mail to each voting member of the Academy a copy of the appellant's notice of appeal and his supporting statement, if any, and a copy of the Board of Director's statement.

l. A vote of three-fourths (3/4) of the members present and voting at the Annual Business Meeting shall be required to overrule the action of the Board of Directors in regard to censure, suspension or expulsion of a member.

m. The Ethics Committee shall formulate internal Rules and Procedures, designed to facilitate the expeditious, fair, discreet, and impartial handling of all complaints or matters brought before it. The Rules and Procedures, and any subsequent deletions, additions or amendments thereto, shall be subject to the approval of the Board of Directors.

SECTION 6 – SUSPENSION OF MEMBERS

Members who have been suspended from membership may apply for reinstatement once the period of suspension is completed. A suspended member will not be required to pay dues during the period of suspension. If reinstated, the required dues payment will be the annual dues less the pro-rated amount for the period of suspension.

American Society of Public Administrators
Code of Ethics

I. SERVE THE PUBLIC INTEREST
Serve the public, beyond serving oneself. ASPA members are committed to:

1. Exercise discretionary authority to promote the public interest.
2. Oppose all forms of discrimination and harassment, and promote affirmative action.
3. Recognize and support the public's right to know the public's business.
4. Involve citizens in policy decision-making.
5. Exercise compassion, benevolence, fairness and optimism.
6. Respond to the public in ways that are complete, clear, and easy to understand.
7. Assist citizens in their dealings with government.
8. Be prepared to make decisions that may not be popular.

II. RESPECT THE CONSTITUTION AND THE LAW
Respect, support, and study government constitutions and laws that define responsibilities of public agencies, employees, and all citizens. ASPA members are committed to:

1. Understand and apply legislation and regulations relevant to their professional role.
2. Work to improve and change laws and policies that are counterproductive or obsolete.
3. Eliminate unlawful discrimination.
4. Prevent all forms of mismanagement of public funds by establishing and maintaining strong fiscal and management controls, and by supporting audits and investigative activities.
5. Respect and protect privileged information.
6. Encourage and facilitate legitimate dissent activities in government and protect the whistleblowing rights of public employees.
7. Promote constitutional principles of equality, fairness, representativeness, responsiveness and due process in protecting citizens' rights.

III. DEMONSTRATE PERSONAL INTEGRITY
Demonstrate the highest standards in all activities to inspire public confidence and trust in public service. ASPA members are committed to:

1. Maintain truthfulness and honesty and to not compromise them for advancement, honor, or personal gain.
2. Ensure that others receive credit for their work and contributions.
3. Zealously guard against conflict of interest or its appearance: e.g., nepotism, improper outside employment, misuse of public resources or the acceptance of gifts.

4. Respect superiors, subordinates, colleagues and the public.
5. Take responsibility for their own errors.
6. Conduct official acts without partisanship.

IV. PROMOTE ETHICAL ORGANIZATIONS

Strengthen organizational capabilities to apply ethics, efficiency and effectiveness in serving the public. ASPA members are committed to:

1. Enhance organizational capacity for open communication, creativity, and dedication.
2. Subordinate institutional loyalties to the public good.
3. Establish procedures that promote ethical behavior and hold individuals and organizations accountable for their conduct.
4. Provide organization members with an administrative means for dissent, assurance of due process and safeguards against reprisal.
5. Promote merit principles that protect against arbitrary and capricious actions.
6. Promote organizational accountability through appropriate controls and procedures.
7. Encourage organizations to adopt, distribute, and periodically review a code of ethics as a living document.

V. STRIVE FOR PROFESSIONAL EXCELLENCE

Strengthen individual capabilities and encourage the professional development of others. ASPA members are committed to:

1. Provide support and encouragement to upgrade competence.
2. Accept as a personal duty the responsibility to keep up to date on emerging issues and potential problems.
3. Encourage others, throughout their careers, to participate in professional activities and associations.
4. Allocate time to meet with students and provide a bridge between classroom studies and the realities of public service.

APPENDIX C

American Society of Crime Laboratory Directors Code of Ethics

The Amercian Society of Crime Laboratory Directors recognizes the existence of ethics issues arising from activities unique to managers, such as hiring, training and supervising subordinates, establishing procedures for evidence handling and analysis, and providing quality assurance. These management responsibilities may have a profound effect on the integrity and quality of the work product of a crime laboratory, yet are not generally addressed in the ethics codes of other forensic science associations.

Therefore, as members of the Amercian Society of Crime Laboratory Directors, we will strive to foster an atmosphere within our laboratories which will actively encourage our employees to understand and follow ethical practices. Further, we shall endeavor to discharge our responsibilities toward the public, our employers, our employees and the profession of forensic science in accordance with the ASCLD Guidelines for Forensic Laboratory Management Practices.

APPENDIX D

American Society of Crime Laboratory Directors Guidelines for Forensic Laboratory Management Practices

INTRODUCTION

The American Society of Crime Laboratory Directors is a professional organization of managers and supervisors employed in forensic laboratories. We are the holders of a public trust because a portion of the vital affairs of other people has been placed into our hands by virtue of the role of our laboratories in the criminal justice system. The typical users of forensic laboratory services are not in a position to judge the quality of our work product or management for themselves. They must rely on the expertise of individual professional practitioners and the standard of practice maintained by the profession as a whole.

The purpose of this document is to provide guidelines for the conduct of managers and supervisors of forensic laboratories so as to safeguard the integrity and objectives of the profession. These are not immutable laws nor are they all inclusive. Instead, they represent general standards which each manager and supervisor should strive to meet. Laboratory managers must exercise individual judgment in complying with the general guidelines in this document. The guiding principle should be that the end does not justify the means; the means must always be in keeping with the law and with good scientific practice.

Adopted 1987, Revised 1994.

RESPONSIBILITY TO THE EMPLOYER

Employers rarely have the ability to judge the quality and productivity of their forensic laboratory. Therefore, the employer relies upon the forensic manager to develop and maintain an efficient, high quality forensic laboratory.

Managerial Competence

Laboratory managers should display competence in direction of such activities as long range planning, management of change, group decision making, and sound fiscal practices. The role(s) and responsibilities of laboratory members must be clearly defined.

Integrity

Laboratory managers must be honest and truthful with their peers, supervisors and subordinates. They must also be trustworthy and honest when representing their laboratories to outside organizations.

Quality

Laboratory managers are responsible for implementing quality assurance procedures which effectively monitor and verify the quality of the work product of their laboratories.

Efficiency

Laboratory managers should ensure that laboratory services are provided in a manner which maximizes organizational efficiency and ensures an economical expenditure of resources and personnel.

Productivity

Laboratory managers should establish reasonable goals for the production of casework in a timely fashion. Highest priority should be given to cases which have a potentially productive outcome and which could, if successfully concluded, have an effective impact on the enforcement or adjudication process.

Meeting Organizational Expectations

Laboratory managers must implement and enforce the policies and rules of their employers and should establish internal procedures designed to meet the needs of their organizations.

Health and Safety

Laboratory managers are responsible for planning and maintaining systems that reasonably assure safety in the laboratory. Such systems should include mechanisms for input by members of the laboratory, maintenance of records of injuries and routine safety inspections.

Security

Laboratory managers are responsible for planning and maintaining the security of the laboratory. Security measures should include control of access both during and after normal business hours.

Management Information Systems

Laboratory managers are responsible for developing management information systems. These systems should provide information that assists managers and the parent organization in decision making processes.

RESPONSIBILITY TO THE EMPLOYEE

Laboratory managers understand that the quality of the work generated by a laboratory is directly related to the performance of the staff. To that end the laboratory manager has important responsibilities to obtain the best performance from the laboratory's employees.

Qualifications

Laboratory managers must hire employees of sufficient academic qualifications or experience to provide them with the fundamental scientific principles for work in a forensic laboratory. The laboratory manager must be assured that employees are honest, forthright and ethical in their personal and professional life.

Training

Laboratory managers are obligated to provide training in the principles of forensic science. Training must include handling and preserving the integrity of physical evidence. Before casework is done, specific training within that functional area shall be provided. Laboratory managers must be assured that the employee fully understands the principles, applications and limitations of methods, procedures and equipment they use before beginning case work.

Maintaining Employee's Competency

Laboratory managers must monitor the skills of employees on a continuing basis through the use of proficiency testing, report review and evaluation of testimony.

Staff Development

Laboratory managers should foster the development of the staff for greater job responsibility by supporting internal and external training, providing sufficient library resources to permit employees to keep abreast of changing and emerging trends in forensic science, and encouraging them to do so.

Environment

Laboratory managers are obligated to provide a safe and functional work environment with adequate space to support all the work activities of the employee. Facilities must be adequate so that evidence under the laboratory's control is protected from contamination, tampering or theft.

Communication

Laboratory managers should take steps to ensure that the employees understand and support the objectives and values of the laboratory. Pathways of communication should exist within the organization so that the ideas of the employees are considered when policies and procedures of the laboratory are developed or revised. Communication should include staff meetings as well as written and oral dialogue.

Supervision

Laboratory managers must provide staff with adequate supervisory review to ensure the quality of the work product. Supervisors must be held accountable for the performance of their staff and the enforcement of clear and enforceable organizational and ethical standards. Employees should be held to realistic performance goals which take into account reasonable workload standards.

Supervisors should ensure that employees are not unduly pressured to perform substandard work through case load pressure or unnecessary outside influence. The laboratory should have in place a performance evaluation process.

Fiscal

Laboratory managers should strive to provide adequate budgetary support. Laboratory managers should provide employees with appropriate, safe, well-maintained and calibrated equipment to permit them to perform their job functions at maximum efficiency.

RESPONSIBILITY TO THE PUBLIC

Laboratory managers hold a unique role in the balance of scientific principles, requirements of the criminal justice system and the effects on the lives of individuals. The decisions and judgments that are made in the laboratory must fairly represent all interests with which they have been entrusted. Users of forensic laboratory services must rely on the reputation of the laboratory, the abilities of its analysts and the standards of the profession.

Conflict of Interest

Laboratory managers and employees of forensic laboratories must avoid any activity, interest or association that interferes or appears to interfere with their independent exercise of professional judgment.

Response to Public Needs
Forensic laboratories should be responsive to public input and consider the impact of actions and case priorities on the public.

Professional Staffing
Forensic laboratories must hire and retain qualified personnel who have the integrity necessary to the practice of forensic science. Verification of academic, work experience and professional association credentials is essential.

Recommendations and References
Professional recommendations of laboratories and/or analysts should be given only when there is knowledge and an endorsement of the quality of the work and the competence of the laboratory/analyst. Referrals of clients to other professional colleagues carry a lesser degree of endorsement and are appropriate when a laboratory is unable to perform the work requested.

Legal Compliance
Laboratory managers shall establish operational procedures in order to meet constitutional and statutory requirements as well as principles of sound scientific practice.

Fiscal Responsibility
Public laboratories should be managed to minimize waste and promote cost effectiveness. Strict inventory controls and equipment maintenance schedules should be followed.

Accountability
Laboratory managers must be accountable for decisions and actions. These decisions and actions should be supported by appropriate documentation and be open to legitimate scrutiny.

Disclosure and Discovery
Laboratory records must be open for reasonable access when legitimate requests are made by officers of the court. When release of information if authorized by management, all employees must avoid misrepresentations and/or obstructions.

Work Quality
A quality assurance program must be established. Laboratory managers and supervisors must accept responsibility for evidence integrity and security; validated, reliable methods; casework documentation and reporting; case review; testimony monitoring; and proficiency testing.

Responsibility to the Profession
Laboratory managers face the challenge of promoting professionalism through the objective assessment of individual ability and overall work quality in forensic sciences. Another challenge is dissemination of information in a profession where change is the norm.

Accreditation
The Laboratory Accreditation Board (ASCLD/LAB) provides managers with objective standards by which the quality of work produced in forensic laboratories can be judged. Participation in such a program is important to demonstrate to the public and to users of laboratory services the laboratory's concern for and commitment to quality.

Peer Certification

Laboratory managers should support peer certification programs which promote professionalism and provide objective standards that help judge the quality of an employee's work. Meaningful information on strengths and weaknesses of an individual, based on an impartial examination and other factors considered to be important by peers, will add to an employee's abilities and confidence. This results in a more complete professional.

Peer Organizations

Laboratory managers should participate in professional organizations. They should encourage employee participation in professional societies and technical working groups which promote the timely exchange of information among peers. These societies prove their worth to forensic science, benefiting both the employee and employer, through basic training as well as continuing education opportunities. Personal contacts with other agencies and laboratories with similar interests are also beneficial for professional growth.

Research

When resources permit, laboratory managers should support research in forensic laboratories. Research and thorough, systematic study of special problems are needed to help advance the frontiers of applied science. Interaction and cooperation with college and university faculty and students can be extremely beneficial to forensic science. These researchers also gain satisfaction knowing their work can tremendously impact the effectiveness of a forensic laboratory.

Ethics

Professional ethics provide the basis for the examination of evidence and the reporting of analytical results by blending the scientific principles and the statutory requirements into guidelines for professional behavior. Laboratory managers must strive to ensure that forensic science is conducted in accordance with sound scientific principles and within the framework of the statutory requirements to which forensic professionals are responsible.

1. AGENCY SPECIFIC DOCUMENTS

Each grant requires that applicants complete specific forms. Federal grants may include an application for federal assistance, a worksheet disclosing the geographic area that will be affected by the proposal, assurances that the applicant complies with federal statutes governing the use of federal funding such as employee and environmental regulations, and certifications that the applicant complies with regulations regarding lobbying and drug-free workplace requirements.

2. PROPOSAL SUMMARY

In a succinct manner, the summary should stand alone to describe the proposed project. The summary should include project goals and objectives and the methodology to be employed to achieve them.

3. PROGRAM NARRATIVE

The program narrative builds upon what was presented in the Proposal Summary. The organizational introduction, problem statement, project objectives, program design, and program evaluation are detailed in a concise manner. The organizational introduction should include the names and titles of the key persons that will undertake the project tasks. The problem statement should cite the issue to be solved with the program and why it is a concern to the community. The project objectives should include a timeline of major events to be accomplished within the grant period. The program design should outline the strategy that will be employed in order to achieve the objectives. Finally, the program evaluation should detail how the program's success will be evaluated.

4. BUDGET

The following budgetary detail is taken from the Budget Detail Worksheet included in the United States' National Institute of Justice grant solicitation. In addition to the worksheet, the NIJ requires a budget narrative to describe how the expenses are necessary to accomplish the goals of the proposal.

A. Personnel
i.   List name and title of employees participating in project.
ii. List salary rate and percentage of time devoted to project.
iii. Compute cost for each employee involved in project.

B. Fringe Benefits
i.   List name and title of employees participating in project.
ii. List actual fringe benefits costs such as retirement and unemployment compensation or use established formula.
iii. Compute cost for each employee involved in project.

C. Travel
i. List travel costs for project personnel including purpose of travel (e.g. receiving or providing training).
ii. Indicate basis of cost computation (e.g. 5 employees to two-day training course in "location" at $X airfare, $X lodging, etc.)
iii. Include statement indicating travel policies that will be followed.

D. Equipment
i. List non-expendable items that will be purchased and cost of items.
ii. Explain why purchase of equipment is necessary for project.
iii. Include statement describing procurement policy to be used.

E. Supplies
i. List expendable items to be purchased and consumed during the project and cost of the items.

F. Construction
i. Generally, construction costs are not allowable in federal grants but minor repairs or renovations may be included if approved by the granting authority.
ii. List purpose for the construction, description of work, and cost.

G. Consultants/Contracts
i. Include statement describing procurement policy to be used to choose project consultant.
ii. List name of consultant, service to be provided, fee and estimated time to be spent on the project.
iii. List consultant expenses that will be paid in addition to fees.
iv. List product or service that will be obtained by contract and cost of product or service.

H. Other Costs
i. List items not included elsewhere in budget worksheet (e.g. facility expenses to include rent and utilities).

I. Indirect Costs
i. Indirect costs are only allowable in federal grants if approved by the granting authority.

5. APPENDICES
Among the items to be included in the appendices are resumes of key personnel, letters of cooperation from other agencies, and final reports from prior grants.

INDEX